Microsoft

Office Professional 2013
for Touch Devices Plain & Simple

Katherine Murray

Published with the authorization of Microsoft Corporation by:
O'Reilly Media, Inc.
1005 Gravenstein Highway North
Sebastopol, California 95472

ISBN: 978-0-7356-7203-1

1 2 3 4 5 6 7 8 9 TI 8 7 6 5 4 3

Printed and bound in Canada.

Microsoft Press books are available through booksellers and distributors worldwide. If you need support related to this book, email Microsoft Press Book Support at *mspinput@microsoft.com*. Please tell us what you think of this book at *http://www.microsoft.com/learning/booksurvey*.

Acquisitions and Developmental Editor: Kenyon Brown
Production Editor: Kristen Borg
Editorial Production: Kim Scott
Technical Reviewers: Joli Ballew, Andrew Couch, Andy Pope, and Darren Lloyd
Indexer: Ron Strauss
Cover Design: Twist Creative • Seattle
Cover Composition: Karen Montgomery
Illustrator: S4Carlisle Publishing Services

To every person like me who wilts in the office on beautiful summer afternoons, yearning to get outside. This book is for you!

Contents

8   Working with shared documents in Word 2013 187

9   Designing, editing, and saving a worksheet in Excel 2013 211

10   Using Excel 2013 for data analysis **245**

11   Creating, animating, and saving a presentation in PowerPoint 2013. . . . . **265**

12 Collaborating and finishing your presentation 301

13 Organizing your research with OneNote 2013 321

Acknowledgments

Wow, what a great project! When your work involves multiple projects with multiple teams, sometimes things go smoothly and sometimes not. This was truly a dream project from start to finish, flowing easily from one stage to the next. I hope you'll experience that happy result as you try the techniques and explore the tasks in this book.

Everything couldn't have gone as well as it did without the contributions and expertise of the following people:

- Kenyon Brown, senior editor, for inviting me to think about an Office 2013 book for touch devices in the first place, and for being a great source of support and encouragement all the way through;

- Kristen Borg, production editor, for her clear communication skills and expert but friendly management style—she kept things moving well!;

- Joli Ballew, Andrew Couch, Andy Pope, and Darren Lloyd, technical reviewers, for testing all the tasks and processes and making sure the text was accurate;

- Kim Scott, designer, for a smooth and wonderful project all the way through, and for a great-looking layout;

- Bob Russell, Dianne Russell, and Ron Strauss—copy editor, proofreader, and indexer—for helping to ensure the text was as clear as possible and that you would be able to find what you need easily;

- And to Claudette Moore, my agent, for her great ability to focus on the details, her good humor, and her continual support.

About this book

1

Ah, sweet freedom! Gone are the days when you were chained to your desk, drafting a report while a perfect afternoon slips away outside your office walls. Today, the chances are good that you have a touch device like a tablet or a smartphone you can grab and take with you on the go. This means that you can work anywhere you like—the park, a sidewalk café, or rooftop—confident that you'll still be able to finish your report, review a worksheet, perfect a presentation, or keep up with your email, no matter where you are.

Microsoft Office 2013 is the first version of the Office suite designed specifically with touch-device users in mind. Now, Office has a Touch Mode as well as the traditional mouse and keyboard approach, and you can easily navigate your documents and work on projects with nothing more than your touch device.

This book shows you how to get the most out of Office 2013 on your touch device. You'll find out how to master the basics quickly and focus on the things that matter most to you.

In this section:

- Plain talk about Office 2013
- The Plain & Simple approach
- What's new in Office 2013 for touch devices?
- Big features in Office 2013
- What you'll find in this book
- A few assumptions
- Before we begin

Plain talk about Office 2013

Simple is good, even when technology isn't so simple. When you're trying to learn how to do a new task or you need to solve a problem—right now—you don't need long, laborious descriptions or convoluted examples. You want to go straight to the information you need, and you want it to be clear.

Microsoft Office Professional 2013 for Touch Devices Plain & Simple is written in plain language, so there's no "computer-speak" or technical jargon to get in the way of what you're trying to learn. Simple examples reflect the types of things you're likely to want to do with Office 2013, and the information provided is factual, to the point, and clear. What's more, each task includes an image with numbered steps that show you just what to do and the order in which you need to do it.

The Plain & Simple approach

If you're the type of person who likes to get the straight scoop on new tools and tasks, this is your book. One of the great things about the *Plain & Simple* series is that it helps you explore—in an easy-to-follow, visual format—just what you need to master the tasks you're most interested in learning. The goal of *Microsoft Office Professional 2013 for Touch Devices Plain & Simple* is to teach you all the basics, quickly and efficiently, so that you can get busy using your touch device to review, create, share, and collaborate with others on projects that inspire you. You'll find friendly, focused steps, clear and colorful illustrations, and tips and notes along the way to

help you get the most out of the program you're using without giving you a lot of information you don't need. The following features will help you along the way:

- You can read the book in any order that makes sense to you—just start in a section that explains what you want to learn.

- Steps provide the quickest and best way to accomplish a particular task.

- Screenshots show at a glance where to find the features you need on your screen.

- "Tips" give you valuable information that go along with the covered task.

- "See Also" notes direct you to other parts in the book where similar or complementary tasks are covered.

- "Try This" exercises encourage you to experience a technique yourself by using the steps in the section.

- "Cautions" warn you of potential problems or preventive measures that you can take to avoid trouble down the road.

Microsoft Office Professional 2013 for Touch Devices Plain & Simple gives you just what you need so that you can use your touch device and master major tasks in this latest version of the Microsoft Office suite.

What's new in Office 2013 for touch devices?

This development cycle has been a big one for Microsoft, first with the creation and release of Windows 8, and now with Office 2013 close on its heels. When Windows 8 launched in the fall of 2012, it brought users a new way to work with their operating system that places a great deal of emphasis on touch. Whether you're using a touch device or a touchscreen, you can flick, swipe, pinch, and tap your way through folders, files, and applications.

Office 2013 builds on the touch capabilities of Windows 8. In fact, some of the more important goals set by the Office development team was to bring about a great touch experience for touch device and touchscreen users. Specifically, they focused on how well the application responds to your touch, how accurately you can choose tools, text, objects, and options in a touch interface, and how easily you can type on the touchscreen.

Quick response to your touch

In Office 2013, the emphasis on touch responsiveness means that the program you're using responds instantly to your touch. This could mean your text reflows as you drag a picture from one place to another or a tab on the ribbon appears instantly after you tap it.

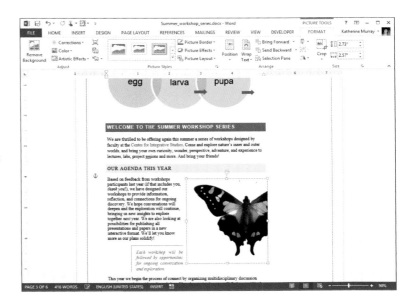

Making sure touch is on target

Touch accuracy is about getting the touch focus correct so that when you tap a tool, you're selecting the tool you intended to select. Office 2013 enhances the accuracy of touch by giving you a touch mode for window display that offers more space around tools on the ribbon and in minibars. This means tapping the tool you want is easier and more accurate, and you'll have fewer "near misses" when you inadvertently select an unwanted item.

Typing flexibility on a touchscreen

Now with Office 2013 you can add content on your touch device without connecting a keyboard, thanks to the onscreen keyboard selections. Windows 8 gives you several different keyboard options; you can choose to display a standard, split, or extended keyboard along the bottom half of your touch device screen. The split keyboard groups the keys along the outer edges of the touch device, which is perfect if you're working with the touch device as you go and are adding comments or content with your thumbs.

Touch mode enabled   More space in the ribbon

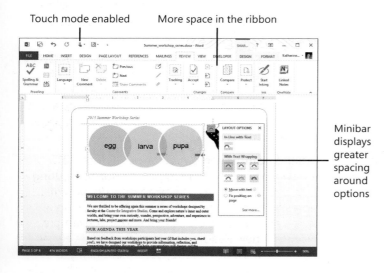

Minibar displays greater spacing around options

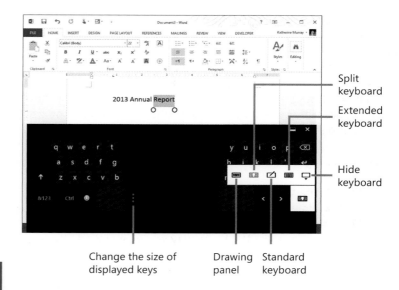

Split keyboard

Extended keyboard

Hide keyboard

Change the size of displayed keys

Drawing panel

Standard keyboard

> **TIP** You can ensure that you have access to all the latest features in Office 2013 by keeping your apps up to date. Swipe in from the right to display the Windows 8 charms, tap Settings and tap Change PC Settings to display PC Settings. Scroll down and tap Windows Update. Ensure that your system is set to check for updates and install them automatically.

Big new features in Office 2013

Office 2013 includes many new features that make it easier than ever to work wherever and whenever you want and with whomever you choose. Because the latest version includes a seamless connection with the cloud (assuming that you have an Internet connection), you can easily work on files, sharing them among various devices as well as multiple people on your team.

Windows 8 is a big part of the new Office 2013 design, although the program runs on both Windows 7 or Windows 8 computers. Windows 8 offers a new, high-color interface designed to be navigated by touch. Windows 8 offers a modern, clean interface and runs Start screen apps in full-screen, without the traditional windows you've been used to in earlier versions of the operating system. When you launch an Office 2013 app—which might be Word 2013, Excel 2013, PowerPoint 2013, and so on—the app will open on your Windows 8 Desktop, and will have a familiar window-based appearance. These windows are the traditional windows you are used to, and offer options to minimize, restore, and so on.

Some of the big changes you'll see in Office 2013 include these:

- **Install the version that makes sense for you** Microsoft offers more than one way to get and use Office 2013. You can opt to purchase and install Office 2013 on your computer in much the same way you've installed Office in the past, or you can get Office 2013 as part of a subscription to Office 365, which includes a suite of cloud services such as email, storage, SharePoint team sites, Microsoft Lync 2013, and more.

- **Save seamlessly to the cloud** Whether you're using Office 2013 as part of Office 365 or using it as a traditional desktop program, you have the option of saving files directly to the cloud, where you can access and work on your files from anywhere, using any compatible device with web access.

- **Work with Office apps** You can work with Office apps even if you're using a device that doesn't have Office. Office on Demand is a service available through Office 365 subscriptions with which you can stream Office on a computer that doesn't have Office installed.

- **Keep it social** Social media was on the rise when Office 2010 first appeared on the scene, but it is a way of life today. Office 2013 connects to social media services, making it possible for you to share and use photos and files, connect with your contacts, ask questions on social media sites, and more.

- **An enhanced computing experience** Office 2013 includes new features that can improve your computing experience, whether you're reviewing new documents, taking notes that you want to review later, or giving a presentation at a large business meeting. For example, Word includes a new Reading Mode that adjusts easily to the size of your screen, live layout functionality that reflows your document as you move objects on the page, and "peeks" that help you to get the information you need without leaving your current view.

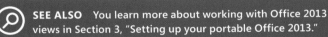

SEE ALSO You learn more about working with Office 2013 views in Section 3, "Setting up your portable Office 2013."

Which editions of Office 2013 are available?

Technology continues to change the way we live and work, and Office 2013 editions reflect different working styles for different types of users. Here's a quick overview of the different editions.

If you're a big fan of cloud technology and love the idea of working on files from anywhere, using any compatible device, you will like the subscription-based Office model available through Office 365. There are several subscription plans available so that you can choose the one that fits what you want to accomplish. Office 365 Home Premium is designed for home users and consumers who want to use Office on up to five computers and devices. Office applications include Word, PowerPoint, Excel, Outlook, OneNote, Access, and Publisher. Other Office 365 subscriptions cater to small business and enterprise. In addition, a version of Office

for Mac is available through Office 365. Office on Demand is also available through the Office 365 edition, which makes it possible to stream Office live so that you can work on computers that don't even have Office applications installed.

If you prefer the more conventional method of installing Microsoft Office on your computer and using it as a standalone suite of programs (although you can still save your files to the cloud if you choose), you can purchase and install Microsoft Office 2013.

If you use a device with an ARM processor running Windows RT, your device will come equipped with Office on Windows RT. This edition includes Word, Excel, PowerPoint, and OneNote and is provided by the manufacturer. It's not something you can buy separately and install.

What you'll find in this book

Microsoft Office Professional 2013 for Touch Devices Plain & Simple is designed so that you don't need to read the sections in any particular order; instead, simply jump in to the section that offers the answers you seek. You'll find that the book is organized to offer shared tasks and topics first; the ensuing sections explore individual apps.

Section 2, "The touchable Office 2013: navigation basics," starts the process by focusing on how to use touch to navigate Windows 8, how to start Office 2013, and how to customize the app tiles on the Windows 8 Start screen. You also find out about the touch techniques you'll use most often, find out how to display and choose the On-Screen Keyboard you want to use, and discover how to get help in Office 2013. Section 3, "Setting up your portable Office 2013," also focuses on common tasks you'll use in all your Office 2013 apps. You learn how to choose an Office background, select an Office theme, and connect social media services and accounts to your Microsoft Account. You'll also learn how to find and open apps, move among open apps, add Office apps from the Windows Store, review your documents, worksheets, and presentations, and change the ribbon display.

Section 4, "Staying in touch with Outlook 2013," shows you how to launch Outlook, navigate the Outlook window, add email accounts, add contacts, set up teams and groups, read and respond to mail, use Quick Steps to manage your mail, flag mail for follow-up, and organize your mail. Section 5, "Updating your schedule and managing your tasks," spotlights your appointments and to-do lists, helping you display and add to your calendar, schedule meetings, share your calendar, and create, manage, and mark tasks as complete in Outlook 2013.

Section 6, "Connecting right now with Lync 2013," introduces you to Lync 2013, showing you how to start Lync, add contacts, send and respond to instant messages, and make phone, audio, and video calls. You also learn how to set up an online meeting, invite participants, and host the meeting using a whiteboard and shared desktops.

In Section 7, "Creating and saving a document in Word 2013," you learn how to navigate the Word window, start a new document, add your own content, apply a theme, format your content, insert bookmarks and pictures, flow your text, and search and replace text. You'll also find out how to create tables, add headers and footers, insert sidebars and quotes, and save and export Word content. Section 8, "Working with shared documents in Word 2013," focuses on the collaboration features offered in Word. Here, you'll learn how to share your documents, collaborate with others in the cloud, turn on and work with tracking, add and respond to comments, open and edit PDFs, and compare documents.

Section 9, "Designing, editing, and saving a worksheet in Excel," introduces you to Excel 2013 and gives you the lay of the land in the Excel window. You find out how to create a new worksheet, add worksheet data, apply a theme, insert pictures, add a chart, save and share a workbook, and export worksheet data. Section 10, "Using Excel 2013 for data analysis," shows you how to apply conditional formatting, add sparklines, work with formulas and functions, analyze data trends by using PowerView Reports, and filter your data by using slicers.

Section 11, "Creating, animating, and saving a presentation in PowerPoint 2013," teaches you about creating, editing, and formatting a new presentation. You learn to choose a slide layout, work with master slides, add text and pictures, insert video, add sound effects, animate slide elements, add transitions, and save the presentation file. Section 12, "Collaborating and finishing your presentation," shows you how to comment on the presentation, share it with others, preview the presentation, time your delivery, print presentation materials, use Presenter View, broadcast the presentation online, and save the presentation as a video.

Section 13, "Organizing your research with OneNote 2013," introduces you to digital note-taking by bringing you on a tour of the OneNote window and showing you how to create a notebook, open existing notebooks, create sections, add note pages, use page templates, manage pages and sections, file unfiled notes, insert side notes, add notes in audio or ink, clip notes from the web, and much more.

Section 14, "Creating, reviewing, and touching up publications with Publisher 2013," helps you learn how to create your own publications—newsletters, flyers, brochures, invitations, and more—by using Publisher templates. You see how to flow text, insert pictures, arrange and layer objects, share your publication, and review and comment on your files.

Section 15, "Creating a web app with Access 2013," introduces you to a great new feature in Access 2013 with which you can create and publish a web app that collects data from others and gives you the capability to manage your information easily. You'll learn how to find your way around the Access window, create and edit a data table, add data, launch and use the web application, work with different views, and work with a team site in Access 2013.

A few assumptions

I wrote this book with a few assumptions in mind. First, I'm assuming that you've already installed Office 2013 on your touch device, or, your touch device came with the suite preinstalled. If you haven't yet installed Office 2013, you can install the software easily by purchasing and downloading it from *www.microsoftstore.com*, by downloading it from Office 365 if you subscribed to that service, or by installing it from the CD in the packaged software you purchased.

I'm also assuming that you're interested in the most popular Office 2013 applications: Word, Excel, PowerPoint, Outlook, OneNote, Access, Lync, and Publisher. You might be using either Office 365 Home and Family, Office 2013 ProPlus, or Office 2013.

I'm further assuming that for the most part you're familiar with computer basics, although I do cover touch navigation techniques in Section 2 and call your attention to techniques that may differ depending on whether you're using a touch device or a traditional desktop or laptop computer.

Additionally, although you'll find some brief bits of information here that touch on Office 2013 RT, the focus on this book is the version of Office 2013 running on Windows 8 touch devices based on the Intel processor. This means that the full range of app features are available to you and will be covered here as applicable to the section focus.

If you're using a touch device equipped with an ARM processor, you'll have Office 2013 RT: The apps in Office 2013 RT are similar to those you'll find in the standard Windows 8 version of Office 2013, with a few exceptions: macros, add-ins, and other third-party apps don't work in Office RT. Another missing piece: Office Home & Student 2013 RT also doesn't include Outlook but instead uses a Windows RT email app. Additionally, some specific features in individual apps—auto-synching to SkyDrive, audio recording in OneNote and PowerPoint, and grammar checking languages in Word—aren't available in Office RT.

Finally, I'm assuming that you are most interested in finding out how to use Office 2013 on your touch device in the most expedient way. You can also connect a traditional keyboard or dock your touch device and use a mouse, as well, but for the most part the techniques in this book focus on those you can accomplish by using touch.

Before we begin

The primary goal of *Microsoft Office Professional 2013 for Touch Devices Plain & Simple* is to help you to learn the tasks you most want to accomplish in Office 2013 by using your touch device. Hopefully, along the way you'll discover new features you're excited to try; learn how to connect to friends, family, and colleagues you haven't talked with in a while; and find out how great it can be to have the freedom and flexibility to work anywhere, anytime, with anyone you choose.

Office 2013 gives you the chance to be productive on the go, keep projects moving even when you're out of the office, and be creative about how and when you complete your important tasks. I hope you'll enjoy exploring all the possibilities in Office 2013 as much as I enjoyed writing this book for you.

And, because the best way to learn about Office 2013 is to begin putting it through its paces, grab your touch device, power up, and let's get started!

The touchable Office 2013: navigation basics

2

Chances are that you purchased a touch device because you like to work on the go. You probably also enjoy the touch capabilities of your smartphone and you wanted to be able to navigate your computer by using similar gestures and techniques. Pinch to zoom, tap to select, tap and hold to display options. Nice.

Office 2013 is the first version of Microsoft Office that is truly "touchable." Now, thanks to Touch Mode, you can easily navigate the Office ribbon, choose tools in minibars and galleries, and select content on the screen using only touch. You can also use the On-Screen Keyboard to type additional content, add notes, or edit the current file. This chapter introduces you to the various touch techniques you'll use to navigate Office 2013 on your touch device.

In this section:

- Starting Office 2013 on your touch device
- Starting Office 2013 on your Windows 8 phone
- Learning the Office 2013 screen
- Using the ribbon
- Displaying minibars
- Modifying the ribbon display
- Working with the Backstage view
- Touch techniques for everyday use
- Using the new Touch Mode
- Single-tapping to select an item
- Tapping and holding an item
- Swiping the screen to view content
- Spreading and pinching to zoom in and out

Starting Office 2013 on your touch device

As soon as you begin using Windows 8, you are sure to notice how easy it is to start an app from the Start screen. With just a tap, you can be working with the Office 2013 app of your choice. After you launch the Office 2013 app from the Start screen, it opens on the Windows Desktop, where you can create, enhance, and share the files you create. You can pin your favorite Office 2013 apps to the Windows Desktop taskbar if you like so that you can launch the programs directly from there. You can also create a shortcut on the Windows desktop if you prefer to launch the apps that way.

Start Office apps from the Windows 8 start screen

1 Swipe to display the app tiles on the far right side of the Start screen.

2 Tap the Office 2013 app that you want to launch.

   The application opens on the Windows 8 desktop.

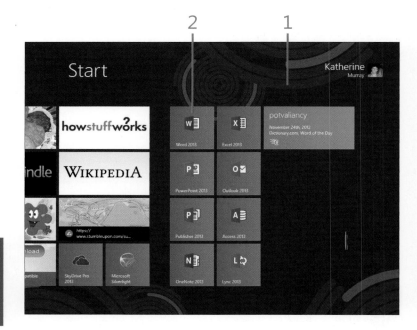

> ✓ **TIP** If you're using Office 2013 on a touch device running Windows 7, you begin by tapping the Start button in the lower left corner of the Windows 7 desktop. Next, click All Programs, navigate to the Microsoft Office 2013 folder, and then launch the application that you want to use.

> ✓ **TIP** You can also display all apps by flicking up on the Windows 8 Start screen and tapping All Apps. If you know which app you want to start, you can also type the name (such as Word or Outlook) on the On-Screen Keyboard to display the app tile. Tap the tile to start the app.

Add Office 2013 to the desktop

1 On the Windows 8 Start screen, swipe to the far right side of the Office app tiles.

2 Swipe down on the tile of the Office 2013 app that you want to add to the desktop taskbar.

3 At the bottom of the Start screen, tap Pin To Taskbar.

4 Scroll to the left and tap the Desktop tile.

The Windows desktop appears.

5 Tap the Office 2013 app icon on the taskbar to launch the program.

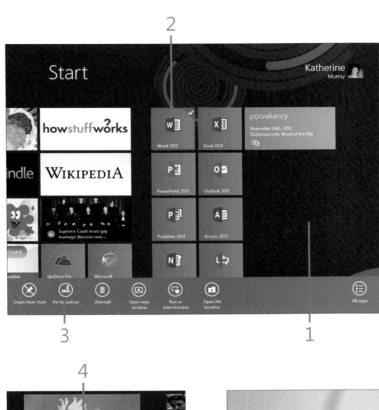

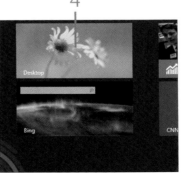

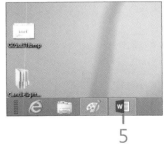

> ➔ **TRY THIS** If you prefer to keep your taskbar clean, you can create a desktop shortcut to the Office 2013 apps that you want to start from the Desktop, as well. On the Windows 8 Start screen, type the name of the app that you want to add as a shortcut. Flick down on the app tile in the results screen and tap Open File Location. Tap and hold the program name and then, on the shortcut menu that appears, tap Create Shortcut. Tap Yes when you are prompted to add the shortcut to the desktop. Repeat these steps for each shortcut you want to add.

From computer to touch device to phone

One of the great things about Office 2013 is that you can easily work with files on a variety of devices. You might start at the office, creating a report in Word. You leave for a meeting and find that you're stuck waiting for your 3 P.M. appointment. While you wait, you can open the file on your touch device and review a section that doesn't feel quite right. Later than evening you think of a way to improve the section; no problem, you can open the file on your phone, move a few paragraphs around, and resave the file to the cloud, all in a matter of minutes.

Depending on the way in which you purchase and install Office 2013, you are able to download and install the software on multiple computers. If you subscribe to Office 365, you can install Office 2013 on up to five computers. If you install Office 2013 Professional Plus, you can download Office to your primary computer and then log on to your SkyDrive Pro account by using your Microsoft Account to access and work with Office files on your touch device. If you're using a Windows 8 Phone, Office Mobile is already installed, which means that you are able to open and edit your Office 2013 files without installing anything at all. Nice.

Starting Office 2013 on your Windows 8 phone

Office Mobile is already installed on your Windows 8 phone, which means you can tap the Office tile and get started working on your Office 2013 files whenever you choose. You can both start new files on your phone and work with files you've created and saved to the cloud. Office Mobile automatically connects to your SkyDrive account. This means that any saved files that are associated with the Microsoft Account with which you log on to your phone will be visible in the Office Hub.

Start Office on your phone

1 On the Start screen of your Windows 8 Phone, swipe left to display the apps list.

2 Tap Office.

The Office Hub appears.

> **✓ TIP** You can pin Office 2013 to your phone's Start screen by tapping and holding the Office app tile. The option Pin to Start appears. Tap it to add the tile to the bottom of the tiles on your Windows 8 Phone Start screen.

Explore the Office Hub

1 Tap the location where the file you want to use is stored.

2 Alternatively, swipe left to display the Recent files list.

Tap to create
a new folder

Search for a
specific file

Office on Demand

With Office on Demand, you can use Office applications on on which Office isn't installed; for example, a computer in the library, at a business center, or one that you borrowed from a friend. The applications are "streamed" nearly instantly to the computer without being permanently installed on it. After you log off the computer, the applications and documents are no longer available to other users of that device. You can use Office on Demand on a computer that is connected to the Internet and running Windows 7 or later.

If you installed the Office 365 Home Premium Preview, you can create a new document using Office on Demand by going to *www.office.com*. Next, sign in with your Microsoft account and then, on the My Office tab, click the icon for the application that you want to use (located under Create New). Click Create. You will be able to start working on your new document within seconds—even before the all of the features have finished streaming. You can also access existing documents by using Office on Demand either from *www.office.com* or from SkyDrive. Just sign in with your Microsoft Account and open the document in which you want to work. The document will initially open in its Web App, but you can open it in the full application from the Web App.

If you installed the Preview version of Office 365 Small Business Premium or Office 365 Enterprise, you can use Office on Demand by logging on to your account at *www.office365.com* on a computer that doesn't have Office installed. Then, go to SharePoint and open the file with which you want to work, selecting the option to edit the document in its application.

Open an Office file on your phone

1 Scroll through the list of recent files to display the file that you want to open.

2 Tap the file to open it.

3 Alternatively, if you want to start a new Office file, at the bottom of the screen, tap the New button.

Learning the Office 2013 screen

One of the first things you'll notice about Office 2013 is the clean, uncluttered look of the screen. The Office development team wanted to make the its interface so easy to use that you can naturally find tools when you need them and simply let them disappear when you don't.

Another new aspect to the Office 2013 design is that when you're working with an Office app on your touch device, you won't see any window borders, which gives you a maximum amount of work to navigate on-screen. Here are some of the most important tools you'll be using regularly in the various Office apps:

- The **ribbon** contains groups of tools related to specific tasks you perform with the program.

- The **Quick Access Toolbar** is customizable so that you can add often-used tools and access them easily as you work. This is also where you'll find the Touch/Mouse Mode tool, with which you can switch seamlessly between using touch or using the mouse to navigate.

- **Tabs** present tools on the ribbon in an organized fashion, according to function. Tap the appropriate tab to display the tools related to the task at hand.

- **Contextual tabs** appear only when certain items or objects are selected in a file, offering tools and options related to that object (which could be text, an image, a chart, or other elements).

- Clicking the File tab displays **the Backstage view** where you perform file management chores and set program options.

(continued on next page)

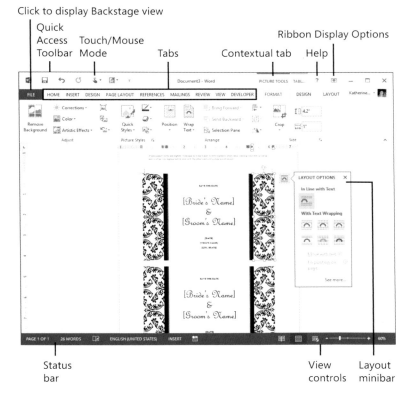

Click to display Backstage view

Quick Access Toolbar

Touch/Mouse Mode

Tabs

Contextual tab

Ribbon Display Options

Help

Status bar

View controls

Layout minibar

- **Help** displays the help window for the application you are using.

- **Minibar** controls are small palettes of tools related to the selected item that you can display and hide as needed. There are various minibars. (You can see the Layout mini-bar in the screenshot on the previous page.)

- Using the **Ribbon Display Options**, you can choose how much of the ribbon you want visible while you work. You can choose to auto-hide the ribbon, show only the tabs, or show the tabs and commands (which is the entire ribbon).

- With the **View** controls, you can change the way the file is displayed on the screen.

- The **status bar** gives you information about the current document. In the screenshot on the previous page, the status bar at the bottom of the Word document shows the number of pages and words and the language in use.

Using the ribbon

The ribbon gives you all the tools you need to create, work with, and share the files you create with Office 2013. In addition to the tabs you see by default in your current Office 2013 application, *contextual tabs* appear when you select certain types of objects on your page, making available specialized tools for the object that you selected.

Begin by tapping the tab you need. The tabs along the top of the ribbon will vary slightly depending on which app you're using. In Word, you'll see (from left to right) Home, Insert, Design, Page Layout, References, Mailings, Review, View, and

Developer tabs. Each tab offers a different set of tools related to specific tasks. When the ribbon is displayed in touch mode, all tools appear with an extra amount of space surrounding them so that you can easily tap the one you want.

Some tools on the ribbon present additional options and display a menu when you tap them. You can also display traditional dialog boxes for some groups of tools—for example, the Paragraph group on the Home tab in Word 2013—when you tap the small dialog launcher in the lower-right corner of the tool group.

Use the ribbon

1 With an Office 2013 app open on the screen, tap any tab to the right of the Home tab.

2 Tap an option in a group that displays a drop-down arrow (the down-facing triangle icon). This tells you that there are additional options that will appear when you tap the tool.

3 Tap the tool or option that you want to select.

(continued on next page)

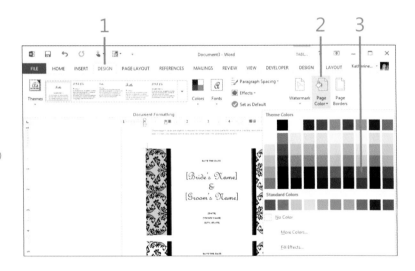

Use the ribbon *(continued)*

4 Tap a dialog launcher (the small square-looking icon in the lower-right corner of a tool group) to open a dialog box with additional options related to that group of tools on the ribbon.

5 In the dialog box that opens, choose the options and settings you want.

6 Tap OK to save your changes.

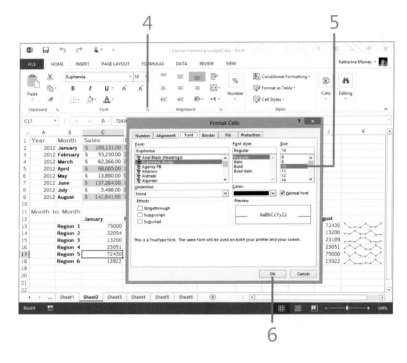

✓ **TIP** You can also easily hide and redisplay the ribbon at will, using the new Collapse The Ribbon tool (which alternately turns into the Pin The Ribbon tool when you tap a tab after the ribbon is hidden).

Displaying minibars

Minibars are a great new feature in Office 2013 that offer the options you need based on the object you've selected on the page. For example, if you tap an image, a minibar of image editing and formatting tools appears. If you choose a table, a different minibar displays options for editing, updating, and enhancing the table.

Display minibars

1 In your Office 2013 document, select some content such as a chart, cells, or a picture.

2 Tap the minibar icon near your selection.

3 If categories appear, tap the one that reflects the task you want to accomplish.

4 Tap your choice.

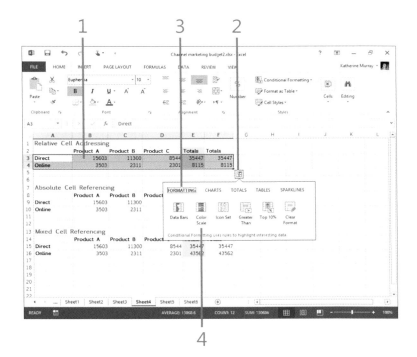

Modifying the ribbon display

Some people are fans of the ribbon, and some aren't. When the ribbon first appeared—in Office 2007—some folks were concerned that it took up too much space on the screen. Others felt it was clunky or confusing. In Office 2013, developers have tried to arrive at a happy medium. Now, you can use the Ribbon Display Options tool in the upper-right corner of the screen to set the ribbon to display the way you like it.

You can select three different ways to display the ribbon. First, you can auto-hide the ribbon so that it disappears while you're working on your file. If you want to display the ribbon so that you can select a tool, you simply tap the top of the application window. Choose Show Tabs if you want to hide most of the ribbon but leave the tabs showing. When you want to choose a tool, simply tap the tab you want to display, and the ribbon appears. The last option, Show Tabs And Commands, displays the full ribbon with tabs and tools at all times.

Change ribbon options

1 In the upper-right corner of your Office 2013 app, tap the Ribbon Display Options button.

2 On the menu that appears, tap Auto-Hide Ribbon.

   The ribbon, Quick Access Toolbar, and status bar all disappear; only your current file is visible on the screen.

(continued on next page)

Change ribbon options (continued)

3 To return to the ribbon display, in the upper-right corner, tap the ellipses (...).

4 On the menu that appears, tap Show Tabs to hide all but the tabs at the top of the ribbon.

5 To choose a tool, tap the tab you want to view, and the ribbon appears.

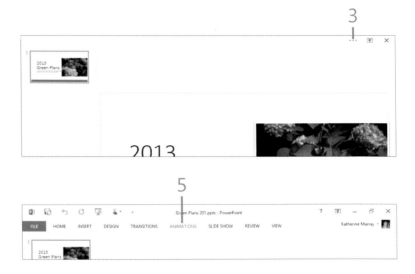

TIP If you've chosen any "hide" option, after you tap a tab and the ribbon appears, you can tap the Pin The Ribbon tool on the far right side of the ribbon to keep the ribbon visible without changing the Ribbon Display Options again.

Working with the Backstage view

Most of the tabs across the top of the ribbon display tools you can use to work in your Office files. The one exception is the File tab. When you tap the File tab, the Office 2013 app you're using displays Backstage view, which contains all the tools you need to work with the file itself, with your Microsoft account, and with your Office preferences. In Backstage view, you might open, save, password protect, or share your file, and you can also set program options, choose an Office background or theme, and connect different social media services to Office 2013.

Use the Backstage view

1 With an Office 2013 file open on the screen, tap the File tab.

By default, the Info tab is displayed.

2 Tap the relevant tab to carry out what you need to do with the file in the Backstage view.

3 Review and update file properties by clicking the Info tab.

4 Check the status of your Microsoft Account, connected services, and subscriptions by tapping Account.

5 Tap Close to exit the current file.

6 Tap the Options tab to display a dialog box in which you can set program options for whichever Office 2013 app you're using.

7 Return to the document display by tapping the back arrow.

> ✔ **TIP** You can change some of the properties shown in the right panel of the Info tab of the Backstage view. Tap either the Add A Tag or Add A Title link to display a text box in which you can then type the information you want to add.

> 🔍 **SEE ALSO** You learn how to personalize the look of Office 2013 by choosing an Office Background and Office Theme in Section 3, "Setting up your portable Office 2013."

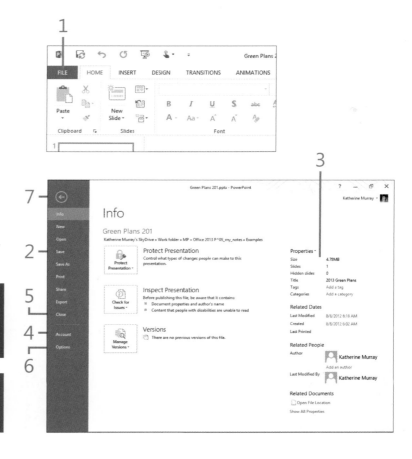

Touch techniques for everyday use

The touch responsiveness of Office 2013 was one of the focal points of development team, as was making sure that the elements on the screen were large enough targets for most people to touch successfully. This led to a number of changes in the user interface that you'll notice on your touch device:

- The new Touch Mode enhances the appearance of the Office 2013 screen—including the ribbon, dialog boxes, and other interface elements—by adding space around the tools and elements, creating larger touch targets.

- The Quick Access Toolbar is larger so that you can easily tap the commands on it.

- The height of the status bar has been increased.

- The mini-toolbars are expanded, offering more space.

- The handles on objects like pictures and charts are larger, making them easier to select and manipulate.

> ✓ **TIP** If you're mobile, how mobile are you? Will you be using one hand or two to hold your device? Do you need to use your thumbs to navigate on the screen, or will one hand be free to tap and swipe? When you use Office 2013 on a touch device, you can choose the type of On-screen Keyboard you want to use. You can display the keyboard on a Windows 8 touch device by tapping in a text box or by tapping the keyboard icon on the taskbar of the Windows 8 Desktop. After the keyboard displays, you can choose from among several different styles.

Using the new Touch Mode

One of the new features that make Office 2013 touch-friendly is Touch Mode. The development team at Microsoft recognized that fingers are not as slender as a mouse pointer, so they included this option, which increases the amount of space between tools and commands on the ribbon and in lists and dialog boxes. This makes it easy for you to tap what you want without inadvertently selecting the wrong item.

Turn on Touch Mode

1 On the Quick Access toolbar, tap the Touch/Mouse Mode button.

2 On the menu that appears, tap Touch.

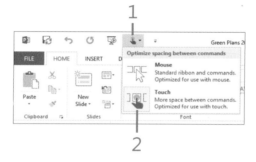

Single-tapping to select an item

What could be easier than a single tap? If you've ever tapped someone on the shoulder, pushed the button on an ATM, or dialed a cell phone, this action is as natural to you as breathing.

Single-tap the screen

1 Open the Office 2013 application that you want to use and locate the desired tool or command.

2 Tap the item once, quickly. Office 2013 responds to the touch by displaying the tab, selecting the tool, or completing the action the tap initiated.

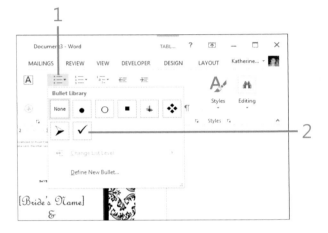

Tapping and holding an item

The tap-and-hold technique on touch devices is similar to right-clicking your mouse or trackpad. When you tap and hold your finger on an item, a square appears around the point of contact. Windows 8 interprets that gesture as you wanting to know more about the item you selected. When you release the touch, either a shortcut menu or the On-Screen Keyboard appears so that you can take further action.

Tap and hold

1 Press and hold your finger on the screen element that you want to select. This might include a word, a title, a tool, an object, or another screen element.

A square appears around the place where you touched.

2 Release your touch.

If you tapped text, the text is selected and the formatting mini-bar appears. If you tapped a tool with options, a shortcut menu appears, presenting additional options or commands from which you can choose.

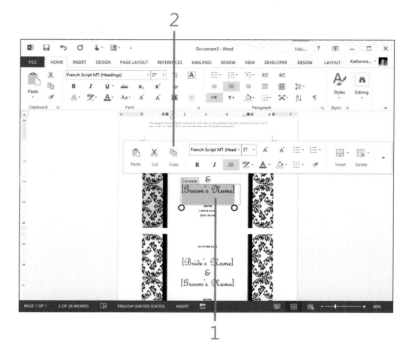

Swiping the screen to view content

Swiping the screen right and left is a similar gesture to the one you use to turn the page of a real, hold-in-your-hands book. You can display content off the right edge of your screen by swiping your display to the left, and you can display content off the left edge of your screen by swiping the display to the right.

Swipe the screen

1 Open a file that contains more data than can be displayed on the screen.

2 Swipe up from the bottom of the file window to scroll content into view.

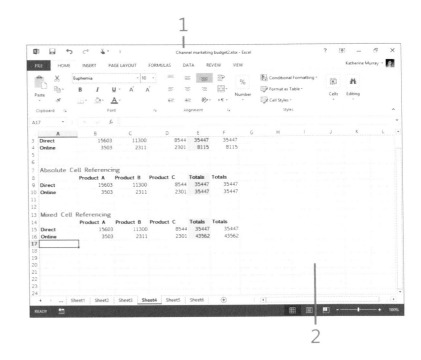

> ⚠ **CAUTION** If you're having trouble swiping up from the bottom of the screen, make sure you are starting your gesture inside the file window. If the taskbar appears, for instance, and you swipe up on that, you won't get the desired result you're looking for.

Spreading and pinching to zoom in and out

If you have ever used a smartphone, you're likely already familiar with this gesture. On your touch device, you can easily enlarge or reduce the size of the display by by spreading your thumb and finger apart on the display or pinching your thumb and finger together, respectively .

Enlarge and reduce the screen

1 To enlarge the content display of your file, position your fingers on the screen and spread them apart.

The screen enlarges the area you selected.

(continued on next page)

Enlarge and reduce the screen *(continued)*

2 To reduce the the size of content displayed on your screen, put two fingers on the screen and move them toward each other in a pinching motion. The screen reduces as you move your fingers on the screen.

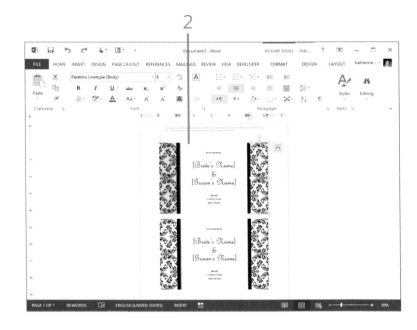

Choosing your On-Screen Keyboard

The On-Screen Keyboard will appear automatically whenever you tap in an area of the screen where you can add information. You can choose from a number of keyboards so that you can enter text or values in the manner that is most comfortable for you.

You'll find the keyboard selection tool in the lower-right corner of the keyboard. Tap it to display a pop-up bar of keyboard choices. You can choose from a standard keyboard, a split keyboard, a drawing palette, or an extended keyboard that includes the Windows key, Alt keys, and Ctrl keys.

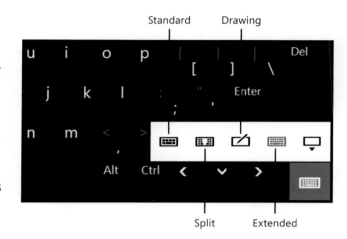

TIP   If the On-Screen Keyboard won't appear, tap the keyboard icon on the taskbar.

Setting up your portable Office 2013

3

Technically, Office 2013 is ready to use on your touch device as soon as you install the software (either from Office 365 or from your Office 2013 Professional installation discs). It's a good idea to take some time at the start to set up your preferences, make sure your accounts are connected, and that you understand how to do some of the basics, like opening, saving, closing, and printing files.

This section introduces you to the various tasks you'll need as you set up your preferences in Office 2013. You'll also find out how to get help, complete basic file tasks, and work with multiple apps open on the screen at once.

In this section:

- Managing your Microsoft Account
- Choosing an Office background
- Selecting an Office theme
- Adding services
- Moving among open apps
- Docking apps
- Adding Office apps from the Windows Store
- Opening, saving, and closing files
- Sharing files with others
- Previewing and printing files
- Getting help

Managing your Microsoft Account

Your Microsoft Account (formerly known as your Windows Live ID) keeps track of your program preferences, templates, program choices, and more as you work with Office 2013 on different computers and devices. Your Microsoft Account makes it possible to bring your Office experience with you when you travel because it keeps track of your settings and makes them available on whatever computer or device you use to log on next.

You'll enter your Microsoft Account information when you install Windows 8 for the first time, but you can change it and modify your account settings at any time by tapping the Settings charm and then displaying PC Settings. Next, tap Users and then tap the More Account Settings Online link to see other settings affiliated with your Microsoft Account. You can change your name, email address, personal information, and password. You can also add security information for the various devices you plan to use with your Microsoft Account. By choosing the categories on the left side of the Microsoft Account screen, you can also change the notifications you receive from Microsoft, change permissions and settings for various accounts linked to your Microsoft Account, and review and update your transactions and billing information.

If you want to instruct Windows 8 to stop using your Microsoft Account at log on, you can tap Switch To A Local Account on the Users screen of PC Settings. This changes your account settings so that they remain on your local computer only. But, be aware that by doing this, your preferences—like templates, color schemes, and more—won't be synced across the various devices you use. Additionally, your files won't be saved to SkyDrive by default.

In Office 2013, you can set up your Office 2013 account the way you want it on the Account tab of the Backstage view. First you can change the Microsoft Account you're using to sign in to Office 2013—and switch accounts if you like—and review your account settings and change your account photo. You can also find information about which Office 2013 installation you're using.

Change your account settings in Microsoft Office

1 With an Office 2013 app open on the screen, tap the File tab to display the Backstage view.

2 In the upper-right corner of the window, tap the drop-down arrow to the right of your user name.

A list appears, showing your name and account email address and giving you access to your account settings.

3 If you want to change your photo, tap Change Photo.

This takes you to your profile online, where you can tap Change Pictures and then choose a new photo from your computer. Click Save.

4 Back in the Backstage view in your Office 2013 app, if you want to add information about yourself, tap About Me.

5 If you tap Account settings, the Account tab of the Backstage view is displayed, showing your User Information, connected services, and the Office background you've selected.

6 If you want to switch the account you're using, tap Switch Account.

> ⚠️ **CAUTION** It is possible to close your Microsoft Account if you'd like, but be aware that this means your account information—including your ID and password and all your contacts—will be deleted, as well. You also won't be able to use that account to sign in to any other Microsoft services. If you decide you do want to close your Microsoft account, in the upper-right corner of the Office app that you're using, tap the profile down-arrow and tap About Me. Your online profile appears in your web browser. Tap your name in the upper-right corner and choose Account Settings. On the Overview tab of your Microsoft Account page, tap Close Account. Verify that you have the right account, enter your password, and then tap Next. Finally, choose Deactivate Your Hotmail Account and tap Close Account.

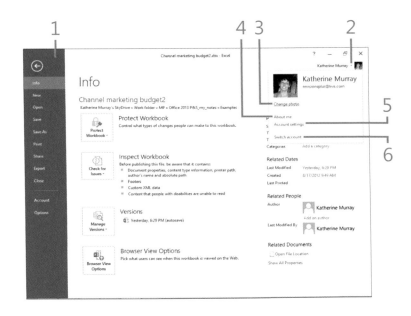

Checking your Office 2013 account

In addition to checking your Microsoft Account settings, you can also check your Office 2013 account settings on the Account tab in the Backstage view. In the Product Information area, tap Manage Account.

If you've subscribed to Office 2013 through Office 365 and downloaded and installed the software, the Office Desktop Apps screen appears, showing you the name of the computer on which your Office 2013 version is installed, which operating system version you're using, and the date on which you installed it.

You can use the links on this page to deactivate an Office 2013 subscription or to install the latest version of Office 2013.

Choosing an Office background

Now, you can personalize the look of your Office apps by adding a new Office background to the screen display. You can choose from a set of ready-made background designs that add just a touch of subtle design to your Office apps. You'll see when you try it that the choice isn't a big commitment and doesn't make a huge change; you'll simply see a new design in the upper-right corner of your app window.

Choose an Office background

1 Launch an Office app and tap the File tab to display the Backstage view.

2 Tap Account.

3 Tap the Office Background drop-down arrow. A list containing 14 background styles appears.

4 To preview a background, tap and hold the item that you want to view. The style appears in the upper-right corner. Tap the background that you want to keep.

Selecting an Office theme

Office 2013 also gives you the ability to choose different display schemes so that you can further personalize the way you work with your favorite apps. Office 2013 gives you three choices:

- White is the default theme, displaying the ribbon as white and tools and options in dark text on a white background.

- Light Gray colors the ribbon and the bordering areas using a light-gray hue, leaving the page area white.

- Dark Gray changes the color in the Backstage view to a deep gray and displays dark gray in the areas surrounding the ribbon and page areas. The ribbon is displayed in a light-gray color so that you can see tools clearly.

Choose an Office Theme

1 On the ribbon, tap the File tab to display Backstage view.

2 Tap the Account tab.

3 Tap the Office Theme drop-down arrow to display a list of themes.

4 Choose the theme that you want to apply.

5 Tap the back arrow to return to the Office app display and see how the theme has changed the screen appearance.

Adding services

You can easily connect Office 2013 to your favorite web services so that you can use files and connections you've already created in other online accounts. For example, if you've stored thousands of photos in Flickr, you can access those photos and use them in your Microsoft Word 2013 documents or your Microsoft PowerPoint 2013 presentations simply by adding

Flickr to your Connected Services. That saves you the trouble of manually downloading the photos to your computer and then adding them to your Word document. You can also add other popular social media accounts like Facebook, LinkedIn, Twitter, and YouTube so that you can share contacts, documents, videos, and more.

Add services

1 Open the Office app that you want to use and tap the File tab to display the Backstage view.

2 Tap the Account tab.

3 In the Connected Services area, review the services.

(continued on next page)

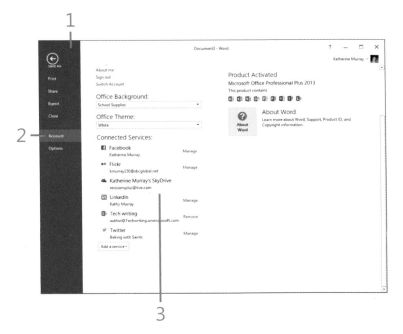

Add services *(continued)*

4 Tap Add A Service.

A menu appears on which you can choose to add a service with which you can incorporate Images & Videos or by which you can save your documents in the cloud.

5 Tap the option that you want. A list of the available services displays beside it.

6 Choose the service that you want to add.

Office 2013 adds the service and makes it available on the Account tab in the Backstage view.

TIP Are you wondering how Office 2013 knows about the services to which you've subscribed? If you connected the People app or the Photos app in Windows 8, Office 2013 is also able to "see" those connections as part of the app sharing features in Windows 8. This ultimately saves you time and trouble and gives you easy access to files you have stored in various places online. You can control the permissions you grant these other sites so you're only sharing the amount and type of information you want to share.

Changing services

You can later remove or manage the services you added to Office 2013. Tap the service you want to change and notice the link provided on the right. Some services give you the choice of removing the service; other services present the option to manage it.

Removing a service that displays Remove as a link is a simple matter: just tap Remove. Office then asks you to confirm the deletion. When you tap Yes, the service is removed.

If the service you want to change displays the Manage link, when you tap it, your Microsoft Account page appears, showing you the permissions you have granted to that service. You can remove some of the services if you like by clearing the corresponding check box. (For example, if you want to stop sharing with LinkedIn, you can tap to clear the Share To LinkedIn check box.) Then, tap Save to keep your changes. If you want to remove the service completely, scroll down to the bottom of the list and tap Remove This Connection Completely.

Moving among open apps

When you're using Office 2013 with Windows 8, you can easily work with several apps open at any one time. You can cycle through them by dragging them in from the left side of the screen or using the thumbnails panel to tap the app you want to use. The great thing about the way Windows manages memory is that only the active program—the one you're currently viewing on your screen—is actually using power; the rest of the apps are in suspended mode until you select them. But, the apps wake up so quickly that you'll never know they weren't fully at the ready, waiting for you to use them.

Move among open apps

1 On the Windows 8 Start screen, open several Office apps with which you want to work by tapping the appropriate app tiles.

(continued on next page)

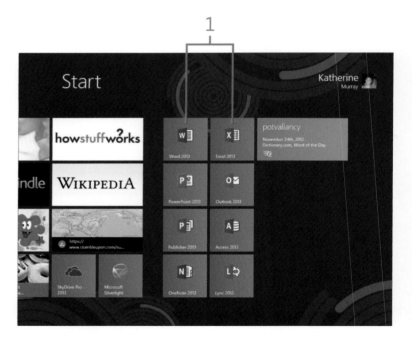

Move among open apps *(continued)*

2 Swipe in from the left side of the screen. The next open app appears.

3 Alternatively, swipe in slightly from the left and swipe up toward the upper-left corner of the screen. The thumbnails panel appears, showing thumbnails of all your open apps.

4 Your open Office app will appear in the Desktop tile. Tap it to display your Office app.

2

> **TIP** When you are flicking apps in from the left side of the screen, you'll discover that Windows 8 shows only one Desktop app in the rotation. So if you want to work with a Desktop app that isn't appearing when you flick in from the left, go to the Desktop and tap the desired app in the taskbar.

Docking apps

Windows 8 makes it easy for you to dock open apps on the screen so that you can do two things at once if you choose. For example, you might be working with a shared document in Word 2013 while you're instant messaging one of your coauthors in the Messaging app, which is docked along the right side of your screen. That way you can easily review the document and ask your coauthor questions while you work. When you dock and app in place, you can still cycle through other open apps by dragging them in from the left edge of your screen.

Dock apps

1 Display the first app that you want to appear on your screen.

2 Swipe from the left to display the app you want to dock on the screen.

3 Swipe the screen toward the top of the window. The app is docked along the side of the screen. You can scroll through apps as normal in the other app area.

4 When you're ready to remove the docked app, tap the divider and drag it to the right.

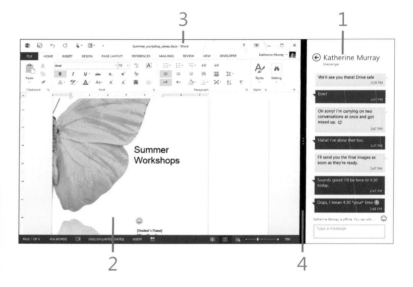

⚠ **CAUTION** If you are having trouble getting apps to dock on your monitor, check your screen resolution. Microsoft announced that you need a widescreen monitor to use docking successfully, and although some touch device screens still qualify, you need to have your screen resolution set to 1366×768 before your docking will "stick."

✓ **TIP** If you find yourself working with the Windows 8 desktop more than the Windows 8 Start screen, you might want to add your Office 2013 apps to the taskbar so that you can launch them easily from the desktop. Start by displaying the Windows 8 Start screen. Scroll to the far right and display the Office app tiles. Swipe downward on the app that you want to add to the taskbar. Tap Pin To Taskbar. The app will now be available on the taskbar when you display the Windows 8 Desktop.

Adding Office apps from the Windows Store

On the Insert tab of Word 2013, Microsoft Excel 2013, Microsoft Outlook 2013, and PowerPoint 2013, in the Apps group, you'll find the Apps For Office tool. The first time you tap this tool, you'll notice that the list is empty. But when you tap See All, Office displays a gallery of featured apps and provides a link with which you can go online to view other apps that are available.

Add an Office app

1 In Word, Excel, Outlook, or PowerPoint, on the ribbon, tap the Insert tab.

2 In the Apps group, tap the drop-down arrow on the Apps For Office button.

3 On the menu that appears, tap See All. The Apps For Office dialog box opens, displaying two tabs: My Apps and Featured Apps. Tap Featured Apps to see a gallery of available apps.

4 Tap the that app you want to add.

The app appears in the task pane on the right side of your application window. A small exclamation point appears in the upper-left corner of the task pane.

(continued on next page)

Add an Office app *(continued)*

5 Tap the exclamation point.

The Office app lets you know that the app is from the Windows Store and will have access to the contents of your document. If that's okay with you, tap Start. You can also tap See Details to get more information. If you decide not to install the app, tap the close button.

6 After you tap Start, the app installs and opens in the Task pane. To begin using the app, enter your information as prompted.

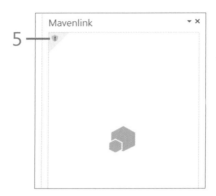

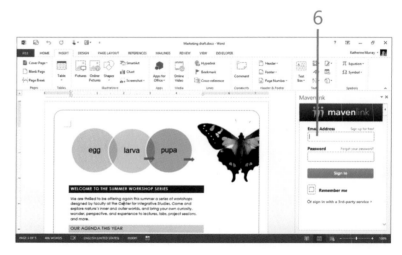

Opening files

Many of the basic tasks you'll perform in your Office programs will be similar from app to app. For example, the procedure for opening a file in Word, Excel, PowerPoint, and Microsoft Publisher is identical from app to app. You can easily open the file by using the new Start screen that appears when you launch the Office app you want to work with. If you're already working with an Office app and want to begin a new file, you can tap the File tab and choose New to start the process.

Open a new file

1 Launch the Office app that you want to use.

2 On the app Start screen, tap Blank Workbook (or Document or Presentation) to open a new, blank file.

3 Alternatively, tap the Search field and enter a type of template for which to search.

4 Scroll through the results list.

5 Tap the template that you want to use as the basis for the new file.

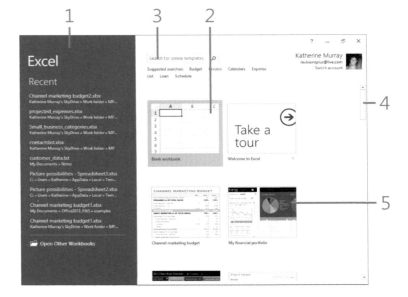

✓ **TIP** What is a template? A template is a ready-made file that can comprise one or several pages and include images, placeholder text, and special layouts. When you start a new file based on a template, the format and layout are already done for you, and you can simply add your own text and images to complete the file.

Open an existing file

1 Launch an Office app. The Start screen for that app appears.

2 In the Recent list, tap the file that you want to open.

3 If you don't see the file you want in the list, choose Open Other Documents (or Workbooks, Presentations, or Publications).

4 In the center column, choose the location where the file is stored.

5 Tap the folder in which the file is stored.

6 Alternatively, tap Browse.

(continued on next page)

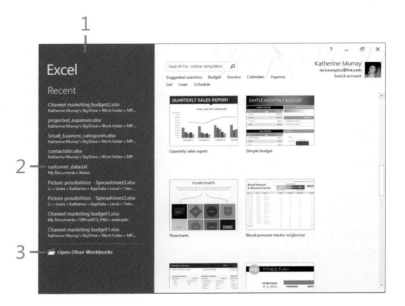

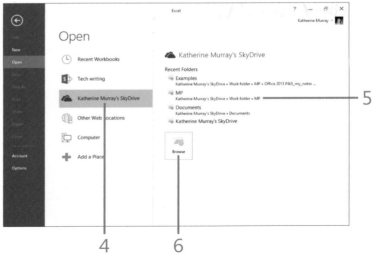

Open an existing file *(continued)*

7 In the Open dialog box, navigate to and tap the file you want to open.

8 Tap Open.

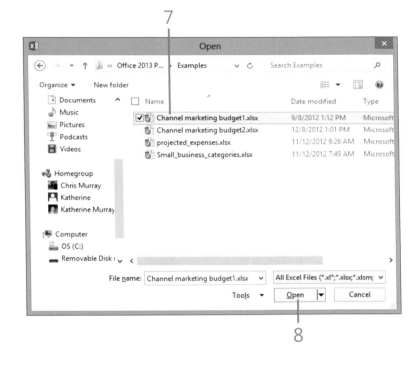

TIP A jump list makes it easy for you to open a file that you've recently used or move quickly to a file that is still open in Office 2013. When you tap and hold (and then release) the Office 2013 icon (after the square appears) in your Windows 8 taskbar, a thumbnail or a list of open or recently used files appears. You can move directly to the file you want by tapping it.

Tagging files

You can add tags to your files to help categorize them and make them easier to find in searches. You might add the name of your project as a tag or use the name of the team leader so that when you search for that word or phrase, all files tagged with it appear in your search results. To add a tag to a file, tap the File tab to display the Backstage view. In the panel on the right side of the Info tab, tap the Add A Tag prompt. In the text box that appears, type one or more tags, separating multiple tags with commas. After you're done entering tags, tap outside the text box to save them with your file.

Saving files

By default, Office 2013 saves your files to the cloud, which is great if you're an avid SkyDrive or SharePoint user, but it might leave you a bit cold if you prefer to keep all your files as close as possible. Luckily, the setting is easy to change, and you can choose to save your files—by default or otherwise—wherever you choose. Saving to the cloud is easier than you might think, and it does give you the extra benefit of being able to share your files easily and work on them no matter what device you are using or where you happen to be.

Save to the cloud

1 Finish working on your Office file and then tap the File tab to display the Backstage view.

2 Tap the Save As tab.

3 In the center column, choose the SkyDrive location.

4 Tap the folder in which you want to save the file.

5 Alternatively, tap Browse and then, in the Save As dialog box, navigate to the SkyDrive folder you want.

6 Tap Save to save the file.

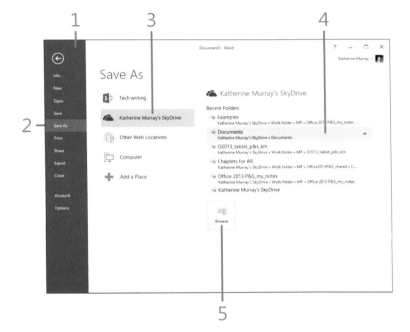

Add a new place to save

1 In the Backstage view, tap the Save As tab.

2 In the center column, choose Add A Place. Office 2013 displays two cloud locations that you can choose for the new place.

3 If you are an Office 2013 subscriber and use SharePoint Online to store, organize, and share your files, choose Office 365 SharePoint.

4 If you prefer to use your SkyDrive account, select SkyDrive. You are prompted to sign in to the account, and Office adds it to the locations column in the center of the Save As screen.

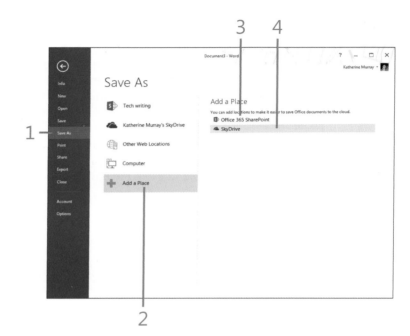

Save files to your touch device

1 Complete the file that you want to save and then tap the File tab to display the Backstage view.

2 Tap the Save As tab.

3 In the center column, tap Computer.

4 Choose the folder to which you want to save the file.

5 Alternatively, tap Browse and then, in the Save As dialog box, navigate to the folder where you want to save the file and tap Save.

6 Type a name for the file.

7 Tap Save.

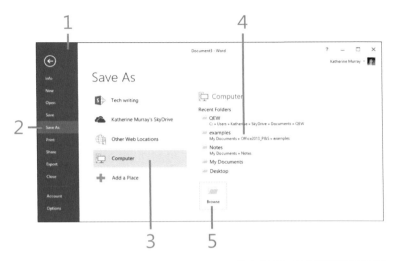

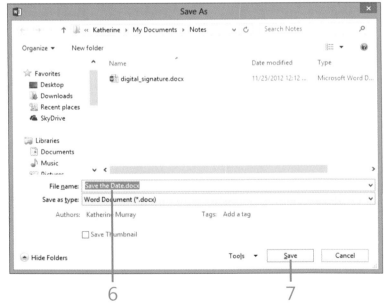

Closing files

Closing a file is a super-simple task. And if you forget to save it first, don't worry: Office 2013 will prompt you to save it before it closes so that you won't lose any work.

Close a file

1 With the file open on the screen that you want to close, on the ribbon, tap the File tab to display the Backstage view.

2 Tap Close.

> → **TRY THIS** There are two additional simple ways to close a file. One way is to tap the close button (the X) in the upper-right corner of the app window. The other way is to use the Windows 8 method and swipe down from the top of the screen, dragging the app all the way to the bottom of the screen. The app window becomes smaller and then finally disappears, which lets you know that the file is closed.

Inspecting your files

Office 2013 includes a tool called the Document Inspector that helps you to ensure that your files are ready to share with others. Tap the Info tab in the Backstage view, tap Check For Issues, and then tap Inspect Document.

The Document Inspect dialog box appears, listing all the items the tool will search for during the inspection. You can clear the corresponding check box for any items you don't want to search for and then tap Inspect. The Inspector looks for the items you selected and lets you know if anything worrisome is found. You can then make changes and run the Document Inspector again to make sure the file is ready to share.

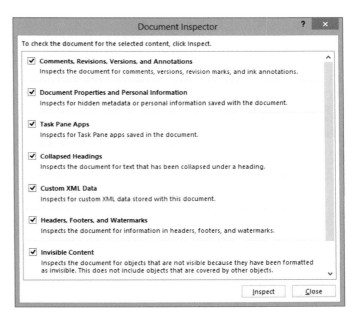

Sharing files with others

Not long ago, when you wanted to share a file, you had to put it on a disk and physically hand it to another person. Today, thankfully, sharing a file can be literally as easy as saving it.

Office 2013 makes it possible for you to invite others to access your file, and then you can choose the way you want to share it easily, with no fuss and no bother.

Invite others to share your file

1 In your Office 2013 app, on the ribbon, tap the File tab to display the Backstage view.

2 Tap the Share tab.

3 Choose Invite People.

If you haven't saved the file to the cloud previously, the Office app will prompt you to do that.

4 Choose Save to Cloud.

The Save As dialog box opens, in which you can choose the location in the cloud where you want to save the file.

(continued on next page)

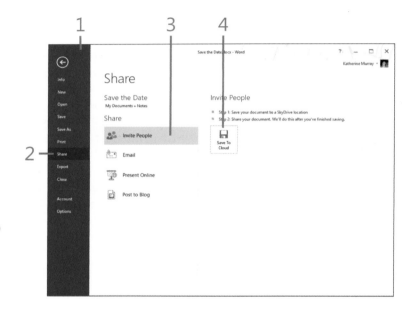

TIP   You can tap the Address Book icon to the right of the email address line to choose recipients from your contacts list.

Invite others to share your file (continued)

5 Tap the place where you want to save the file.

6 Tap the folder where you want to file to be stored. When the Save As dialog box appears, tap Save.

Office saves your file to the cloud and displays the Share tab with additional options by which you share the file with others.

7 Enter the email addresses of the people with whom you want to share the file.

8 Choose the permission level that you want to assign to the invited people. You can choose between Can Edit and Can View.

9 Type a message to go along with your invitation.

10 Tap Share.

The Office 2013 app displays a message that the file is being sent and then displays the recipient's information at the bottom of the screen so that you can easily see who has access to the shared file.

5   6

7

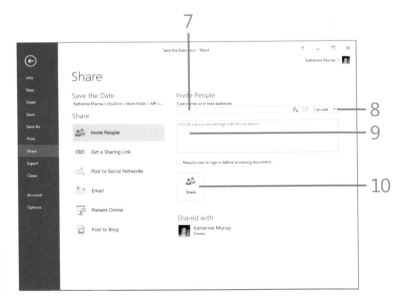

8

9

10

TIP If you want to ensure that those who are viewing or editing your file log on before they can access the file you've shared, select the Require User To Sign-In Before Accessing Document check box.

Send your file via email

1 On the ribbon, tap the File tab to display the Backstage view and then tap the Share tab.

2 Tap Email. Email options appear in the right panel.

3 Tap the way you want to save the file.

If you send the file as an attachment, the Office file is attached to the email message. If you send a link (which becomes available only if you've previously saved the file to the cloud), you can copy the link to the file and insert it in the body of the email message. Send As PDF and Send As XPS save the file to PDF or XPS format and attach the file to the email message. Send As Internet Fax uses a fax service to send the message as a fax.

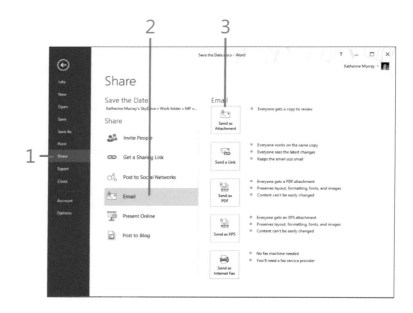

TIP A fax service is a third-party vendor that will likely charge you a fee for faxing the file. After you choose Send As Internet Fax, a message box appears, informing you know that Office will open a browser page on which you can locate a provider to use to send the fax.

Previewing and printing files

No matter which Office app you are using, previewing and then printing your file is straightforward. You choose Print from the Backstage view, and you can set all your print options and preview what your document will look when printed, all in the same screen.

Preview and print files

1 On the ribbon, tap the File tab to display the Backstage view and then tap the Print tab.

2 Choose the printer that you want to use.

3 Tap to select the pages that you want to print.

4 Choose one or two-sided printing.

5 Select the paper size.

6 Choose portrait or landscape orientation for your printed file.

7 Tap to preview other pages.

8 Scroll through the previewed document.

9 Enter the number of copies that you want to print.

10 Tap Print to print the file.

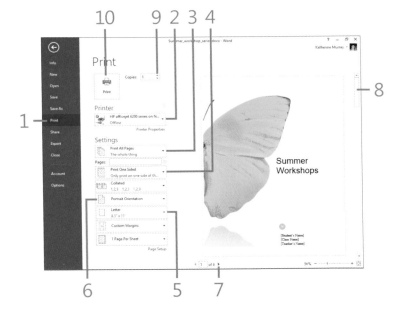

TIP If you choose two-sided printing, Word and Publisher will display the previewed file as it would appear if images appear on both sides of the page. This helps you see whether text or pictures will show through on the other side of the page so that you can make adjustments before you print. Pretty neat, eh?

Export your files

Office 2013 now includes an easy-to-use export tool that you can use to share your Office 2013 data with non-Office applications. You'll find the Export tab in the Backstage view. On this tab, you can create a PDF/XPS file with the exported data or change the file type and export the information in the file format you need to import it into your other program.

Simply choose the format you want to use for the exported file and tap the Create button to begin the process. In the Publish As dialog box, choose the folder where you want to store the exported file and enter a file name if necessary. Tap Publish to finish the task.

Translating file content

Today it's not unusual to be working with teammates on different continents, and while that brings the great benefit of enabling groups of people to combine their strengths to work together effectively, it can also pose a challenge: how will we understand each other?

Office 2013 includes translation tool that help you translate on the fly, whether you're receiving files that need to be translated or translating files you plan to send to others. You'll find the translation tools in the Language group on the Review tab. You can use the Language tool to set your language preferences and choose the language you want to use in your document, Help screens, and ScreenTips. Use Translate to convert selected text or the entire document.

You can also turn on the Mini Translator, which appears like a minibar near the content you select, offering a translation in the language you have selected and giving you the option to copy the translation, hear it read aloud, or look up additional information.

If you choose to translate the entire file, Office 2013 will display a message box, asking your permission to send the file over the Internet to be translated by Microsoft Translator. Tap Send if that's okay with you; tap Don't Send if you decide not to translate the page after all. If you tap Send, Office 2013 displays a new window with the contents of the translated file. If you choose Don't Send, you are returned to your document.

Getting help

Help in Office 2013 is only a tap away, no matter which app you are using or what you might be doing with it. You'll find the Help tool in the upper right corner of your application window. When you tap the Help tool, Office displays a Help window that you can use to search for specific help, choose a popular help category, or browse through articles and training options related to the main features and functions in your app.

Get help

1 In your current Office 2013 apps, in the upper-right corner of the screen, tap the Help button (the question mark).

2 Tap to enter a word or phrase you want to search.

3 Tap the Search button (the magnifying-glass icon).

(continued on next page)

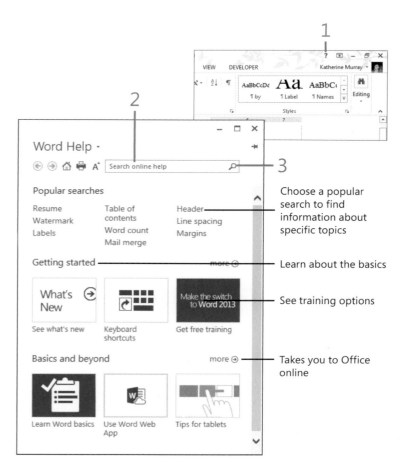

Get help *(continued)*

4 Scroll through the list that appears if necessary.

5 Tap the title of the article that you'd like to view.

(continued on next page)

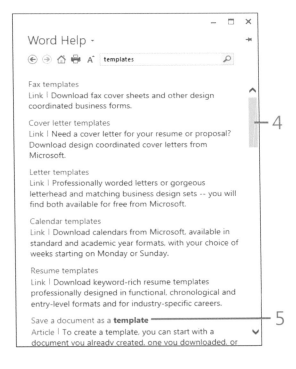

TRY THIS You can choose whether you want to search for help online or access the Office help files installed on your computer. Tap the drop-down to the right of the Help title at the top of the Help dialog box. By default, the help displayed is from Office.com. If you want to change that, tap Help from Your Computer, and the Office program searches the help information on your computer and displays results according to the search text you entered.

Get help *(continued)*

6 Read through the article.

7 Tap Print if you want to print the article for future reference.

8 Tap the Close button to exit Help.

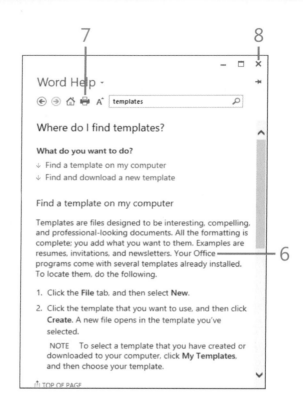

Setting Office 2013 preferences

You can display the program options for a specific Office application by tapping File and then tapping the Options tab in the Backstage view. The Options dialog box appears with choices related to the application you're using. Chances are good that the default options already set in Office 2013 will work well for most files you create. The tabs available in the Options dialog box will vary slightly from app to app. Here's a quick rundown of the types of preferences you can set:

- On the General tab, verify that all of the items are selected in the User Interface Options to ensure that you get the maximum amount of onscreen help at any given time. These options control whether you can see the previews of choices before you choose them.

- The Display tab contains selections about the items that appear on the screen while you work. These might include formatting marks and page display options, such as whether white space appears between pages in Print Layout view. On the Display tab you can also choose printing options, such as whether you want to print drawings, background colors and images, document properties, hidden text, and more.

- On the Proofing tab, you can choose the way you want Office 2013 to correct spelling and grammatical errors.

- On the Save tab, you select the defaults for the files you create. You can also choose the way you want Office 2013 to handle AutoRecover options and where you want to save files by default. If you are using the subscription version of Office 2013, your files are set

to save automatically to your SkyDrive account. If you want to change this, you'll change the setting on the Save tab of the Options dialog box.

- On the Language tab, you can choose the languages that you want to use with Office 2013.

- The Advanced tab presents options for a variety of tasks related to the specific app. You might see editing options; cut, copy, and paste choices; image size and quality choices; options for charts; and document display, printing, and saving choices.

- On the Customize Ribbon tab, you can add, hide, or reconfigure the tabs on the Office 2013 ribbon. Note that when you change the ribbon, it is altered only for the app you're using when you make the changes. You can also reset and even export or import your ribbon changes.

- The Quick Access Toolbar tab makes it easy for you to add tools to the Quick Access Toolbar, which appears in the upper-left corner of your app window.

- The Add-ins tab shows you all the add-ins that have already been added to your Office 2013 application You can also manage additional add-ins here.

- The Trust Center tab gives you information about your privacy and security as you use Office 2013. You can make additional choices to set Trusted Publishers, Trusted Locations, and more.

Staying in touch with Outlook 2013

4

If you love having access to email on your smartphone, the chances are good that you're already familiar with the techniques you need to tap your way through messages, send responses, work with contacts, and more. Now, thanks to Microsoft Outlook 2013, you can put all those touch techniques to good use on your touch device.

Your most common email task is probably receiving and sending email messages, but you'll also need to work with your calendar to set appointments, add and organize contacts so you can reach the people you want to reach, and perhaps add tasks, notes, and more to help you stay on track. This section focuses on Outlook 2013 and provides a broad set of features for managing your contacts, calendar, and tasks. The most common thing people use Outlook for, however, is sending and receiving email. You can use Outlook to send relatively simple messages in plain text, or you can use it to send highly formatted messages containing different font types and formatting, images, and other elements.

After you set up at least one email account in Outlook, you can start sending and receiving email and configure it to work in a way that reflects your preferences.

In this section:

- A first look at Outlook 2013
- Getting started with Outlook 2013
- Adding mail accounts
- Reading and responding to messages
- Adding contacts
- Editing contacts
- Adding contact groups
- Managing your mail by using Quick Steps
- Flagging mail for follow-up
- Categorizing your mail
- Moving messages to folders

A first look at Outlook 2013

In many ways, Outlook 2013 resembles your other Office apps, thanks to the presence of the ribbon and the new modeless design. However, Outlook's interface is also very different from other apps, offering the tools and views you need to receive and send mail, add and manage contacts, set appointments and work with your calendar, and create and assign tasks. Here's a quick look at the primary tools you'll be using in Outlook 2013.

Mail

The Mail window is where you'll find your Inbox and other email folders as well as the commands you commonly use to send and receive email, organize email, view and work with the Address Book, and work with email in other ways.

Calendar

The Calendar window shows you what you have planned for the day, week, or month. You can easily create new meetings and events in the Calendar folder, view other peoples' calendars, share your calendar, and organize your upcoming events.

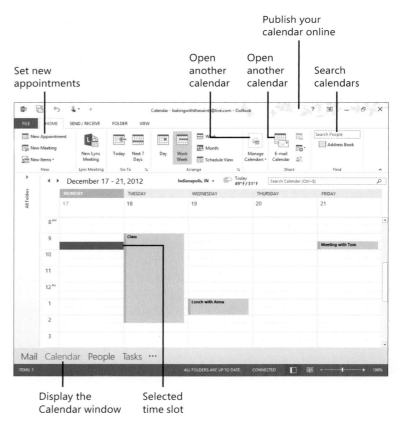

Publish your calendar online

Set new appointments

Open another calendar

Open another calendar

Search calendars

Display the Calendar window

Selected time slot

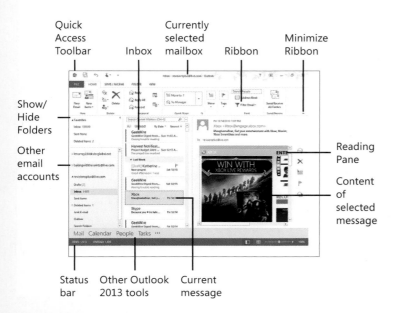

Quick Access Toolbar

Inbox

Currently selected mailbox

Ribbon

Minimize Ribbon

Show/ Hide Folders

Other email accounts

Reading Pane

Content of selected message

Status bar

Other Outlook 2013 tools

Current message

People

The People window works much like the Contacts window in previous versions of Outlook 2013. You use the People window to view and manage your contacts.

Tasks

If you like to work with to-do lists and keep track of what you need to accomplish, you'll like working with the Tasks window. And, if you are using Exchange Server as the back-end for Outlook, you can also create and assign tasks to others.

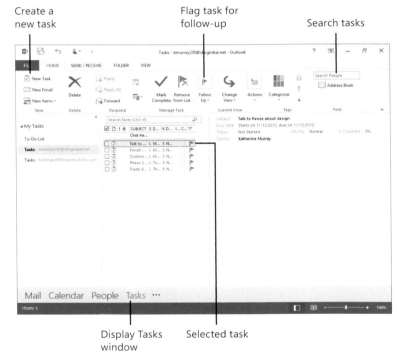

Choose a contact list

Contacts in the current list

Change current view

Edit contact information

Selected contact

Send email to contact

Create a new task

Flag task for follow-up

Search tasks

Display Tasks window

Selected task

Notes and more

In addition to the main tools provided by Outlook 2013—Mail, Calendar, People, and Tasks—you'll find additional tools by tapping the ellipses (...) to the right of Tasks in the Outlook window. When you tap this, an option list appears, offering you four additional choices: Navigation Options, Notes, Folders, and Shortcuts.

- Choose Navigation Options to select the items that you want to display in the Outlook navigation bar. You can display or hide Mail, Calendar, People, Tasks, Notes, Folders, and Shortcuts. You can also reorder the items so that they appear in the order that best fits the way you like to work.

- Tap Notes if you want to display the Notes window and open a small note on the screen so that you can capture a thought, web address, or other piece of information.

- Choose Folders to display the Folder pane.

- Tap Shortcuts to display in the panel on the left side of the Outlook window the shortcuts you are currently using with Outlook 2013.

Getting started with Outlook 2013

You'll find an Outlook 2013 app tile on your Windows 8 Start screen. The first time Outlook starts, the program prompts you to set up an email account. A wizard guides you through the steps to connect Outlook to your mailbox so that you can begin receiving and sending email messages.

Start Outlook

1 On the Windows 8 Start screen, tap the Outlook 2013 app tile.

The first time you start Outlook, the Welcome To Outlook 2013 screen appears, giving you the opportunity to set up your email address. When you start Outlook 2013 subsequently, the Mail window will appears automatically.

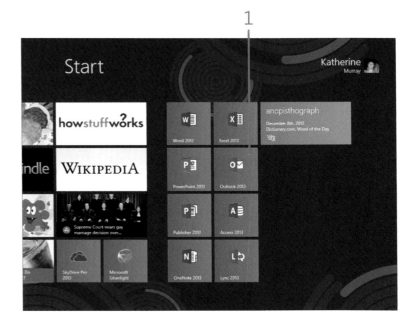

Set up an email account

1 If this is the first time you're starting Outlook, a wizard will open and ask you whether you want to set up an email account. Tap Yes.

2 Tap Next.

3 On the Add Account page of the wizard, type your name.

4 Type your email address.

5 Type and confirm your password.

6 Tap Next. Outlook sets up the account and displays a final screen to inform you that the task is completed. Tap Finish to open your new email account in Outlook.

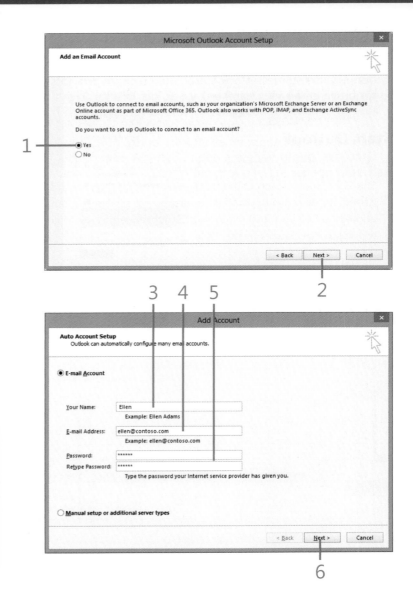

> ⚠ **CAUTION** Unfortunately, setting up email isn't always this easy. For example, if you're adding a Google mail account, you might get an error message stating that an encrypted connection is not available and prompting you to tap Next to try again. If you get this error, follow the steps outlined on the webpage *http://email.about.com/od/outlooktips/qt/et_get_gmail.htm* to set up Google mail with your Outlook account. Similarly, you might have trouble setting up Yahoo!, AT&T, Verizon, or Time Warner accounts. Search those sites for further information on how to set up your email account manually in Outlook.

Adding more mail accounts

After you've created your primary account, you can easily add additional accounts so that you can access your email in one place. On the ribbon, tap the File tab to display the Backstage view to start the process. If you don't see the File tab, click the ellipsis button at the top of the Outlook 2013 window.

In the Account Information screen (click the Info tab), tap Add Account. This opens the Add Account dialog box, in which you can enter your name, email address, and password as you set up the new account.

Tap Add Account

Reading and responding to messages

Probably the first thing you'll want to do with Outlook 2013 is check and respond to your mail. Email has become so much a part of our lives that we are used to having access to it no matter where we are. Outlook makes it very easy for you to read your messages quickly and respond to them when you choose.

Read and reply to a message

1 Tap the Inbox folder for the email account that you want to view.

2 In the Inbox, tap a message header.

3 Preview the message in the Reading pane.

4 Tap Reply.

(continued on next page)

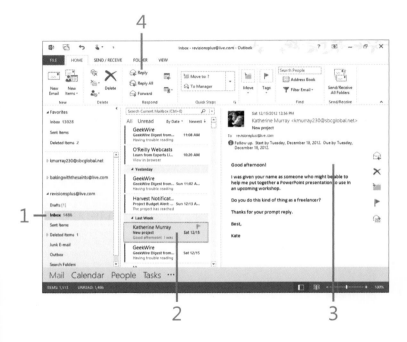

> **✓ TIP** When you are working with Outlook 2013 in touch mode, a set of quick-touch tools appears along the right side of the window display. You can tap the tools to carry out common Outlook tasks quickly. Choose from Respond, Delete, Move, Follow Up, and Mark As Unread.

> **✓ TIP** If your ribbon doesn't appear unless you tap the ellipsis button at the top of the window, your ribbon is set to auto-hide. You can change the ribbon setting by tapping a ribbon tab and tapping the Pin The Ribbon tool on the far right side of the ribbon to keep it displayed while you work with Outlook.

Read and reply to a message *(continued)*

5 Type your reply.

6 Tap Send to deliver the message.

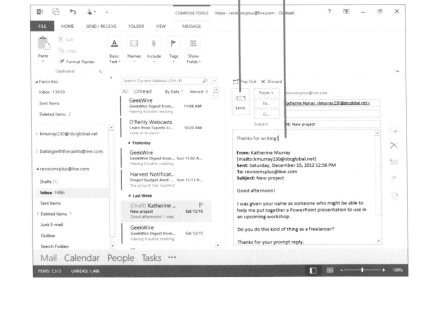

TIP If you prefer to open an email message and work with it in its own window, in the Reading pane, at the top of the message, you can tap Pop Out. If you don't see this, just double-tap the message header in the Inbox pane The message opens on the screen and you can tap Reply and respond to it as you like. When you're finished writing your response, tap Send to deliver the message.

Tweaking the Outlook window

You can easily change the way the Outlook 2013 window looks so that the tools are arranged just the way you like them. Here are some of the ways in which you can customize the look of Outlook (note that all of these are done on the View tab on the ribbon):

- Collapse and redisplay the Folder pane by tapping the arrow located on the right side of the pane.

- To change the way messages are displayed, in the Current View group, tap Change View.

- To change the elements displayed in the Mail view, in the Layout group, tap Folder Pane, Reading Pane, or To-Do Bar.

- To change how much you see of each message before you open it, in the Arrangement group, tap Message Preview.

- To hide the ribbon, tap Collapse the Ribbon. To redisplay the ribbon, tap a tab name, and to keep the ribbon displayed, tap Pin The Ribbon.

- To change the way the ribbon is displayed as you work, in the upper-right corner of the Outlook window, tap the Ribbon Display Options button.

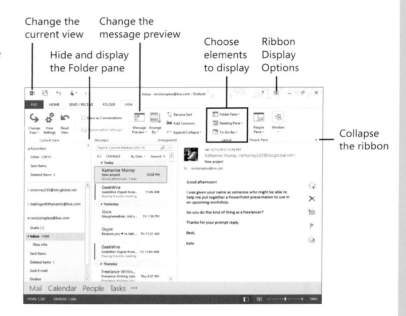

Change the current view

Change the message preview

Hide and display the Folder pane

Choose elements to display

Ribbon Display Options

Collapse the ribbon

Adding contacts

Gathering contact information for friends, colleagues, and family members used to be a pretty slow event. You might write down a phone number, ask for a business card, or copy an email address from something someone shared. Today, you can easily add whole lists of contacts from your social media accounts such as Facebook and LinkedIn with just a few clicks. When you want to add a new contact manually, Outlook 2013 makes that easy for you, as well.

Add a new contact manually

1 In the Outlook window, tap People.

2 On the Home tab, in the New group, tap New Contact.

(continued on next page)

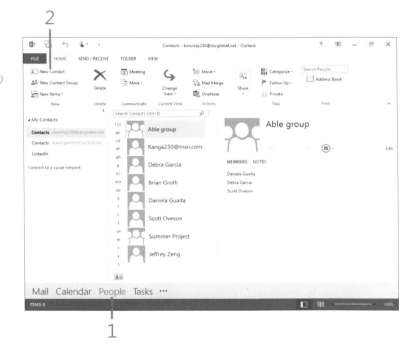

Add a new contact manually (continued)

3 Type the contact's full name.

4 Type the contact's company name.

5 Type the contact's job title.

6 Type the contact's email address.

7 Type the contact's website address.

8 Add phone numbers as needed.

9 Add a physical address.

10 On the ribbon, tap Save & Close.

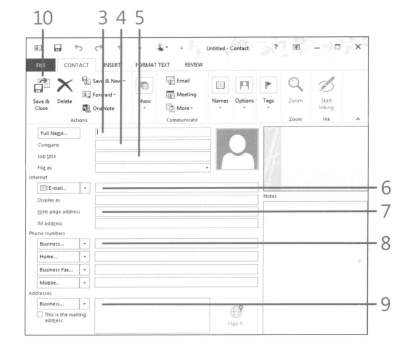

Editing contacts

The nature of working with people is that things change. We're forever adjusting something—getting a new email address, changing a mobile phone number, moving to a different job or different position, or updating our profile pictures. You can edit the contacts you've added to Outlook 2013 so that you're always working with the most accurate information available.

Edit a contact

1 Tap the contact that you want to edit.

2 Tap Edit.

(continued on next page)

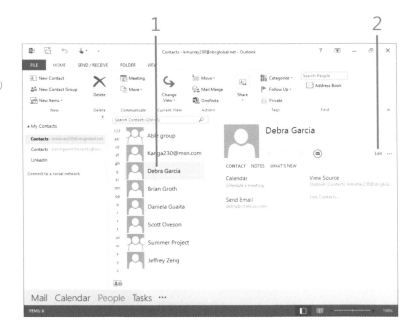

Edit a contact *(continued)*

3 Edit the contact name as needed.

4 Edit other existing fields as needed.

5 Tap to add a new email address.

6 Tap to add phone or IM information.

7 Tap Save to keep the changes.

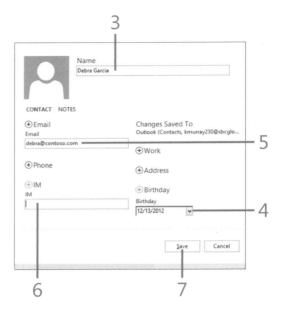

Adding contact groups

Today, we often work in teams—both permanent teams and teams that come together for a specific period of time. You can easily create contact groups in Outlook 2013 that include the email addresses of contacts related to a specific project or company. Then, when you want to send a message to the group, you can choose the group as you would a regular contact, and the group name is added to the To line of your email address.

Add a contact group

1 On the Home tab, in the New group, tap New Contact Group.

2 Type a name for the group.

3 Tap Add Members.

4 Choose From Outlook Contacts or From Address Book.

(continued on next page)

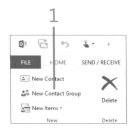

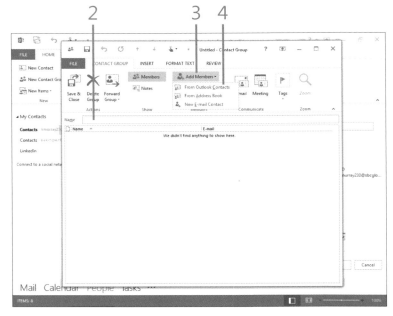

Add a contact group (continued)

5 In the Select Members dialog box, choose existing contacts by tapping the names of those whom you want to include.

6 In the lower-left corner of the dialog box, tap Members.

7 Tap OK.

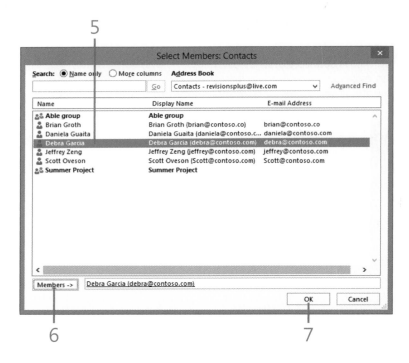

Add new members to the group

1 Display the contact group by locating the group name in your People list and double-tapping it.

2 In the Members group, tap Add Members.

3 On the menu that appears, tap New Email Contact.

4 In the Add New Member dialog box, type the contact's name.

5 Type the contact's email address.

6 Tap OK.

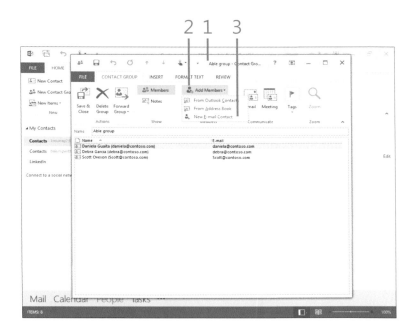

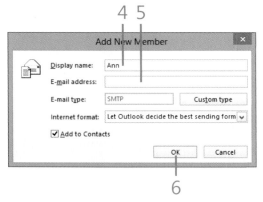

> ⚠️ **CAUTION** When you tap Remove Member from the Members group on the Contact Group tab, be forewarned: Outlook doesn't ask you to confirm the deletion; the contact is removed immediately. So before you get carried away deleting folks from your group be sure to double-check the ones you plan to delete. (If you do delete someone accidentally, don't worry—you can use Add Members to return them to the group.)

Working with people views

In the Current View group on the Home tab, Outlook 2013 gives you a number of ways to view your contact information. By default, contacts are shown in People view, showing each individual's profile picture (if your contacts are connected to your social media account) and listing their names.

You can also choose to display your contacts in Business Card view, which shows each person's name, picture, title, and email address, as well as the social media account on which the contact is listed. Choosing the Card view displays all contacts with information only and no pictures. Selecting the Phone view lists your contact names with the phone numbers you've entered as part of the contact entries.

In the People view, tap the Change View tool on the View tab to expand your view options and then tap the view that you want to apply.

> ✓ **TIP** Locating the contacts you need is a simple task in Outlook. You can use the search Contacts box to locate contacts by typing just a few characters of a name. You can also use the search tools and Advanced Find to refine your search. Tap the Search Contacts search box and type the text you'd like to find. The center pane shows results that match the search criteria.

Managing your mail by using Quick Steps

Quick Steps are convenient, ready-made procedures that you can apply to your mail in a single tap, and Outlook 2013 will organize your mail in the manner you selected. Quick Steps help you to create, send, reply to, and organize your mail quickly, with a minimum of steps. In addition to the Quick Steps that are built-in to Outlook, you can create your own custom Quick Steps and streamline the tasks you find yourself doing repeatedly.

Set up and use a Quick Step

1 In your Inbox, tap the email message that you want to use. (You'll need to be in the Mail window.)

2 On the Home tab, in the Quick Steps group, tap Move To.

3 In the First Time Setup dialog box, tap the Move To Folder drop-down arrow.

4 If you want to specify a folder where the mail will be stored auto-matically when you choose the Move To Quick Step, in the list that appears, tap Other Folder.

5 Or, if you want Outlook to prompt you to choose the folder each time you select the Move To Quick Step, tap Always Ask for Folder.

(continued on next page)

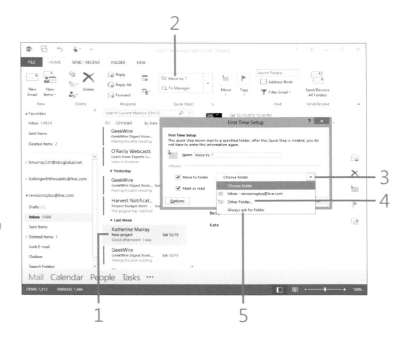

Set up and use a Quick Step (continued)

6 If you choose Other Folder, the Select Folder dialog box opens. Tap the arrow if necessary to show the folders in the email account you want to use.

7 Tap the folder to which you want to move the mail.

8 Alternatively, if you want to add a new folder, tap New, type a name for the new folder, and then tap OK.

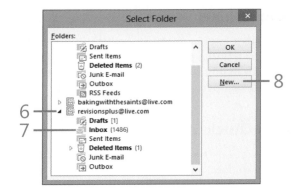

✓ TIP Depending on which Quick Step you choose, Outlook will prompt you to provide different types of information to set it up for the first time. For example, when you tap To Manager for the first time, Outlook asks you to enter the email address of your manager. When you choose Team Email (you might need to tap the arrow in the Quick Steps group to show these additional options), Outlook prompts you to choose the members of your team that should receive the email.

Manage Quick Steps

You can review the different Quick Steps Outlook 2013 offers, duplicate them, create new ones, remove the ones you don't need, or return all Quick Step settings to their defaults by using the Manage Quick Steps dialog box.

On the right side of the Quick Steps list, tap the drop-down arrow to display a full list of Quick Steps. At the bottom of the list, tap Manage Quick Steps. In the Manage Quick Steps dialog box, select the Quick Step you want to work with and then choose whether you want to edit, duplicate, or delete the Quick Step. You can also change the order of your Quick Steps in the listing that's displayed on the Home tab—this can come in handy if you use some Quick Steps more than others and want to put those at the top of the list.

When you're finished making changes to your Quick Steps, click OK to save your changes and close the Manage Quick Steps dialog box.

Flagging mail for follow-up

Here's an easy way to make sure that you don't miss a message for which you need to follow up. You can flag the message so that you can easily return to it later and take the action you need to take. If you're still concerned that you might miss it, you can set a reminder so that Outlook 2013 lets you know it's time to take on that flagged message.

Flag mail

1 Tap the message that you want to flag for follow-up.

2 On the ribbon, tap the Home tab.

3 In the Tags group, tap Follow Up.

4 Choose the time to assign to the flag.

5 Alternatively, tap No Date if you don't want to set an end date for the message.

> **TIP** If you want to mark a message as complete—for example, if you've responded to a customer's technical question—you can tap Follow Up in the Tags group and tap Mark Complete. Outlook adds a green checkmark to the message in your Inbox so that you know the message needs no further action from you.

> **TIP** Some Outlook features, such as the Follow Up feature in the Tags group or the Add Reminder feature may might be available if you are using accounts other than Outlook or Microsoft email accounts.

Add a reminder

1 With the flagged message still selected, tap Follow Up a second time.

2 On the menu that appears, tap the Add Reminder command.

3 In the Custom dialog box, verify that the Reminder check box is selected.

4 Choose a date for the reminder.

5 Choose a time for the reminder.

6 Tap OK.

The reminder is added in your Tasks list and will prompt you according to the date and time you specified.

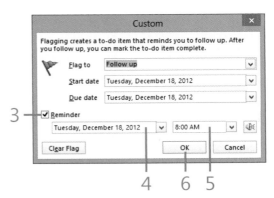

TIP You can view the reminders as well as the messages you've flagged or follow up by tapping the Tasks button along the bottom of the Outlook window. This displays the Tasks view, where your flagged items appear in the center column of the window.

Categorizing your mail

These days, email messages come from everywhere. You might receive some related to projects, others related to causes you support. Some will arrive from friends and family, and others deliver advertisements to your Outlook 2013 Inbox. How can you keep all the mail straight so that you can be sure to respond to the ones that are most important? One answer is to categorize mail from senders who matter most to you. You can assign a color category to messages so that you can see at a glance which ones are the most pressing items in your Inbox.

Categorize your email

1 On the ribbon, tap the Home tab.

2 In the Tags group, tap Categories.

3 On the menu that appears, tap the category that you want to add to your message.

4 Alternatively, you can create a new category and name it. In the Categories list, tap All Categories.

(continued on next page)

Categorize your email *(continued)*

5 In the Color Categories dialog box, tap New.

6 In the Add New Category dialog box, type a name for the new category.

7 Choose a color for the new category.

8 Tap OK.

9 Tap OK to close the Color Categories dialog box to save the new category.

Now you can assign the category to email by choosing it from the Categorize list.

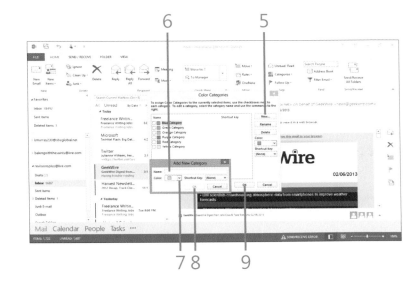

 TIP You can remove the categories you've created by clicking Categorize on the Home tab and choosing Clear All Categories.

Use Quick Click categories

You can also create a Quick Click category for messages if you want to be able to categorize messages with a single tap while you scan your messages.

You can display the Categorize list either by tapping Categorize in the Tags group on the Home tab or by tapping and holding the message you want to categorize. Choose Set Quick Click, and the Set Quick Click dialog box appears. Choose the category you want to apply and choose OK.

Now, you'll be able to categorize your mail by using the category you just selected when you tap the Categories column in your Inbox. If you have the Reading pane displayed in the right side of your Outlook window, you might not be able to see the Categories column by default. To display it, move the Reading pane to the bottom of your window or turn it off completed. To do that, tap the View tab, choose Reading Pane in the Layout group, and then select Bottom or Off. In the Categories column, tap the open box of the messages you want to categorize, and Outlook adds the color category you selected.

Moving messages to folders

If you're like most people, you receive a steady stream of email during the day. It's likely you've already realized very quickly that leaving all your messages in your Inbox isn't a very convenient way to organize the ones you might need later.

Outlook 2013 makes it simple for you to add mail folders so that you can organize messages by project, by people, or by using any other organizational structure that makes sense for you.

Organize your mail with folders

1 On the ribbon, tap the Folder tab.

2 In the New group, tap New Folder.

3 In the Create New Folder dialog box, type a name for the new folder.

4 Select the folder in which you want the new folder created.

5 Tap OK.

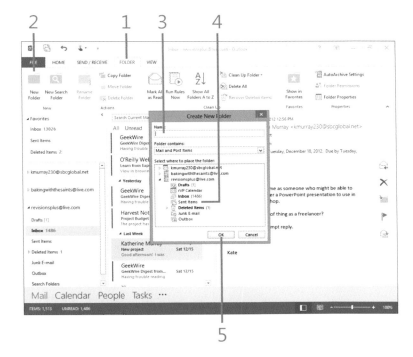

Move mail to the new folder

1 On the ribbon, tap the Home tab.

2 In the Inbox, select a message to move.

3 In the Move group, tap Move.

4 In the list that opens, choose the destination folder to which you want Outlook to move the message.

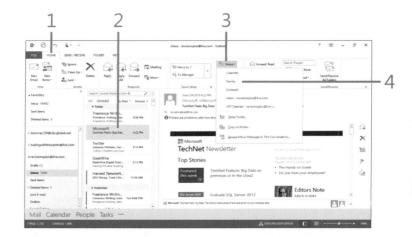

Updating your schedule and managing tasks with Outlook 2013

5

Does your calendar run your life? Most of us walk a fine line between wanting our calendars to give our lives order and rebelling against them as some electronic parental voice that's telling us to do our chores.

With Microsoft Outlook 2013 on your tablet, you can balance your "have-to's" with your "want-to's" and get just the amount of information you need about the day ahead. You can view your appointments for the day on the updating app tile on the Windows 8 Start screen—without a single tap—and update and add information as needed. You can work with team calendars to keep everyone on the same page. You can set up an online meeting, manage tasks, and much more.

This section shows you how to use the Calendar tool in Outlook 2013. You'll find out how to set up appointments and meetings, update your calendar, share it with others, and set calendar options so that it looks and feels the way you want. You'll also learn how to add, update, and mark as finished those tasks you feel are important enough to add to your to-do lists.

In this section:

- Exploring the calendar window
- Opening a calendar
- Creating a new calendar
- Creating calendar groups
- Creating appointments
- Creating meetings and sending invitations
- Changing the look of the calendar
- Sending your calendar by email
- Adding tasks to your to-do list
- Managing tasks

Exploring the calendar window

At the bottom of the Outlook 2013 window are four view tabs: Mail, Calendar, People, and Tasks. The ellipsis to the right of Tasks tab indicates that there are more options available to you; if you tap there, an options list appears so that you can display

Navigation Options or choose to work with Notes, Folders, and Shortcuts. To display Calendar view, simply tap the Calendar tab. You can then navigate the view to display the day or days that you want to view.

Navigate the calendar

1 At the bottom of the Outlook window, tap the Calendar tab.

The Calendar view opens.

2 Tap a date to display that day in the calendar area.

3 On the Home tab, in the Arrange group, tap Day to display a single day.

4 Tap Month to show the entire month.

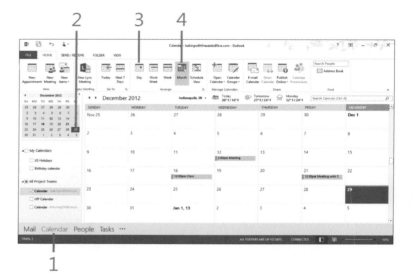

Display your local weather

Now, in Outlook 2013 you can add the local weather report to the top of your calendar. The weather tool shows you what the conditions are in your local area (I suppose it doesn't have to be your own local weather—if you're dreaming about Hawaii, you could display that weather, instead) and shows the high and low temperature along with an image that depicts whether to expect rain, snow, sunshine, or something else.

To add your weather conditions to the Outlook 2013 calendar, tap the drop-down arrow to the right of the current weather location and tap Add Location. Enter your city and state or type a ZIP code of the area you want to see and then tap Search. If prompted, tap your city's name. Outlook searches current weather conditions and displays the weather report for the area you selected at the top of your Calendar window.

Search your calendar

1 In the upper right of the Calendar window, next to the current weather information, tap the Search box.

2 Type the word or phrase that you want to find.

3 If necessary, tap the Search tool. Outlook displays the results in a results list.

4 Double-tap an item to display it in an appointment window. Review the appointment as needed and then tap the close box to dismiss the appointment window.

5 Tap the close box to exit search and return to the calendar window.

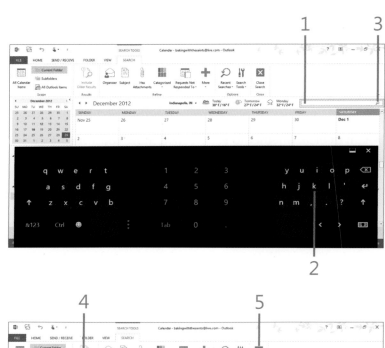

Opening a calendar

If you typically work with more than one calendar, or you want to display calendars others have shared with you along with your own, you can use the Open Calendar tool in the Manage Calendars group on the Home tab to locate, open, and display the new calendar in Outlook 2013.

Open a calendar

1 At the bottom of the Outlook window, tap the Calendar tab.

2 On the Home tab, in the Arrange group, tap Open Calendar.

An options list appear so that you can navigate to the calendar that you want to open.

3 Tap your choice in the list.

Choosing From Address Book or From Room List opens the Select Names dialog box in which you can choose the name of the contact with the calendar that you want to view. Tap From Internet if you want to open a calendar that is currently saved with an online calendar tool.

(continued on next page)

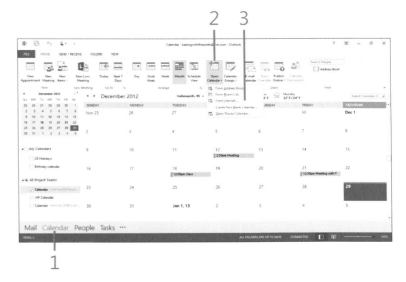

Open a calendar *(continued)*

4 If you choose From Address Book or From Room List, choose the person in the Address Book list of the Select Names dialog box or in the New Internet Calendar Subscription dialog box, enter the web address for the calendar that you want to view. If you selected From Internet, type the web address where the web calendar is stored.

5 Tap OK.

Outlook adds the calendar to your My Calendars list and displays it in the calendar area.

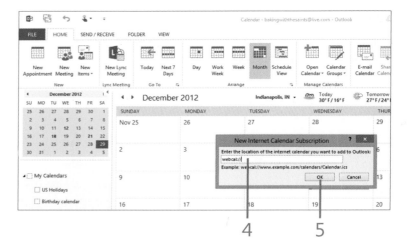

Open a shared calendar

1   At the bottom of the Outlook window, tap the Calendar tab.

2   On the Home tab, in the Manage Calendars group, tap the Open Calendar drop-down arrow.

3   On the menu that appears, tap the Open Shared Calendar command.

4   In the Open A Shared Calendar dialog box, tap Name to display the Select Name dialog box.

5   Or, in the text box, type the email address of the person who has shared the calendar.

6   Tap OK.

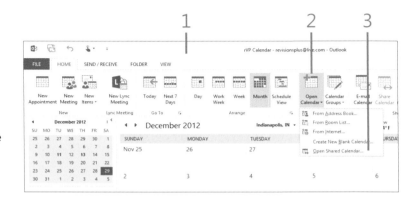

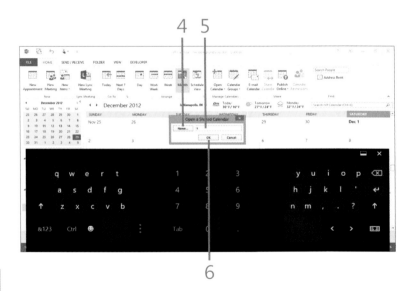

⚠ **CAUTION** If you get the message "Cannot display the folder," make sure that the person who owns the calendar you are adding has turned on sharing for that calendar. Also check to be sure the person is added as an Outlook contact, update any information as needed, and then try again.

Merge calendar display

If you have several calendars displayed in the calendar window, side-by-side, you can easily merge them so that you can see at a glance what your availability looks like for scheduling appointments.

Begin by displaying all the calendars that you want to show in the calendar area. Then, tap and hold the tab of one calendar. When the options box appears, release your touch and the options list appears. Tap Overlay. Outlook combines the calendar with the one next to it. Repeat these steps to overlay additional calendars as you like.

To reverse the process and return the calendar to its own display, tap and hold to display the options list again and tap Overlay a second time.

Creating a new calendar

You can easily start a new calendar in Outlook 2013 if you want to keep some appointments separate. For example, you might want to keep a family calendar that is separate from the one you use at work. You can easily merge the display of the calendars so that you can be sure you're not double-booking yourself. Having a calendar dedicated to non-work events might help you keep your activities straight.

Create a new calendar

1 At the bottom of the Outlook window, tap the Calendar tab. Then, on the ribbon, tap the Home tab.

2 In the Manage Calendars group, tap Open Calendar.

3 On the menu that appears, tap the Create New Blank Calendar command.

4 In the Create New Folder dialog box, tap the Name box and type a name for the new calendar.

5 Tap OK to save the new calendar.

Outlook displays it in your My Calendars list, and you can display it by selecting its check box.

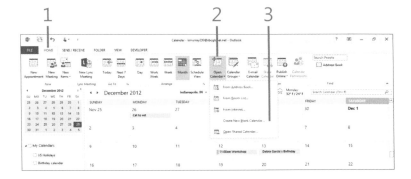

> **TIP** Leave the Calendar Items folder selected when you name the new calendar so that Outlook is able to access and display the new calendar.

Creating calendar groups

If you regularly work with the same group of people—such as a team or a department—you can easily add all the calendars of your group members to your Outlook 2013 calendar so that you can orchestrate meetings and more. A new feature in Outlook called calendar groups makes it simple for you to compare dates and schedule events at a time when everyone is available.

Create a calendar group

1 At the bottom of the Outlook window, tap the Calendar tab.

2 In the My Calendars area, select the check boxes for the calendars that you want to display.

3 On the Home tab, in the Manage Calendars group, tap Calendar Groups.

4 On the menu that appears, tap the Save As New Calendar Group command.

5 In the Create A New Calendar Group dialog box, type a name for the calendar group.

6 Tap OK.

The new group appears in the Folder pane on the left side of the Calendar window.

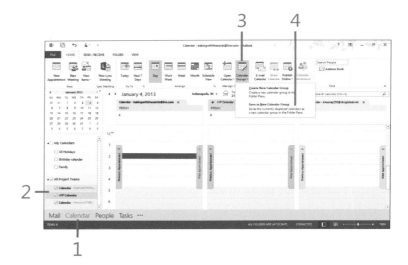

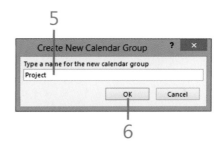

> **TIP** You can also create a new project group without having previously added group members' calendars by tapping Calendar Groups and choosing Create New Calendar Group. The Create New Calendar Group dialog box opens, in which you can name the group. After you type the group name and tap OK, the Select Name: Contacts dialog box opens. Here, you can tap the group members you want to add and tap Group Members to add them to the list. (You can also add the members quickly by double-tapping them.) Finally, tap OK to save the new calendar group.

Creating appointments

New appointments spring up all the time, especially when you're on the road or out visiting clients. You can easily add a new appointment to your Outlook 2013 calendar. You can also add notes about the appointment or even attach files you plan to use during the appointment—for example, a sales presentation you want to share with new customers or an order you need to pass along to a vendor. Before you add a new appointment, make sure you're in a view in which you can see the time slots available, such as Week, Work Week, or Day views, in the Arrange group in the Home tab.

Add a calendar entry

1 Double-tap a time slot on your calendar.

2 Tap the Subject line.

3 Type a word or phrase describing the appointment and, if you like, add location information.

(continued on next page)

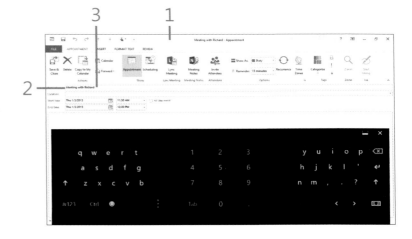

TIP You can also display the new appointment window by tapping New Appointment on the far left side on the Home tab in Calendar view.

Add a calendar entry *(continued)*

4 To change the duration of the appointment, tap the End Time drop-down arrow.

5 In the list that appears, tap the end time for the appointment.

6 Tap the notes area and type any notes related to the appointment.

7 On the ribbon, tap Save & Close to close the appointment and return to Calendar view.

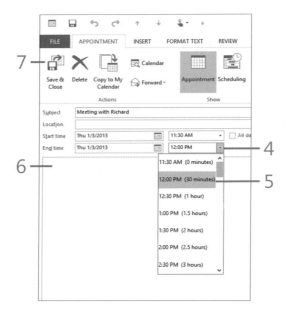

TRY THIS Attach a file to an appointment in your calendar. Double-tap an appointment, tap the Insert tab, and then, in the Include group, tap Attach File. Choose the file you want to add to the appointment, tap Insert, and Outlook adds the file icon to the notes area of the appointment so it will be there when you need it.

Scheduling recurring appointments

In addition to adding appointments and meetings to your Outlook 2013 calendar, you can set up scheduled events that repeat on a regular basis. You can choose to repeat an appointment daily, weekly, monthly, or yearly. If you prefer you can select the day of the week on which you want the appointment to recur, and you can choose the start and end date for the recurrence, as well.

Select the entry on your calendar that you want to turn into a recurring item and then, on the Appointment tab, in the Options group, tap Recurrence. The Appointment Recurrence dialog box opens, in which you can choose how often you want the event to recur and enter the number of weeks you want the recurrence to continue. If you want the item to recur on a particular day of the week, tap your choice. Select a start and end date and tap OK to save your settings.

If you want to change the recurrence of an item later, simply tap the item on the calendar and tap Recurrence. In the Appointment Recurrence dialog box, change the settings as needed and tap OK to save your changes.

Creating meetings and sending invitations

If you're the one who needs to set up and invite others to meetings, you can use your tablet to take care of that task in Outlook 2013, as well. You can easily set up the meeting appointment and then invite the individuals whom you want to attend.

Send meeting invitations

1 At the bottom of the Outlook window, tap the Calendar tab, and then tap a time slot for the meeting.

2 On the Home tab, in the New group, tap New Meeting.

A new meeting appointment opens on the screen.

(continued on next page)

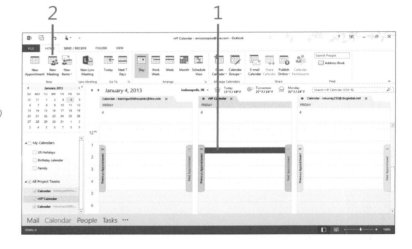

Send meeting invitations (continued)

3 Type a subject for the meeting.

4 Type a location.

5 Enter notes or agenda topics for the meeting.

6 Tap To.

7 In the Select Attendees dialog box, tap the name of a person whom you want to invite.

If you want to invite a person who isn't in your address book, you can simply type the person's email address in the To line of the meeting invitation.

8 Tap Required, Optional, or Resources, depending on the role the person will play in the meeting. Repeat until you've invited all participants that you want to include.

9 Tap OK.

10 Tap Send.

The invitation is sent as an email message to those in the To box, and recipients can tap Accept, Tentative, Decline, or Propose New Time to indicate their availability.

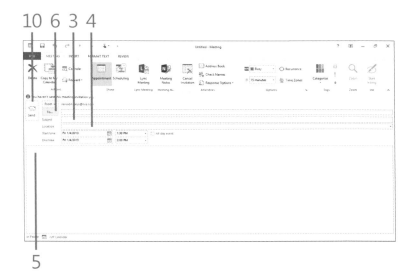

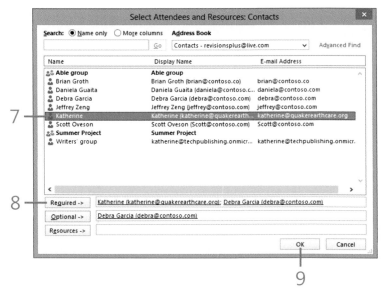

Changing the look of the calendar

Outlook 2013 offers a pretty-clean looking calendar and you might be happy with it just the way it is. But, if you'd like to change the colors or hide or display elements on the screen, you can do that easily, too.

For example, by minimizing the Folder pane along the left side of the window, you will gain more room for appointments on your calendar. You can also display a Daily Task List and a To-Do bar that can remind you about upcoming tasks and meetings during your day, making it easier to connect with favorite people.

Change the calendar color and scale

1   At the bottom of the Outlook window, tap the Calendar tab and then tap the View tab.

2   In the Color group, tap Color.

3   In the Gallery that opens, choose a color.

4   In the Arrangement group, tap Time Scale.

5   Choose the time increment that you want to show in the calendar window.

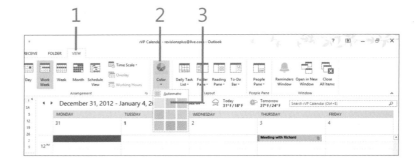

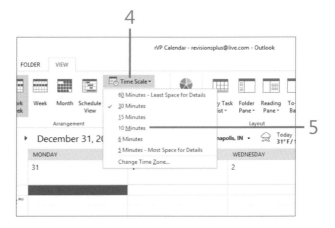

Change the layout of the calendar window

1 On the ribbon, tap the View tab and then, in the upper-right corner of the Folder pane, tap the Minimize arrow to reduce the pane to a vertical bar.

2 Alternatively, on the ribbon, in the Layout group, tap Folder Pane and then, in the list that appears, tap Minimized.

3 Tap Daily Task List and then, in the list that appears, tap Normal. Tasks for each day appear at the bottom of the Calendar.

4 Tap To-Do Bar. In the list that appears, choose one of three types of information you can display: Calendar, People, and Tasks. Tap any items that you want to appear in the To-Do bar on the right side of the Calendar window.

TIP You can use the People pane tool in the View tab to control where Outlook gets the contacts that appear in your People view. When you tap People Pane and choose Account Settings, a dialog box opens that lists the social network accounts you are currently using with Outlook. If you don't have any social networks connected, you can tap Next to get started, input the required information, tap Connect, and then tap Close. With that done, you can repeat these steps and then tap More to add a new social network or remove an existing one by tapping the Delete tool on the far-right side of the desired entry in the dialog box. If you want to change the account settings for a particular social media account, tap the Edit icon to the left of the Delete tool for the entry. When you're done making changes, tap Finish to save the new settings. You can view the new changes by tapping at the bottom of the Calendar window.

Sending your calendar by email

You can easily send any calendar that you create in Outlook 2013 by email so that others can see at a glance what your schedule looks like. You'll find the E-mail Calendar tool in the Share group on the Home tab.

Send a calendar by email

1   At the bottom of the Outlook window, tap the Calendar tab and then, on the Home tab, in the Share group, tap E-Mail Calendar.

2   In the Send A Calendar Via E-Mail dialog box, choose a date range.

3   In the Details section, tap the list box and then choose the level of calendar detail to share.

4   Tap OK. (If there are no appointments for that time frame, tap Continue.)

(continued on next page)

1

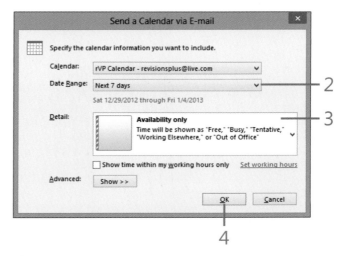

2

3

4

Send a calendar by email *(continued)*

5 Address the email.

6 Add a note, if desired.

7 Tap Send.

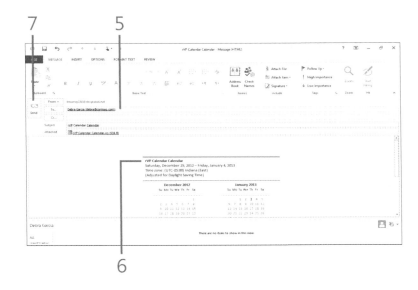

Adding tasks to your to-do list

If you're a list maker, you will love task tools in Outlook 2013. You can easily add the items you need to accomplish and display the tasks in your To-Do bar, in Tasks view, or in the Quick Task list.

Create a task

1 At the bottom of the Outlook window, tap the Tasks tab and then, on the Home tab, in the New group, tap New Task.

2 Type a subject for the task.

3 Choose a start date.

4 Choose a due date.

5 Choose a status.

6 Add optional notes.

7 On the ribbon, tap Save & Close.

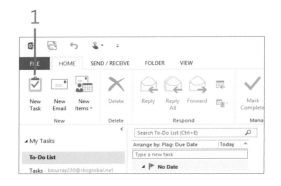

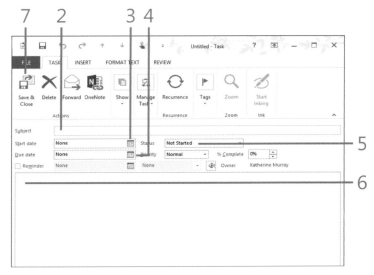

Set task properties

1 In Tasks view, in the task list, tap the task that you just created.

2 View properties for the selected task in the right pane of the window.

3 Tap the lock icon to mark the task as private so that others can't see it.

4 Tap the exclamation point icon to set the task priority to High.

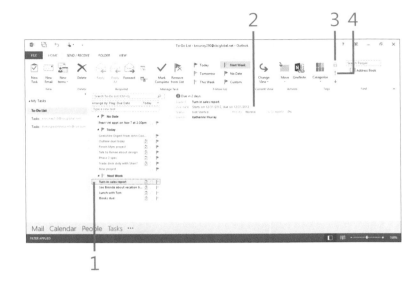

Managing tasks

There's no rule that says you have to do all tasks yourself. You can assign tasks to others, as well. This way, you can share the workload and make sure your team stays focused on everything it needs to accomplish.

Assign a task

1 At the bottom of the Outlook window, tap the Tasks tab and then double-tap a task to open it.

2 On the Task tab, in the Manage Task group, tap Assign Task.

3 Type a recipient for the task or tap To and choose a recipient.

4 Adjust the due date, if needed.

5 Select this option to keep an unassigned copy of the task in your own Tasks folder.

6 Select this option to receive a status report when the assignee marks the task as Completed.

7 Tap Send.

The person you sent the assignment to receives the notification as an email message, and when she chooses Accept, you will receive a notification by email of the acceptance. Outlook then records the assignment in your task list.

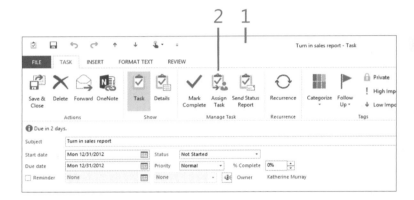

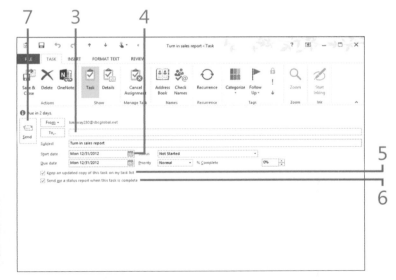

> **TRY THIS** After you've finished a task you can easily mark it as completed. That will remove the task from the active task list and show you that you're crossing items off your list. Tap the task you have finished and then, on the Home tab, in the Manage Task group, tap Mark Complete.

Connecting right now with Lync 2013

6

Microsoft Lync 2013 is Microsoft's answer to real-time communication that ties together your collaborative and in-the-cloud work. Using Lync, which is available with Office 2013 Professional Plus or in Office 365 Small Business, ProPlus, or Enterprise subscriptions, you can have in-the-moment conversations, hold online meetings, share files, and work collaboratively. Lync is also available as a service that you can add to your existing Office 365 subscription, no matter which plan you have.

Lync is available in several versions, which means you can use it anywhere. It's available as a Lync Mobile app for phones of all types, downloadable through Office 365, installable as part of Office 2013 Professional Plus, and accessible as a Lync Web App. So, if you need to stay in touch with your team wherever you are, Lync makes it easy for you.

In this section:

- Launching and signing in to Lync
- Getting started with Lync
- Learning the Lync window
- Personalizing your Lync info
- Adding and managing contacts
- Instant messaging friends and colleagues
- Making calls by using Lync
- Setting up an online meeting
- Hosting your meeting

New features in Lync 2013

Lync 2013 includes new features throughout its various communications capabilities. If you've used Lync before, in this new version you'll find new ways to view your contacts and new ways of launching and working in meetings. In addition to new meeting-hosting features, you can use one-tap responses in your meeting invitations, read through tabbed conversations, create your own meeting room, and predetermine settings such as whether participants' audio will be muted and video will be blocked. With the new Gallery View, you can see multiple people at once in a video conference, and the new federation to Skype makes it possible for you to instant message and call your Skype contacts. In addition to the whiteboard and desktop sharing features, you can also share a OneNote notebook with others in the meeting so that each of you can capture what you feel is most important in the meeting at hand.

Launching and signing in to Lync

Your first step is to tap the Lync 2013 app tile on the Windows 8 desktop, and Lync springs into life. The Lync window opens, and you'll be prompted for your user name and Microsoft password.

If you select the Save My Password check box, Lync will log you on automatically when you launch Lync in the future.

Start Lync 2013

1 Display the Windows 8 Start screen and swipe to display the far right side of the screen.

2 Tap the Lync 2013 tile.

Lync opens on your Windows 8 Desktop.

(continued on next page)

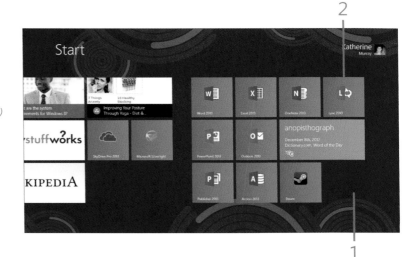

TRY THIS You can personalize your log on so that Lync signs you in showing the status of your availability right from the start. Tap the arrow to the left of the availability setting beneath Sign In As. Tap your choice and Lync displays that status when you are logged on.

Start Lync 2013 *(continued)*

3 In the Sign-In Address text box, type your user ID email address, if needed.

Usually after you sign in the first time, you can skip this step.

4 In the Password text box, type your password.

If you later save your sign in information, you also will be able to skip this step.

5 Tap Sign In.

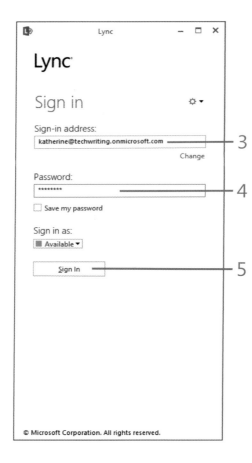

Getting started with Lync

You'll notice right away that Lync 2013 is a different animal from your other Office applications. Most obviously, Lync takes up only a portion of your screen. This is by design; that way you can view other files on your desktop while Lync is open along the left side of the screen. Lync also does not use the ribbon and instead features its own variety of tools and settings optimized for communicating while you're working on other things.

Learning the Lync window

After you log on to Lync 2013, you'll find the Lync window pretty intuitive if you've ever used an instant messaging program before. Using the tools in the Lync window, you can do the following:

- Set your availability for messaging or calls
- Add new contacts
- Make Lync calls
- Update your status so that friends and colleagues can see what you're up to
- Choose a contact with whom you want to communicate
- Set Lync options and preferences
- Organize your contacts

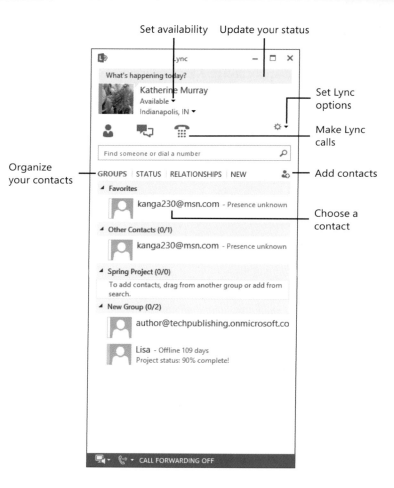

Set availability Update your status

Set Lync options

Make Lync calls

Organize your contacts

Add contacts

Choose a contact

TIP You can personalize your settings by clicking on the Lync options tool and changing your picture, ringtones, file locations, and more.

Display and use the Lync menu bar

1 On the right side of the Lync client window, click the Settings icon.

2 On the menu that appears, tap Show Menu Bar.

The menu bar appears at the top of the Lync window.

3 Tap one of the menus—for this example, tap Tools.

The Tools menu appears.

4 Tap a setting that you want to change.

TIP If you decide later that you'd rather hide the menu bar, you can do that by tapping the Settings button again and tapping Hide Menu Bar.

Use the Quick Lync Bar

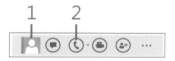

1 Tap the picture of a contact with whom you want to communicate.

A horizontal palette of tools appears to the right of the contact picture. This is the Quick Lync Bar.

2 Tap the tool that you want to use.

You can start an instant messaging conversation, make a phone call, start a video call, or view a contact card to get more information about the contact.

> ✓ **TIP** Tap the More Options button (the ellipsis at the right end of the Quick Lync Bar) to display a list of options you can choose to send an email message, schedule a meeting, copy the contact, move the contact to a different group, or tag the contact so that you will receive status change alerts.

> ⚠ **CAUTION** If you try to log on to Lync and get an error that says, "Can't sign in to Lync because the server is temporarily unavailable," what should you do? This error can be caused by a loss of network/Internet connectivity or by a problem with the Lync server in your organization. Check your network/Internet connection to make sure that you're connected to the web, and if that is okay, contact your IT Support desk or click the service status link on your Office 365 Home page to make sure the Microsoft servers are working properly.

Personalizing your Lync info

Lync 2013 wouldn't be nearly as much fun if you couldn't personalize your experience. But, similar to your favorite social media accounts, in Lync you can update your status, let others know whether you're available to chat, add your own profile picture, display your location, and more.

Update your status

1 Tap in the status area above your account picture in the Lync window.

Initially, it displays What's Happening Today? The On-Screen Keyboard appears.

2 Type your new status.

3 Tap outside the status area to save the change.

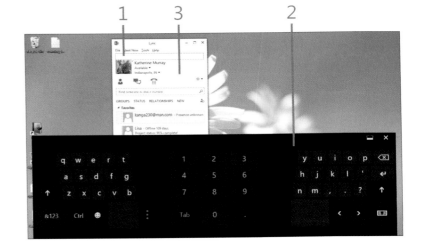

Set your availability

1 Tap the Available button located just below your user name.

2 In the list that appears, tap a different availability setting.

Change your account picture

Lync 2013 displays your account picture in the upper-left corner of the Lync window, and you can easily change the image (and change it often, if you like). Begin by tapping the Settings button (the small gear icon) on the right side of the window. On the menu that appears, choose Tools and then tap Options. In the Lync – Options dialog box, tap the My Picture tab and then tap the Edit or Remove Picture button. (This option might not be available (grayed out) if your administrator has decided not to allow you to change your picture.) If prompted, sign in to your Microsoft Account. The Change Photo screen appears. Tap Browse and then, in the Choose File To Upload dialog box, navigate to the file that you want to use, select it, and then tap Open. The picture is added to the Change Photo screen. Tap Save and then OK to close the Options dialog box. Note that your new picture might not appear immediately. It might take a little while for the picture to be updated on the Lync server.

Specify your location

1 Tap the Set Your Location button, which is located just below the Available button.

If you haven't previously set a location, Set Your Location appears.

2 Using the On-Screen Keyboard, type another location and then press the Enter key.

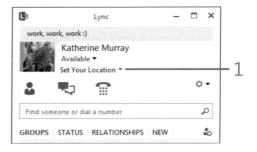

→ **TRY THIS**   Tap the location setting and type a city or place name that reflects your current location. After you've entered a location or two, you can tap the location drop-down arrow and choose the location you want to display from the list that appears. Lync can also remember the location you are working from, so depending on how your network is set up, you might not need to manually enter this information.

✓ **TIP**   You can hide or display location information as you'd like. To hide your location, tap the location drop-down arrow and clear the Show Others My Location check box. The location information will be hidden until you choose to redisplay it by reselecting the check box.

Set your Lync preferences

1 On the right side of the window, tap the Settings button. On the menu that appears, choose Tools and then tap Options.

The Lync – Options dialog box opens.

2 The General tab is displayed by default. Tap a different tab if you'd like.

3 Change the settings on the right side of the dialog box.

4 Tap OK to apply your changes.

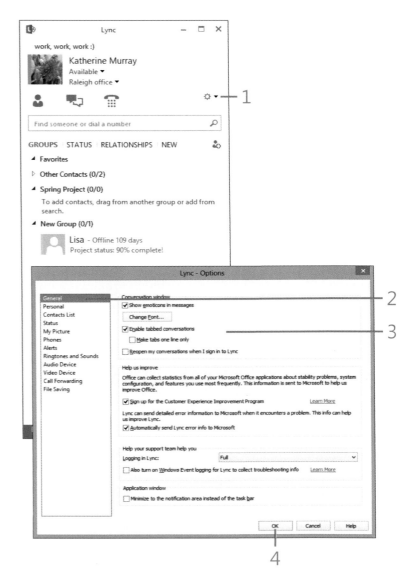

Adding and managing contacts

Lync 2013 makes it easy for you to grow your contacts list and assign contacts to groups so that you can always find who you're looking for easily. You can add new contacts—both within your own workgroup and external to your company—if the right permissions are in place—and assign those contacts to groups.

Add a new contact

1 In the Lync window, tap the Add Contact button.

2 On the menu that appears, tap Add A Contact In My Organization.

3 At the top of the contacts list, tap the search box.

4 Using the On-Screen Keyboard, begin typing the contact's name.

Lync automatically enters what you type in the search text box and displays a list of matching contacts.

(continued on next page)

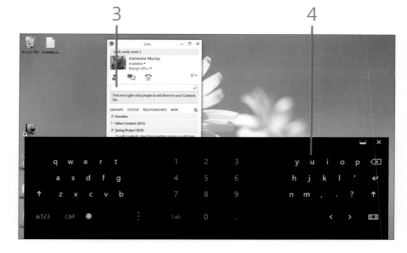

Add a new contact *(continued)*

5 Tap and hold until a rectangle appears on the contact whom you want to add and then release your touch.

6 On the menu that opens, tap Add To Contacts List.

7 On the submenu that opens, tap the name of the group to which you want to add the new contact.

You can add a contact to more than one group if you choose.

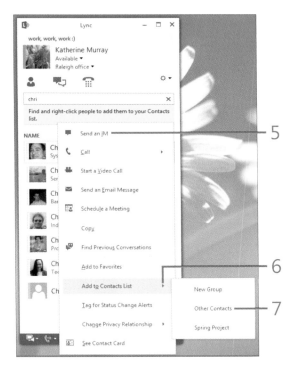

TIP You can create a group of contacts so that you can easily contact everybody at once. Start by tapping the Add Contact button and then tap Create A New Group. In the text box that appears at the bottom of the Lync window, type a name for the group and then tap outside the text box.

Add external contacts

In some cases, your administrator might set up accounts so that you can interact with others outside your organization. If you have the necessary permissions, you can add those contacts so that you can make calls and trade instant messages with them as easily as you do your contacts within your company. Tap Add Contact and then tap Add A Contact That's Not In My Organization. Choose the service used by the contact and enter the contact's messaging ID. Finally, choose a group and select a privacy relationship and then tap OK to save your changes. An invitation that contains a link is sent to the external contact by email, inviting them to join your Contacts list. All the contact needs to do is to click or tap the link to confirm the connection.

View a contact card

1 In your contacts list, tap and hold a contact and then release your touch.

2 On the menu that opens, tap See Contact Card.

3 In the dialog box for the contact, tap the Schedule A Meeting link.

4 Tap a choice here to instant message, call, video call, or email the contact.

5 Tap the Close button to close the contact card window.

TIP By default, Lync tracks your conversations with your contacts. Tap the Conversations button below your location in the Lync window. Scroll down if needed, tap and hold the name for the contact with whom you had a prior conversation and want to find again, and then when the rectangle appears, release your touch and tap Find Previous Conversations from the list that appears.

TIP If you decide you'd rather not be in contact with someone on your list, you can block the contact. Tap and hold the contact name, choose Change Privacy Relationship, and then tap Blocked Contacts. Tap OK to confirm the operation; the contact will no longer be able to see your updates or contact you by using Lync.

TIP You can easily find the contacts you need. Begin by tapping in the Find Someone or Dial A Number text box just below the Lync tool bar. Type the name of the contact whom you want to find. A list of contacts matching what you type appears. Tap and hold the contact for whom you want to display a list of contact options.

Instant messaging friends and colleagues

If you've previously used any kind of instant messaging (IM) program like Windows Live Messenger or the Messaging app in Windows 8, you'll feel comfortable using the instant messaging feature in Lync 2013. The process is simple: Just choose a contact, send a message, and reply to the messages you receive.

Send an instant message

1   In your Contacts list, tap and hold the name of the contact with whom you want to instant message. Release your touch and the options list appears.

2   Tap Send An IM. A conversation window opens.

(continued on next page)

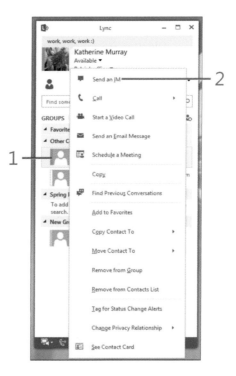

TRY THIS   Use the Quick Lync Bar to start the IM conversation. Tap and hold a contact and release your touch when the square appears around your finger. Choose Send An IM from the options list. Type and send the message.

Send an instant message *(continued)*

3 In the conversation window that opens, use the On-Screen Keyboard to type your message text and then tap the Enter key.

Your message text appears in your conversation window as well as your contact's conversation window. Your contact's typed response will appear below the latest text you sent.

4 Scroll the conversation as needed by using the scroll bar at right.

5 When you're finished with the conversation, In the upper-right corner of the message window, tap the Close button.

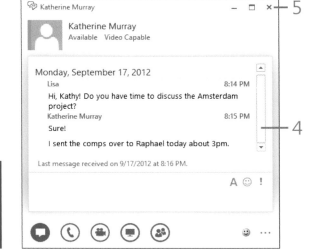

TIP Even after you close the message window, if your contact sends you another one, a notification will appear on your screen so that you can tap and open it. When you tap it, the message window—complete with your previous conversation thread—appears on your desktop.

Respond to an instant message

1 When a contact sends you an instant message, a small notification box appears in the lower-right corner of your screen. Tap the
   picture in the IM request window to open the conversation window
   on your desktop.

2 Type your response in the message area at the bottom of the
   instant message window and tap Enter.

> **TIP** If you do not want to have the IM conversation, you have
> two choices for opting out. Either tap Ignore in the bottom of
> the notification box or tap Options and then select Do Not Disturb to
> change your status. Be aware that if you choose Do Not Disturb, others
> won't be able to instant message you until you change your status.

> **TIP** Some instant messages might be short enough that you
> can read the whole message in the notification box. If the note
> doesn't require a response, you can simply read it and do nothing.
> After a moment, the box will fade from your screen on its own.

Making calls by using Lync

Another popular communication feature in Lync 2013 makes it possible for you to make Internet calls easily. Whether you want to make a traditional voice-to-voice audio call or place a video call with one or more people, Lync makes the entire process simple.

To make a video call, you need a web camera connected to your computer. You can determine whether your contacts are able to participate in a video call because you will see Video Capable listed in the contact information to the right of the contact name.

Make a Lync call

1 In your Contacts list, tap and hold the contact whom you want to call. When the square appears, release your touch. The options menu appears.

2 On the menu that appears, tap Call.

3 On the submenu that appears, choose Lync Call.

A conversation window opens.

(continued on next page)

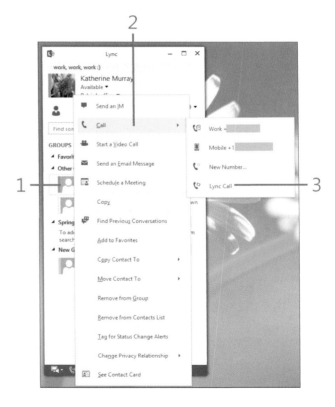

TIP Before you make your first call, check your audio levels to make sure you will be able to hear and be heard during your call. To check your system's capabilities, tap the Settings button (the small gear icon), navigate to the Lync – Options dialog box, and then tap the Audio tab. Use the sliders to adjust the volumes for Speaker, Microphone, and Ringer and and then tap OK. You can also make a test call to ensure that all levels are sufficient before you put them to use.

Make a Lync call *(continued)*

4 Talk normally, using the volume and mute controls on your audio device as needed.

5 Tap the Hang Up button to finish the call.

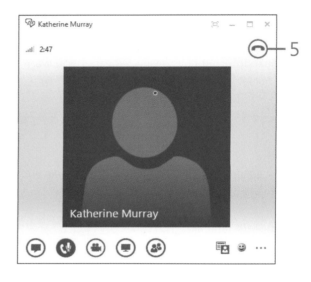

> **→ TRY THIS** You can also use Lync to dial a number that isn't a contact. Tap the Find Someone or Dial A Number text box. Type the number to call and tap outside the text box. Lync places the call and you can begin your conversation when the other person answers. When you're finished, tap Hang Up to end the call.

> **✓ TIP** Get ready to make a video call by making sure Lync sees your webcam. Tap the Settings button (the small gear icon), navigate to the Lync - Options dialog box, and then tap the Video Device tab. Tap Camera Settings. Use the sliders in the Properties dialog box to adjust your camera settings and tap OK twice to save your changes and close the dialog boxes.

Place a video call

1 In your Contacts list, tap the contact whom you want to call and display the options list.

2 Tap Start A Video Call.

3 Talk normally, using the volume and mute controls on your audio device as needed.

4 Tap Hang Up to conclude the call.

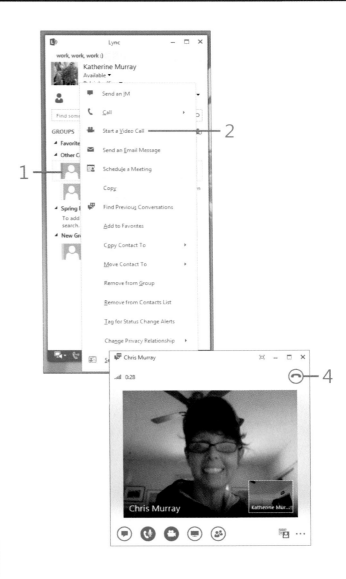

> ⚠ **CAUTION** You might occasionally see error messages such as "Your mic is picking up a lot of noise" in a yellow bar in the conversation window. Tap the Close button at right end of the warning, and make adjustments such as changing the position of your microphone.

Record a call

You might want to record some of your Lync 2013 video calls. For example, if you are conducting an interview or a brainstorming session, you can use Lync to record the call. Begin by tapping the More Options button in the video call window. Tap Start Recording and the recording controls appear in the conversation window.

Tap the Record button. Your video conversation is now being recorded. When you're ready to finish recording, tap Stop. It can take Lync a few minutes to finalize the recorded file. Check the Recording Manager to ensure that Lync has saved the file successfully.

Setting up an online meeting

If you're on the road and need to set up a meeting on the fly, don't worry. Whether you're using your tablet or your laptop, if you're using Lync Online and your administrator has given you the permissions you need to work remotely, you can easily

schedule and meeting with your team from anywhere. You can use Lync 2013 to schedule the meeting and manage it in real time so that no time is lost and you can get moving on items that are important.

Schedule the meeting

1 Tap and hold one of the contacts whom you want to invite to the meeting until the square appears and then release your touch.

2 On the menu that appears, tap Schedule A Meeting.

A Microsoft Outlook appointment window opens.

(continued on next page)

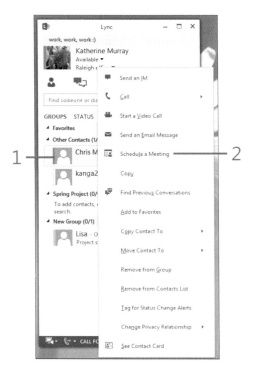

Schedule the meeting *(continued)*

3 Tap the To button to add others to the meeting.

4 Tap in the Subject line and type a subject for the message.

5 Choose a start date and time.

6 Select an end date and time.

7 Type a message to the recipients about the meeting if you like.

8 Tap Send.

The invitation is sent as an email message to those you invited. At the top of the invitation are links with which participants can choose their answer with a single tap.

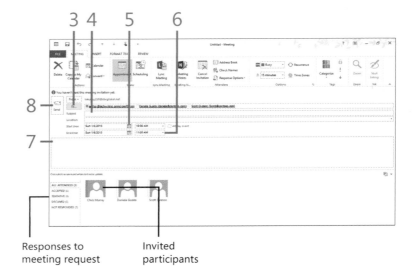

Responses to
meeting request

Invited
participants

✓ **TIP** You can use Lync's Meeting options to choose who you want to attend from the beginning of the meeting and who you want to wait in the lobby before joining. You can also mute all attendees by default when they enter the online meeting, and block video if you choose.

Meet now

1 Start an ad hoc meeting without previous scheduling by tapping the first person whom you want to invite and holding the contact until the square appears. Release your touch.

2 Tap the Settings button.

3 On the menu that appears, tap Meet Now.

The conference call window opens and you can hear Lync making the connection for the meeting.

(continued on next page)

TIP Lync also makes it easy for you to share the great ideas you come up with during your meeting to your OneNote notebook. In the Present window, tap OneNote and tap My Notes (to save the notes in your own personal notebook) or Shared Notes to save the content to a notebook your entire group can use.

Meet now (continued)

4 At the bottom of the conversation window, tap the People button.

The conversation window expands.

5 Tap Invite More People.

The Invite By Name Or Phone Number dialog box opens.

6 Search for the contact by typing a portion of the person's name or phone number if you like.

7 Alternatively, in the displayed list, tap the contact whom you want to add.

8 Tap OK to add the contact to the meeting window.

Lync makes the call and when the person accepts the invitation, he is added to the Lync meeting.

Hosting your meeting

Lync 2013 includes a number of easy to use tools that help you conduct the meeting as you want. First you can use audio, video, and instant messaging to communicate in real time. You can also watch a presentation together, work with a program, brainstorm on a whiteboard, or even create and share a poll to see how everybody's feeling about a particular issue that impacts your team.

Use Lync meeting tools

1   In the meeting window, tap Present. A palette of tools appears.

2   To share your desktop with others on the call, tap Desktop.

3   To launch a particular program, tap Program.

4   To begin sharing a presentation, tap PowerPoint.

5   To display a shared board where all participants can add text and drawings, tap Whiteboard.

6   Tap Poll to create a poll on the fly that asks a question of the group and enables each person to choose his or her answer from a displayed list.

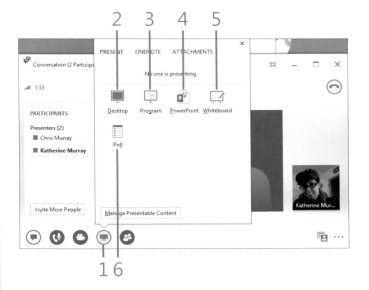

> ✓ **TIP**   Before you can share a program during an online meeting, you need to have the program running on your computer. Open the program and the file that you want to use, if applicable, before you begin your meeting.

> ✓ **TIP**   You can share files with others in your meeting by tapping Attachments at the top of the Present window and then tapping Attach Files in the screen that is displayed. In the Send A File To All Participants dialog box, navigate to the file that you want to share, tap it, and tap Open. Two buttons appear for participants: Accept Sharing Request or Ignore. If they tap Accept Sharing Request, Lync prompts them to open the shared attachment. They can tap Open to view the file you shared.

Creating and saving a document in Word 2013

7

When you first started using your tablet, you might have thought you'd leave the document work for those times you were in the office and could use your keyboard and mouse. Maybe you thought you'd use the tablet for email, browsing, and other tasks you can do easily by touch. But if you're like many of us, after you started using your tablet, you found that you wanted to use it for more and more tasks.

Word 2013 is the program in the Office 2013 suite designed to help you work with documents, no matter what type of device you happen to be using. As one of the most popular word-processing programs in the world, Word makes it possible for you to create, format, enhance, correct, and share documents, short or long. You can prepare a simple report by using one of the many templates Word provides, or you can go it alone and design something unique that is as simple or as complex as you need. And the good news for those of us who are tablet users is that Word, this time around, includes a number of touch features that make the whole process painless on a tablet.

In this section:

- Word 2013: introducing basic touch-friendly features
- Touring the Word window
- Creating a new document and adding content
- Searching and replacing text
- Selecting a theme
- Choosing a style set
- Applying styles
- Formatting your document
- Changing the view
- Inserting pictures and video
- Inserting tables
- Adding headers and footers
- Saving your Word document
- Exporting document content

Word 2013: introducing basic touch-friendly features

Starting Word on a tablet is as simple as a single tap. You scroll across the Windows 8 Start screen to display the Office 2013 app tiles and then tap the Word 2013 tile. Instantly, Word displays the Word Start screen, which gives you all the options you need to create a new file or open an existing one. Whichever you choose, you'll find yourself in the Word window, where you can unleash your creativity and begin working on your document.

All of this happens within a context of touch. Word now includes a number of features that make the touch interface easy for you to navigate and use:

- **Choose to use touch mode**   Word knows you might want to switch between touch and mouse mode, depending on whether you're out in the world with your tablet or using it docked in your workspace. When you choose touch mode, Word adds space around items on the ribbon and the Quick Access Toolbar, making tools easier to select with your not-so-pointy fingertip.

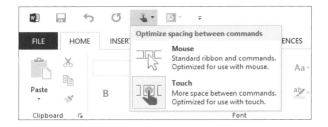

- **Select items easily with touch handles**   When you double-tap items on the screen, Word makes it easy to choose and control them by enlarging selection handles and other controls.

- **Choose your favorite On-Screen Keyboard**   Windows offers you several keyboards from which to choose, each giving you an option of selecting the style that fits the way you like to work. You can choose a standard On-Screen Keyboard, an extended keyboard, or a split keyboard (just in case you're all thumbs).

- **Pinch and zoom**   Word is responsive to your pinch and zoom gestures, so if you have trouble reading something on the screen or you want to zoom out and get a big picture of the overall document, you can easily do this by using a gesture that you probably learned long ago on your smartphone.

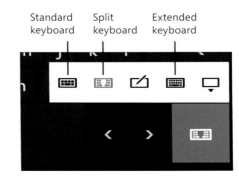

Standard keyboard   Split keyboard   Extended keyboard

Use the Word 2013 Start screen

1 On the Windows 8 Start screen, scroll to the right to display the Office 2013 app tiles.

2 Tap the Word 2013 tile.

The Word 2013 Start screen appears.

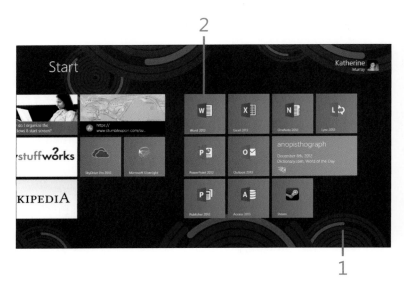

2

1

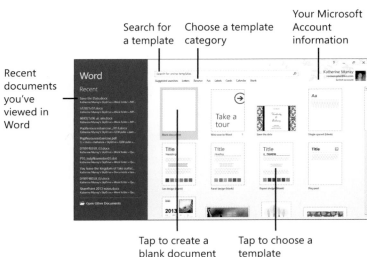

Search for a template

Choose a template category

Your Microsoft Account information

Recent documents you've viewed in Word

Tap to create a blank document

Tap to choose a template

TIP The Start screen is convenient if you want to move directly to a specific document or you often search for templates when you begin to work with Word. But, if you find the Start screen is getting in your way, you can choose to skip it and have Word display a blank document window when you tap the Word 2013 tile on the Windows 8 Start screen. To turn off the display of the Word Start screen, open any document or template, tap the File tab to display the Backstage view, tap the Options tab, and then, in the Word Options dialog box, clear the Show the Start Screen When This Application Starts check box (located from the General tab near the bottom). Tap OK to save your changes.

What's new in Word 2013?

In addition to the new touch-friendly interface, you'll find a number of new features in Word that make reading, designing, and sharing documents easier than ever. Whether you're using Word to review long documents, opening and working with a PDF that a colleague sent you, or sharing a document on SkyDrive or SharePoint, Word makes it easier by offering the following:

- A fresher, cleaner, design.

- Comments and their replies are now displayed in a single comment balloon so that you can read through all comments in a conversational view.

- You documents are now saved online by default in SkyDrive or SharePoint (depending on which version of Office 2013 you have) if you are logged on using your Microsoft Account. You can change this default and save your documents to your local storage, instead. If you are using a local account and not your Microsoft Account, your files will be saved to your computer by default.

- You can use the new Read Mode to read through documents in a natural, easy-to-read view. What's more, Read Mode bookmarks the place where you stopped reading, making it easy for you to return to that spot later.

- The live layout of your Word document causes everything to reflow automatically when you move objects around on the page.

- New alignment guides help you to position your pictures, charts, and diagrams and ensure that they are lined up with text, tables, and more.

- You can open and work with a PDF file in Word, and its content behaves just like traditional Word text, meaning you can edit and reformat the text as needed.

- You can share your Word documents with others, even if they don't have Word installed on their computers by using the new Present Online feature. You can send others a link and they'll be able to view your document online while you work with your document in a meeting or presentation.

Touring the Word window

The new design of Office 2013 provides a fresh, clean palette on which to work with apps such as Word. You will find tools in the various tabs of the Word ribbon along with contextual tools that appear when you select certain types of items on the page.

Choose touch or mouse mode

Tap a tab to see more tools

Tap the tool you want to use

Hide the ribbon

Tap to display the Backstage view

Navigation pane

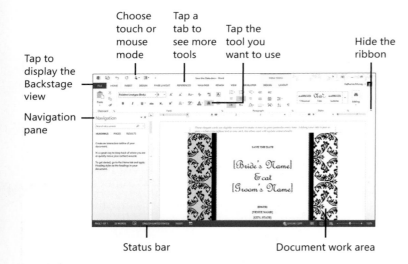

Status bar

Document work area

Creating documents and adding content

In Word 2013, you can start a new document using any of several different ways—all of them simple. In the Word 2013 Start screen, you can choose to open a blank document or use a template to start your design. The Start screen also presents the Recent list, which makes it easy for you to open documents that you've worked on previously.

Start with a blank document

1   On the Windows 8 Start screen, tap the Word 2013 tile to display the Word Start screen.

2   Tap Blank Document.

    The blank document appears on the screen.

3   Begin typing the content for your document.

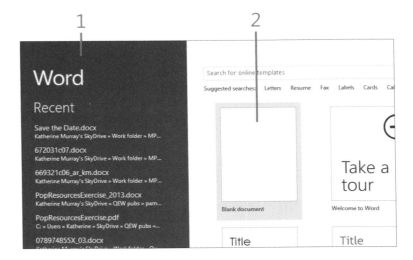

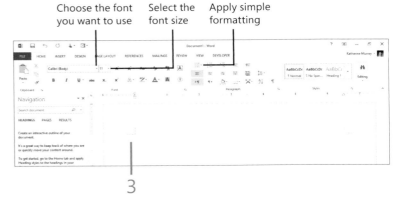

> **✓ TIP**   If you want to start a new blank document when you're already working with Word, simply tap the File tab and then choose New from within the Backstage view. The Word Start screen will appear and you can select Blank Document to get started.

> **→ TRY THIS**   Open a blank document and experiment by tapping and typing a few characters on the screen to find out how quickly Word responds. You can also practice formatting the text you typed by double-tapping a word and then, on the Home tab, choosing a formatting tool.

Start with a template

1 Display the Word 2013 Start screen.

2 In the Search box, enter a word or phrase describing the template that you'd like to find.

3 Tap the Search button.

4 Alternatively, tap a template category.

5 Scroll down to display more templates.

6 Tap the template that you want to use.

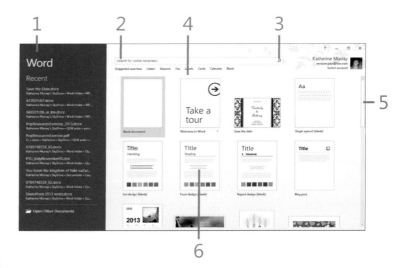

> **TIP** If you choose to search for a template or select a template category, Word displays the Filter By list along the right side of the Start screen. You can use the Filter By list to narrow the search results displayed in the center of the screen. You might narrow the results you received for Fax templates, for example, by choosing a design set you like (such as the Oriel Design Set) or by selecting another characteristic, such as Professional.

> **TIP** Of course not all the documents you'll work with in Word will be brand new; you also need to be able to open documents you've already created. Luckily that's a simple task with the Start screen and Backstage view. In the Word 2013 Start screen, review the list of documents in the Recent list and tap the document you want to open. Or, if you don't see the document you want in the Recent list, tap Open Other Documents. The Open dialog box appears, in which you can choose the location and the folder where the file you want is stored. If you're already working with Word, on the ribbon, tap the File tab to display the Backstage view, tap the open tab, and then, in the center panel, tap Recent Documents to see your recent documents list.

Enter text

1 Tap in the document to display the On-Screen Keyboard.

2 Type your content.

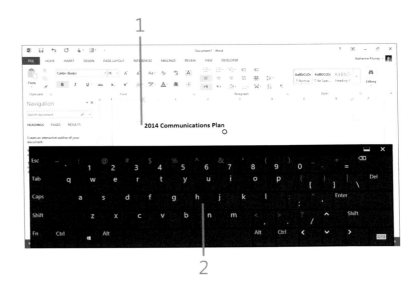

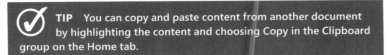

> ✓ **TIP** You can copy and paste content from another document by highlighting the content and choosing Copy in the Clipboard group on the Home tab.

> → **TRY THIS** Type a sentence or two in the blank Word document and, if you're feeling adventurous, experiment with selecting the text by tapping and dragging over the text.

> ✓ **TIP** You can easily add text from another document at the cursor position in your current document. Just tap at the point you want to insert the text, tap the Insert tab, and then tap the Object tool in the Text group. Choose Text From File and then, in the Insert File dialog box, choose the folder where the file is stored. Select the file and tap Insert; the contents of the file are added to your document.

Using the formatting tools to enhance your text

When you select text in your document, Word 2013 displays a minibar of tools with which you can easily apply several commonly used styles and formats to the text. If you choose not to use the formatting minibar, you can also choose the tools by tapping the Home tab and selecting the formatting tool of your choice in the Font or Paragraph groups. You can apply the formatting tools to text you've selected or tap to position the cursor and use the formatting tools to set a new format for text you will type from that point on.

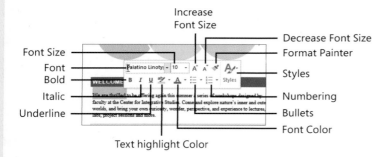

Tools in the formatting toolbar

Use this tool	To do this
Font	Change the font of selected text
Font Size	Adjust the size of selected text
Increase Font Size	Increase the size of selected text by one point size
Decrease Font Size	Reduce the size of selected text by one point size
Format Painter	Copy the formatting applied to selected text
Styles	Display a gallery of styles that you can apply to selected text
Bold	Make selected text bold
Italic	Italicize selected text
Underline	Underline selected text
Text Highlight Color	Add a highlight to selected text
Font Color	Change the color of selected text
Bullets	Add bullets to selected text
Numbering	Add numbering to selected text

Searching and replacing text

Some changes that you need to make in your Word 2013 document might be more far-reaching. Suppose, for example, that you realize after you finish a report that you misspelled a product name throughout. You can easily search for that text and replace it with the correct text by using a simple automated tool.

Find and replace text

1 Display the document that you want to use and then, on the ribbon, tap the View tab.

2 In the Show group, select the Navigation Pane check box.

3 To find all occurrences of a word or phrase in a document, type the text in the Search box.

4 If necessary, tap Results to see where the word is used.

5 Tap a result to go to that place in the document.

(continued on next page)

Search box   2   1

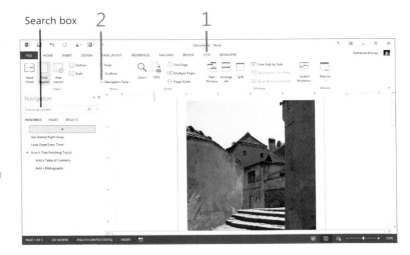

3 4 5

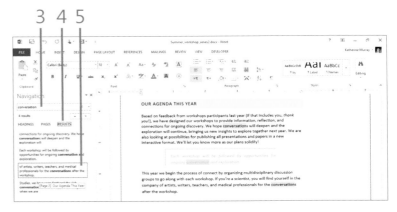

Find and replace text *(continued)*

6 To search and replace text, tap the More drop-down arrow.

7 Choose Replace.

8 In the Find And Replace dialog box, in the Find What box, enter the word or phrase you're looking for.

9 In the Replace With box, type the replacement word or phrase.

10 Tap Find Next and then tap Replace to search for and replace a single occurrence of what you're looking for. Or, tap Replace All to replace all occurrences in the document.

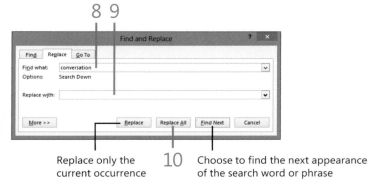

Replace only the current occurrence

Choose to find the next appearance of the search word or phrase

TIP The search and replace feature in Word can replace more than just text items. In the Find And Replace dialog box, tap the More button to display additional search-and-replace choices. You can have Word match the case you enter, locate whole words only, find words or phrases that sound like the one you entered, or find all forms of a word. You can also search for specific formatting, locate special characters, and include or ignore punctuation characters.

Selecting a theme

Word 2013 includes a number of themes that you can use to give your documents a professional, color-coordinated look. These apply a color scheme, preselected fonts, and special

effects to objects on your pages. Out of the box, Word offers you 10 themes, but you can add to those by creating your own if you like.

Choose a theme for your document

1 With any document open, on the ribbon, tap the Design tab.

2 Tap Themes to display the Themes gallery. (Office is the default theme.)

3 In the gallery, tap the theme you want to apply to the document.

Depending on the theme that you select, you might see the font change slightly, as well as the colors and effects used in the document.

Choosing a style set

Whenever you choose a new theme in Word 2013, new style sets come along with it. A style set provides options that affect how certain elements in your document appear; for example, the way your headings look, the types of elements used (borders, boxes, and lines, for example), and the way color is assigned to elements on the page.

Select a style set

1   In an open document, select some text. On the ribbon, tap the Design tab and then, in the Document Formatting group, review the style sets.

2   On the right end of the Style Set gallery, tap the drop-down arrow to see additional style sets.

3   Tap the style set that you want to apply to the selected text.

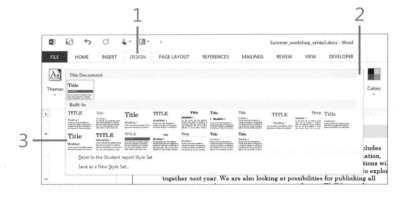

TIP   You can create your own style set. In an open document, change the font and colors for elements as desired. On the right side of the Style Set gallery, tap the drop-down arrow and then tap Save As A New Style Set. In the dialog box, enter a file name for the new style set and tap Save. The new style set becomes available in the Style Set gallery so you can tap it to apply it to the current document.

Applying styles

The styles you assign to the text and paragraphs in your document are available in the Styles gallery on the Home tab, but there are more where those came from. Your business or organization might have its own style sheet with particular styles used for correspondence with customers (you'll learn how to attach a style sheet later in this section). You might want to create or tweak your own styles until you can get just the look you want—and then you can even save those styles so that you can use them consistently in your other documents, as well.

Apply a style to text

1 Tap in or select the text to which you want to apply the style.

2 On the ribbon, tap the Home tab.

3 In the Styles gallery, tap the style that you want to apply.

4 If you want to see additional styles, tap the drop-down arrow on the right side of the Styles gallery.

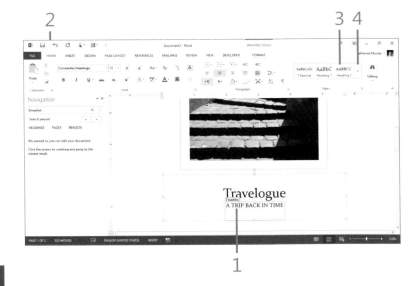

> ✓ **TIP** To display all the styles in a Styles pane along the right side of the document window, on the Home tab, in the lower-right corner of the Styles group, tap the dialog launcher.

> ✓ **TIP** You can easily change the various settings included in a style to achieve just the look you want. Tap the style you want to change and then tap the arrow that appears to the right of the style. Choose Modify to display the Modify Style dialog box, in which you can set the font, size, and formatting for the style.

Managing your styles

As you add styles to your document, you'll need a way of organizing how they appear in the Styles pane. By choosing which styles you want to appear and arranging them in the order you want, you can streamline the amount of time you spend looking for styles and get back to working on the document at hand.

Display the Styles pane by tapping the dialog launcher in the lower-right corner of the Styles group on the Home tab. In the lower right of the Styles pane, tap Manage Styles to display the Manage Styles dialog box. In this dialog box, you can reorder styles, add styles to recommended lists, organize your styles, and even import styles from other documents. Tap OK to save your changes and return to your document.

> ✓ **TIP** The Style Inspector in Word helps you check the styles in your document to make sure that your formatting is consistent throughout. You can also modify styles and make other style selections via the Style Inspector. Start the Style Inspector by tapping the Style Inspector tool in the center of the tools at the bottom of the Styles pane. You can then tap the text that you want to inspect, and Word will display the formatting applied to the selected item. You can choose to reset the formatting, clear all formats, or create a new style as you go.

Formatting your document

Word 2013 makes it easy to you to arrange your text in different formats. Two of the most common formats you will use are bulleted or numbered lists. A bullet list can help you show readers at a glance what's important or memorable about something you're describing in the text. Bullet lists are typically short and sweet—no more than seven to ten bullets—and easy for a reader to review and remember. Numbered lists come in handy when you want to tell your readers about a process. The numbered items provide a step-by-step tutorial (not unlike the steps you're reading in this book).

Create a bulleted list

1 Tap to position the cursor in the document where you want to begin the bulleted list.

2 On the ribbon, tap the Home tab.

3 In the Paragraph group, tap the Bullets tool.

4 Type the text for the first bullet and press Enter.

A new bullet appears, ready for you to enter the second bulleted item.

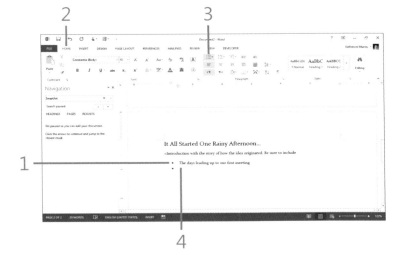

> **TIP** If you want to choose the character used for the bullet or change the bullet style or color, select the drop-down arrow to the right of the Bullets tool. A gallery of bullet choices appears. If you want to create a new bullet, choose Define New Bullet and select your choices in the dialog box that appears. Tap OK to save your settings.

Add a numbered list

1 Tap at the point in the document where you want to begin the numbered list.

2 On the Home tab, in the Paragraph group, tap the Numbering tool.

A number 1 appears at the cursor position.

3 Type the first line in your list and press Enter. A number 2 appears.

4 Continue entering items for the list as needed. Press Enter twice to end the list.

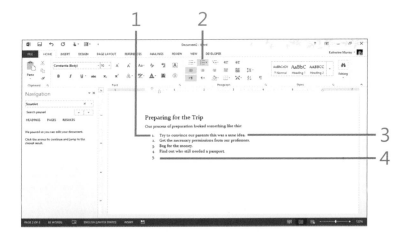

TIP You can easily turn text into a bulleted list or a numbered list after you type it. Just select the text that you want to use and then choose either Bullets or Numbered List. Word formats the list as you selected, assigning one bullet or one numeral to each paragraph. The text is also formatted so that the list aligns and the bullets or numbers hang out to the left of the list items.

TRY THIS Select a few lines of text in your document. (Or, if you haven't yet entered any text, type three brief phrases on three separate lines and select the text.) Choose the Numbered List tool in the Paragraph group. If you want to undo your changes, press Ctrl+Z or tap the Undo tool in the Quick Access Toolbar in the upper-left corner of the Word window.

Formatting and spacing paragraphs

When you apply formats to your paragraphs, you can choose the way the text is aligned, change the spacing before and after paragraphs, adjust the line spacing, and create special indents. Tap in the paragraph you want to adjust and then tap the alignment setting you want to apply in the Paragraph group on the Home tab. You can adjust the spacing before and after paragraphs by tapping in the paragraph and then tapping the dialog launcher in the lower-right corner of the Paragraph group. In the Paragraph dialog box, you can adjust the Before and After values to increase or decrease the amount of space after your paragraphs. Tap OK to save your changes.

> **TIP** If you're trying to center text and find that it's not centering correctly, the ruler can help you see what's going on. Display the ruler by tapping the View tab and selecting the Ruler check box in the Show group. Notice the margin indicators on the horizontal ruler, and check the amount of space available for centering your text. If necessary, you can drag the margin indicator on the right toward the edge of the page to widen the text area of your document and allow for true centering. You can also set tabs by tapping the point on the ruler where you want the tab to appear; this way, you can line up and adjust the text alignment easily by tapping a tab on the ruler and dragging it in the direction you want to adjust.

Changing the view

Word 2013 includes a number of views, making it possible for you to look at your work in different ways, depending on what you need to accomplish. For example, you can use Draft view, which hides pictures and formatting, to enter text quickly. Or you might want to use Outline view if you're just working on the outline of your document.

Word also includes a new view called Read Mode by which you can view the document full-screen, without all the Word control elements and tools to distract you.

Change the view

1 On the ribbon, tap the View tab.

   By default, your document appears in Print Layout view.

2 Tap the view that you want to use.

3 Use the Zoom slider to adjust the display so you see the number of pages you want on the screen at one time, if more than one page exists.

4 Tap to display more than one page on the screen at a time.

5 Tap to display more than one document in the Word window at a time.

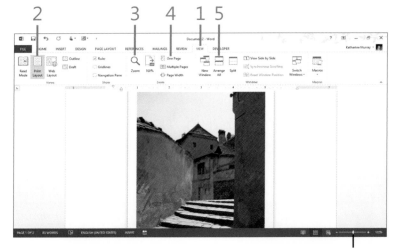

Adjust the Zoom slider to change the size of the display

> **→ TRY THIS** Practice switching among the Word views to find out which view/mode you like best and which Zoom percentage is the most comfortable for you.

Use Read Mode

1 On the ribbon, tap the View tab.

2 In the View group, tap the Read Mode button.

3 By default Read Mode appears in Column layout. At the right edge of the screen, tap the right arrow to display the next page.

4 At the top of the screen, tap View to display viewing and editing options.

5 On the menu that appears, point to Layout.

6 On the submenu that opens, tap Paper Layout.

The display of Read Mode changes so that you use the horizontal scroll bar—rather than the arrows on either side of the colum- nar page—to move through the document. If you prefer Column Layout better, return to that layout by repeating steps 4 through 6, but this time, tap Column Layout.

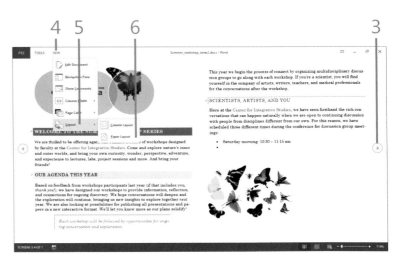

TIP Read Mode offers a number of settings that you can use to customize the display. Tap Navigation Pane to display the Navigation pane on the left side of Read Mode; use other tools in the View tab to add a comments column, change the color of the page, or change the width of columns in Column Layout view. Tap the Esc key to return quickly to Print Layout.

Inserting pictures and video

Today, we expect to see a splash of color, an image or two, or something visually appealing in the documents we read. In Word 2013, you can easily insert and edit photos, choose clip art or photos from online sources, draw shapes, add custom charts, and even take pictures of your screen to include in your document. In addition to adding pictures from your computer, from online storage, or from connected photo-sharing sites, you can also add video clips to your documents that others can watch as they review what you've created.

Insert an online picture

1 Tap to position your cursor at the location in your document where you want to insert a picture. Then, on the ribbon, tap the Insert tab.

2 In the Illustrations group, tap Online Pictures.

(continued on next page)

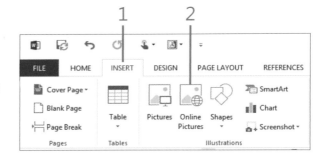

> ✓ **TIP**   After you add a picture to the page, you can use the editing tools in Word to change the brightness and contrast, sharpen up the focus, change the coloring, or even apply artistic effects if you want a special look.

Insert an online picture (continued)

3 In the Insert Pictures dialog box, tap to search Office.com for clip art. You can type the sort of clip art you want to search for first, if you prefer.

4 Type a word or phrase for the type of picture you want to find by using Bing and then tap the Search icon.

5 Tap to choose a picture from an online photo site you've connected to your Office account.

6 Tap to display your SkyDrive folders and choose a picture there.

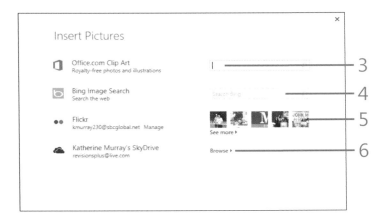

The ways that you can add illustrations in Word 2013

Tab	Tool	Use to
Insert	Pictures	Insert photos, drawings, and other picture files from your local storage device or cloud storage
Insert	Online Pictures	Find images on Office.com, the web, or on your connected picture sites and cloud storage
Insert	Shapes	Draw a variety of shapes on your document page and add a new drawing canvas
Insert	SmartArt	Create a diagram with the color, text, and style you want
Insert	Chart	Add a chart based on numeric and label values
Insert	Screenshot	Insert a screenshot of a current screen image

Edit a picture

1 Tap the picture that you want to change.

2 On the Picture Tools | Format contextual tab, tap Artistic Effects.

3 In the gallery that opens, select the effect that you want to apply to your picture.

Add and play online video

1 Tap to position your cursor at the location in your document where you want to insert a video. Then, on the ribbon, tap the Insert tab.

2 In the Media group, tap the Online Video button.

3 In the Insert Video dialog box, tap in the Bing Video Search and type a word or phrase reflecting the type of video that you want to add. Tap the Search icon or press Enter on your attached keyboard.

4 Alternatively, if you have the embed code from one of your own videos (for example, a video you uploaded to YouTube that you want to include in your Word document), tap the From A Video Embed Code text box and paste the embed code. Tap the Search icon or press Enter on your attached keyboard.

(continued on next page)

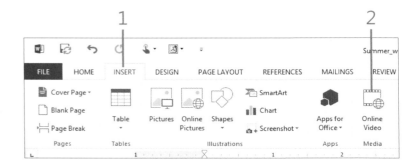

TIP What is a video embed code? Online videos like those you find on YouTube or Vimeo typically offer an Embed option that makes it possible for you to copy the code used so that you can display the video on a webpage or blog. When you tap the Embed button, you will see a link of code you can copy and paste in other tools, like the Video Embed Code option in the Insert Video window in Word 2013.

Add and play online video (continued)

5 Tap the thumbnail of the video you'd like to add.

6 Tap Insert to add the video to your document at the cursor position.

7 You can play the video clip at any point by tapping the Play button at the bottom of the clip.

8 The video clip opens and begins to play. You can use the standard player controls to adjust playback.

Change the topic you're searching for

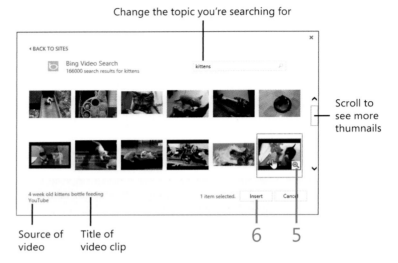

Scroll to see more thumnails

Source of video

Title of video clip

6   5

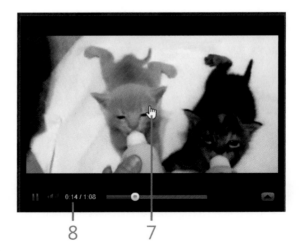

8   7

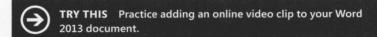

TRY THIS Practice adding an online video clip to your Word 2013 document.

Adding Apps for Office

Apps for Office extends the functionality of Word 2013 by adding apps that bring tools, information, and more right into your line-by-line document work. For example, you might want to add your favorite dictionary as an app in Word. Or, perhaps you regularly fax contracts to others—in this case, adding an app that makes it possible for you to fax from Word is a real time-saving feature.

If you want to add Apps for Office, tap the Insert tab and then tap Apps for Office. In the list that appears, tap See All. A window appears, showing you the apps that are currently available for Word 2013. Tap the app that you want to add and a webpage opens displaying additional information about the app. Tap Add. Tap the close box to close the webpage.

The app appears in a panel along the right side of the Word window. You can close the app by tapping the Close button. In the future you'll be able to start the app by tapping the Insert tab, tapping Apps for Office, and then selecting the app from the displayed list.

Flow text around a picture

1 Select the picture around which you want to flow text.

2 At the upper-right corner of the image, tap the Layout Options button. The Layout Options toolbar appears.

3 In the Layout Options gallery that opens, choose how you want the text to flow around the image.

4 Click to specify whether you want the image to move with the text or remain in one position on the page and have the text reflow around it.

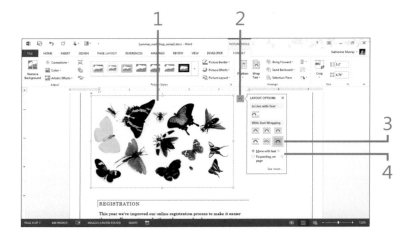

Correcting misspellings

The spelling checker in Word 2013 keeps an eye on the words you type as you type them. You can run the spelling checker when you're finished writing or pay attention to the spelling checker icon in the status bar to see when Word thinks you've got one of more misspelled words. Tap and hold a word that has a red squiggly line beneath it. Release your touch and an options list appears. Select from among the suggested corrections. If the word is spelled correctly, tap Ignore All; occurrences of the word will be ignored by the spelling checker from that point on.

Inserting tables

Word 2013 makes adding tables easy, whether you're using a tablet, laptop, or desktop computer. You can use a table to line up data items so readers can see how the items compare in a side-by-side comparison. The table tools in Word give you a lot of flexibility in the way you create tables in your document. You can draw a table on the page, choose a Quick Table design, or insert a table with the number of rows and columns you want.

Create and modify tables

1 Tap to position your cursor at the location in your document where you want to insert a the table.

2 On the ribbon, tap the Insert tab.

3 In the Tables group, tap Table.

4 On the grid that appears, drag to select the number of rows and columns you want to add to the table. Word displays a preview of the table at the cursor position, showing how the table will look before you tap your choice.

5 Tap in a table cell and type in information. Tap in the adjacent cell.

6 To add a row or column to the table, tap and hold along the left edge of the table. When the square appears, release your touch.

7 In the toolbar that appears, Tap Insert.

8 Tap to add the row or column to the table.

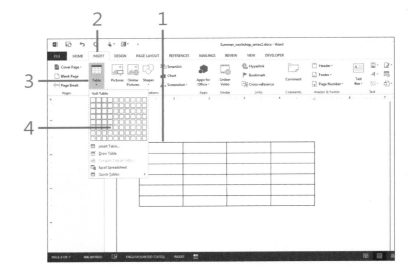

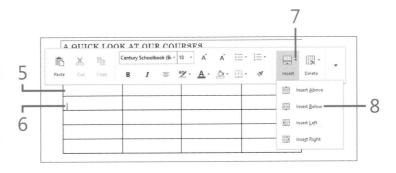

> ✓ **TIP** After you add content to your table, you can format the information by using the various tools on the Home tab. You can also select your text and choose the formatting options that you want to use from the formatting toolbar.

> ✓ **TIP** Tables can be more than text. You can add pictures to tables if that suits what you need for your document. You can also use shading and borders to give your table a professional look.

Changing the table design and layout

When you tap inside a table in your Word document, the Table Tools contextual tabs appear. On the Table Tools | Design tab, you'll find the tools you need to adjust the style of the table and add shading and borders. You'll use the tools in the Table Tools | Layout tab to add, remove, split, and align information in your table cells. You can also sort table data, specify the size for your table cells, remove unwanted lines, and display table properties.

Adding headers and footers

If you're creating a long document, you might want to add headers or footers to help your readers find their way through the document. Word 2013 reserves space at the top and bottom of your document in which you can easily add headers and footers. Word offers a gallery of header and footer styles that you can use to insert predesigned, professional-looking headers and footers for your document. Or, if you prefer, you can create your own from scratch. What's more, you can add page numbers, document information, and even images such as logos. You can also vary the way the headers and footers appear so that they're different on odd and even pages or so that your first page looks different from the rest of your document. Because headers and footers are similar (in every way except the place where they appear on your page), the following tasks apply to both headers and footers.

Insert a header or footer from the gallery

1 On the ribbon, tap the Insert tab.

2 In the Header & Footer group, tap either Header or Footer. A gallery of header or footer styles appears.

3 In the gallery that opens, scroll through to find the style you like.

4 Tap the header or footer that you want to add to the document.

Word inserts the item you selected and displays the Header & Footer Tools | Design contextual tab. You can then add the information you'd like to include in the header or footer.

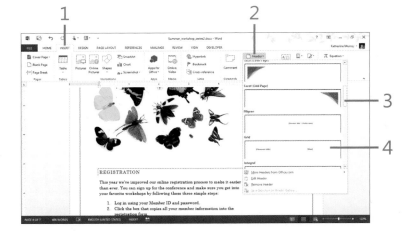

Create your own header or footer

1 Double-tap in the area at the top or bottom of the page.

   Word displays the Header & Footer Tools | Design contextual tab.

2 Type the information that you want to include in the header or footer.

3 On the ribbon, in the Insert group, tap Page Number to add a page number.

4 Tap Date & Time to insert the date and time.

5 Tap Document Info to add document information, such as the author name, file name, file path, or document title.

6 Tap Pictures to insert a picture in the header or footer.

7 Tap Quick Parts to add AutoText, a document property, a data field, or another building block to the header or footer.

8 Tap Close Header And Footer to close the header and footer area.

Saving your Word document

By default, Word 2013 saves your file to the cloud, posting it in your SkyDrive account where you can reach it easily, by desktop, laptop, tablet, and phone. Saving is also an important part of sharing your files, as you'll learn in Section 8, "Working with shared documents in Word 2013." Saving your file can be as simple as tapping the Save icon on the Quick Access Toolbar or you can choose the location and folder where you want the file to be stored.

Save your document

1 On the ribbon, tap the File tab to display the Backstage view.

2 Tap the Save As tab.

3 Tap the location where you want to save the file.

4 Tap the folder in which you want to save the file.

5 Alternatively, tap Browse to display the Save As dialog box.

(continued on next page)

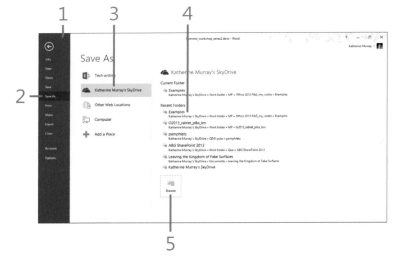

Save your document *(continued)*

6 Choose the folder for the file.

7 Type a name for the file.

8 Tap Save.

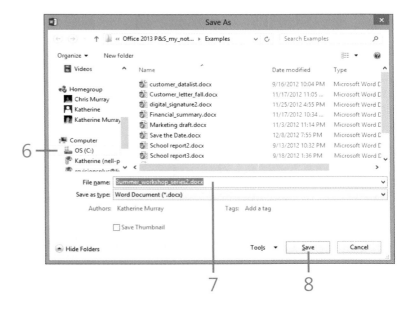

Exporting document content

Word 2013 makes it easy for you to save your file as a PDF or XPS document so that you can share your finished-format file with others without worrying about whether they will make changes to it without your permission. Of course, Word also enables you to open and edit PDF files as though they were native Word documents.

In addition to PDF or XPS format, you can choose another file type to use with the content of your files.

Export as a PDF

1 On the ribbon, tap the File tab to display the Backstage view.

2 Tap the Export tab.

3 Tap Create PDF/XPS Document.

4 Tap the Create PDF/XPS button.

(continued on next page)

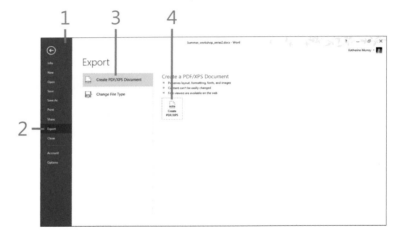

✓ **TIP** You can choose to save your file as a different file type using the Export tool in Word. Tap File to display Backstage view and choose Export. Tap Change File Type and select the file format you want to use in the Change File Type list. Finally, tap Save As, enter a name for the file, and tap Save.

Export as a PDF *(continued)*

5 In the Publish As PDF Or XPS dialog box, type a name for the file.

6 Tap Publish.

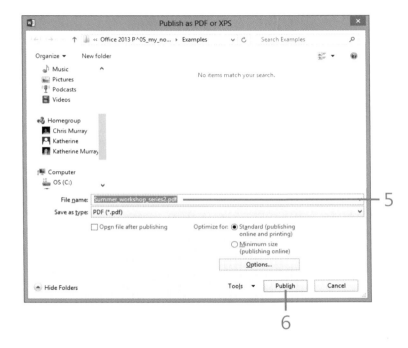

Working with shared documents in Word 2013

8

As you've probably heard by now, collaboration is one of the big features throughout Microsoft Office 2013. The company is aiming to make saving, sharing, and working in the cloud a seamless part of your daily work. You can open, edit, share, comment on, and close files with the focus you need, without ever realizing that the file isn't actually stored on your computer, but is instead in a remote location in a SkyDrive folder. The great thing about this kind of cloud effort is that you can easily share files without worrying whether others are getting the right copy or not, and you can let the program—in this case, Microsoft Word 2013—ensure that all the changes are up to date and reflected in the most recent copy of the file.

Another new and effective collaboration tool in Word 2013 is the new simple markup. This is an improvement of the Track Changes feature, simplifying the view you see after someone has made changes in your document and giving you choices about the way in which you view the changes. Word also adds threaded comments, which displays comments and responses in a single comment balloon, rather than littering your entire page with comment balloons that are really all related to the same question. That's a relief, right?

In this section:

- Understanding the collaboration features in Word
- Sharing your documents
- Collaborating in the cloud
- Contacting coauthors in real time
- Restricting document editing
- Opening and editing PDF files
- Tracking document changes
- Using Simple Markup
- Adding and responding to comments
- Accepting or rejecting changes
- Presenting your document online

Understanding the collaboration features in Word

We learned it in kindergarten, if not before: life is better when you share. Today, increasingly, our jobs ask us to share what we're working on. You need to send a copy of the report to the committee chairperson. The gardening club wants a copy of your latest article. You're drafting a marketing plan and need the input of others in your group.

Word 2013 makes it easy to share your files, whether you're using a tablet, a desktop, or even your phone. You'll find the sharing features you need on the Share tab of the Backstage view.

Using the Word sharing features, you can:

- Save your file to the cloud and invite others to share it

- Choose to create two types of links that you can share with others—one link enables others to view the file; the other allows others to view and edit the file

- Post your file to your favorite social media account

- Send the file to others by email

- Present the document online so that others can go through it with you, even if they don't have Word 2013

- Create and post content directly to your blog

Additionally, the collaboration features that are built in to Word have been enhanced so that you can work together easily. After you save your file to the cloud, you and your coauthors can all work in the file at the same time, and Word keeps track of the changes you're making and synchronizes them all when you close the file.

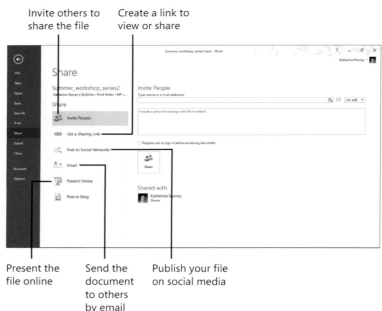

Invite others to share the file

Create a link to view or share

Present the file online

Send the document to others by email

Publish your file on social media

Sharing your documents

When you share your documents, you can do more than work with other people: you can also access your own files easily, using your tablet, desktop, laptop, or compatible smartphone. Wherever you are, if your files are saved in the cloud, you can access the latest version easily.

When you do need to work with others, you can work on the shared document in your own time; the changes will be synchronized automatically, meaning that everyone will have have the most recent changes to the file. And, if you choose to work on the file at the same time as others are using it, no problem—Word synchronizes the changes and even gives you the means to contact each other directly while you work.

Open a shared document

1 On the ribbon, tap the File tab to display the Backstage view.

2 Tap the Open tab.

3 Choose the online location where your shared file is stored.

4 If necessary, tap Browse to look through folders and files in your cloud space.

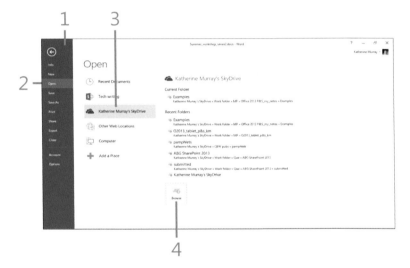

(continued on next page)

Open a shared document *(continued)*

5 In the Open dialog box, tap the folder containing the file you want to use and select the file.

6 Tap Open.

The document opens on your screen. (You might need to tap Enable Editing before you can work on the document.)

7 Word alerts you if other authors are working on the document. Tap the status bar if you want to see the names of the authors or contact them directly.

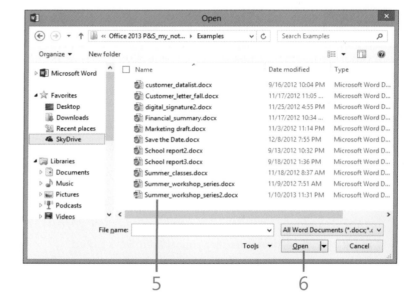

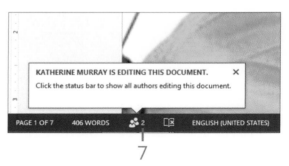

Collaborating in the cloud

While you're working, Word 2013 is busy keeping track of all the changes being made in the file. If someone else makes changes in a particular section, Word displays the changes in a green highlight, making them easy for you to see. Also, if you have Track Changes turned on in your document, you will be able to see what changes were made and who made them. When you save the document, Word informs everyone that an update of the file is available, and when they save their versions of the file, Word synchronizes all the changes and highlights the added text so that each person can see what the others have changed.

Work collaboratively in a document

1 Open a shared document and make the changes that you want to make.

2 Tap a highlighted area in your document that shows where a coauthor has made a recent change. The author's name appears in the box above the highlight.

3 When your coauthor saves changes, Word notifies you that updates are available. Tap Updates Available and save the file as prompted.

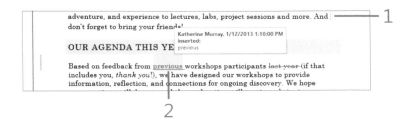

Contacting coauthors in real time

While you're working collaboratively on a project, it's nice to be able to ask a quick question or test out an idea you're thinking of including. Because Word's sharing features shows you the online status of your coauthors, you can easily display the name of your coauthors and contact them by instant message, phone, or email while you work.

Contact your coauthor while you work

1 While you're working in the shared document, tap the authoring indicator in the status bar.

2 The list of current authors appears. Tap the author whom you want to communicate to display the contact information.

3 To send an instant message to the coauthor, tap the Instant Message button.

4 To call your coauthor, tap the Phone button.

5 To start a video call, tap the Video button.

6 To send an email message, tap the email link or the Email button.

7 To set up a new meeting and invite your coauthor, tap the Schedule A Meeting link.

8 Tap the More Options ellipsis to add the contact to your social media or instant messaging contacts.

(continued on next page)

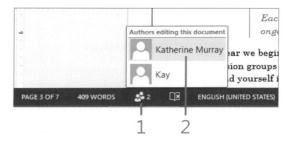

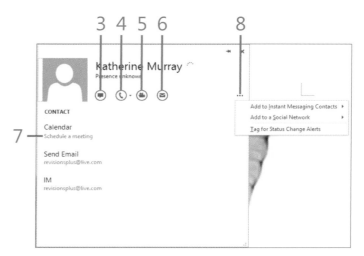

Contact your coauthor while you work *(continued)*

9 If you choose to launch instant messaging, you can dock the messaging window in Windows 8 so that you can work on the document and continue your conversation thread.

10 To create and send a new message, tap the Type A Message text box.

11 To close the docked window when you're done, drag the window divider off the right side of the screen.

Restricting document editing

Just because you're sharing your document with others doesn't mean that you can't have some say over the types of changes they are allowed to make. Word 2013 includes features with which you can limit the changes your coauthors can make in your file. You can limit their formatting choices or choose the kind of editing you'll allow by using the Restrict Editing tool in the Protect group on the Review tab.

Restrict editing

1 On the ribbon, tap the Review tab.

2 In the Protect group, tap Restrict Editing.

   The Restrict Editing pane appears along the right side of your document window.

3 To limit the formatting others can do in your document, select the Formatting Restrictions check box.

4 To control the type of edits other users can make, select the Editing Restrictions check box.

5 Tap the list box and choose the type of editing you want to allow.

6 Tap Yes, Start Enforcing Protection.

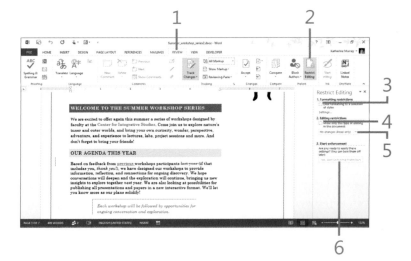

Choose the styles allowed in restricted formatting

1 In the Restrict Editing pane, select the Formatting Restrictions check box.

2 Tap the Settings link.

3 In the Formatting Restrictions dialog box, clear the check boxes corresponding to the styles that you want to restrict.

4 In the formatting section, select the check boxes for the Auto-Format, Theme, and Quick Style items.

5 Tap OK to save your changes.

6 In the Restrict Editing pane, tap Yes, Start Enforcing Protection.

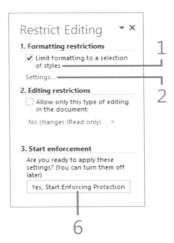

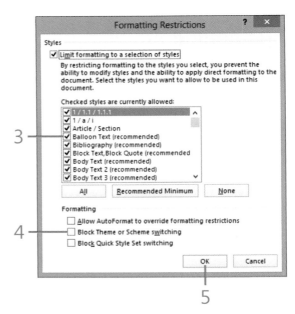

Opening and editing PDF files

You are probably familiar with PDF (Portable Document Files) files, and maybe you've created a few yourself. PDF files have become increasingly popular in the last few years, making it possible for you you to save and share a finished document with others no matter what type of computer they might be using. In the past, however, one of the limitations of PDF files was that you were unable to open and edit them unless you had a special program with which to do it. But now, in Word 2013, you can open and edit PDF files in much the same way that you can work with any native Word document. After you make your changes to the file, you can save it back to PDF format.

Open a PDF file

1 On the ribbon, tap the File tab to display the Backstage view.

2 Tap the Open tab.

3 Choose the place where the PDF is stored.

4 Select the folder in which the file resides.

   The Open dialog box appears displaying the contents of the folder you selected.

5 Alternatively, tap Browse to display the Open dialog box and browse to the folder you need.

(continued on next page)

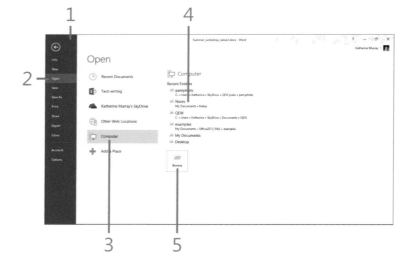

Open a PDF file *(continued)*

6 Tap the PDF file that you want to open.

7 Tap Open.

The document should appear in the Word window in Print Layout view, looking just like a traditional Word document. You can now edit the file as you would any document—all of the tools that you normally have at your disposal in Word are available as you edit the PDF.

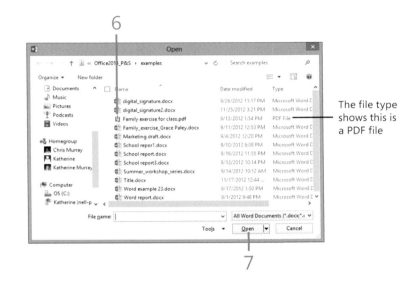

The file type shows this is a PDF file

Save the PDF file

1 When you're ready to save your changes, tap the File tab to display the Backstage view.

2 Tap the Save As tab.

3 Choose the place where you want to save the file.

4 Select the folder in which you want to save it.

5 Alternatively, tap Browse to navigate to the folder.

6 In the Save As dialog box, select the place where you want to save the file.

7 By default, Word will save the edited PDF file as a Word Document. If you want to resave the file in PDF format, tap the Save As Type drop-down arrow.

8 Tap PDF.

9 Tap Save.

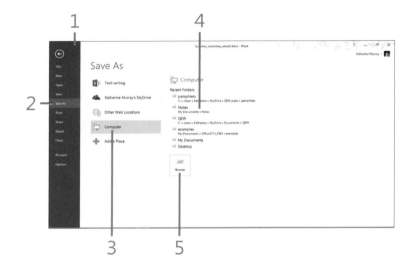

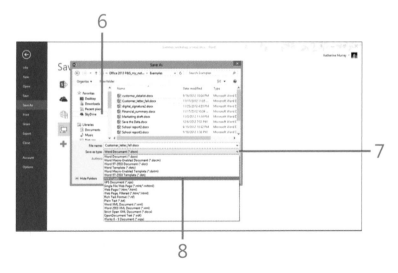

Tracking document changes

The Track Changes feature in Word helps you see what kinds of changes others are making in your shared document. When you turn on Track Changes, Word displays all additional changes made after that point so that you can scan them easily. You can also use Lock Tracking to ensure that tracking remains on. This way, you can rest assured that no one is making changes in your document that you're not seeing.

Turn on Track Changes

1 On the ribbon, tap the Review tab.

2 In the Tracking group, tap Track Changes.

Lock tracking

1 On the ribbon, tap the Review tab.

2 In the Tracking group, tap the Track Changes drop-down arrow.

3 On the menu that appears, tap Lock Tracking.

4 In the Lock Tracking dialog box, in the Enter Password text box, type a password.

5 In the Reenter to Confirm text box, retype the password you entered.

6 Tap OK.

The Track Changes option in the list that appears when users tap Track Changes is now disabled so that the feature cannot be turned off.

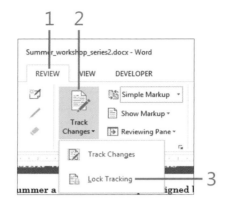

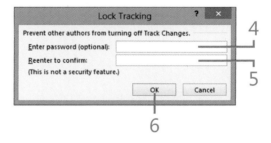

Using Simple Markup

The Track Changes feature has been part of Word for a long time. Traditionally, one of the challenges of viewing the changes in your document is that you can feel overwhelmed with the amount of information displayed on the page. Depending on how many people have reviewed your document and the types of changes they've made, the page you see can be full of comment balloons and multiple colors of edited and inserted text.

How changes are displayed has been simplified in Word 2013. Now, you can choose Simple Markup, which displays a line along the left edge of the document where changes have been made. You can tap the line to display the changes made at that point. You can easily review the changes as you like, without being inundated by changes throughout the document.

Turn on and use Simple Markup

1 On the ribbon, tap the Review tab.

2 In the Tracking group, tap the Display For Review drop-down arrow.

3 In the list of tracking options that appears, tap Simple Markup.

4 To display changes in the document while using Simple Markup, tap one of the vertical bars. To return to Simple Markup, tap the vertical bar a second time.

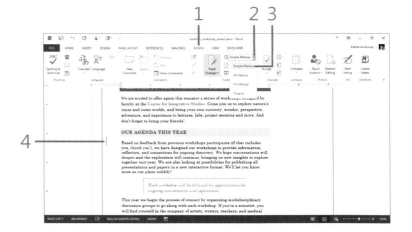

TIP If you're working with a document that has undergone a lot of changing, you might want to display the original document to see how much has changed. You can view the original document—without losing any of your changes—by tapping the Display For Review drop-down arrow in the Tracking group on the Review tab and choosing Original. All markup is hidden and you are able to read through the content as it was originally.

Choose the markup you want to see

1 On the ribbon, tap the Review tab.

2 In the Tracking group, tap the Show Markup drop-down arrow.

3 In the list of markup elements that appears, tap to remove the check mark that appears to the left of any item you want to hide.

4 To change the way balloons are used to show changes in the document, tap Balloons.

5 To display changes made by specific reviewers, tap Specific People and choose the people whose changes you want to review from the list that is displayed.

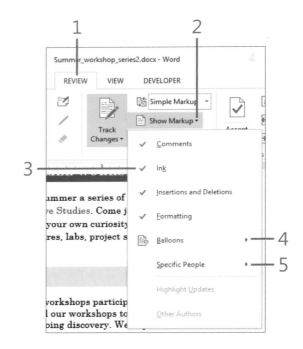

Show and hide the Reviewing pane

If you prefer to work with changes and comments in the Reviewing pane, you can display and hide it easily. On the Review tab, in the Tracking group, tap Reviewing Pane. Two choices appear: Reviewing Pane Vertical and Reviewing Pane Horizontal. Tap the display you prefer.

Adding and responding to comments

Part of working collaboratively on documents means that you need a way to be able to share and respond to ideas sparked by the content. You can use Word 2013 comments to leave notes for other authors and respond to questions and ideas others leave for you. That is fine when you have just a few comments, but if you have a entire team weighing in on a draft of an important report, you could spend all afternoon trying to sort through the hundreds of comment balloons in a 20-page document.

Word adds a simple but elegant fix to the comment-balloon problem. Now, comments are threaded like conversations so that you can read through and respond to a comment in a particular place in the document. Nice.

Add a comment

1 In your document, highlight the text on which you want to comment.

2 On the ribbon, tap the Review tab.

3 In the comments group, tap New Comment.

A comment balloon opens on the right side of the window.

4 Type your comment in the space provided.

5 Close the comment by tapping outside the comment balloon.

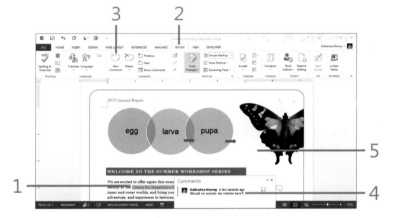

Respond to a comment

1 Display the comment by tapping the comment balloon that appears beside the text.

2 Tap the Reply button to add a new place in the comment for your response.

3 Type your reply.

Word adds your picture and name to the left of the comment.

Delete a comment

1 Display the comment that you want to delete by tapping the comment balloon.

2 On the ribbon, tap the Review tab.

3 In the Comments group, tap the Delete drop-down arrow.

4 On the menu that appears, tap Delete to remove the last comment added in the thread.

5 If you want to remove all comments added, tap Delete All Comments in Document.

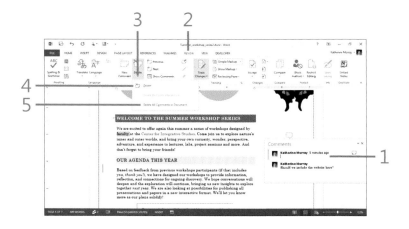

> **TIP** You can easily move from one comment to the next in your document by tapping the Previous and Next tools in the Comments group. You can also open the Comments panel along the right side of your document if you want to read through all comments at once (or prefer this display to viewing comments in balloons).

Accepting or rejecting changes

The whole idea of tracking changes is that you can easily see which changes others have made in your document so that you can choose whether you want to accept or reject the changes when you prepare the final version of the file. In the Changes group on the Review tab, you'll find the tools you need to display changes and decide whether you want to accept or reject the edits made.

Navigate to changes

1 Open a document that has changes made with Track Changes and then, on the ribbon, tap the Review tab.

2 Tap Next Change to find the next change in the document after the cursor position.

3 Tap Previous Change to move to the previous change.

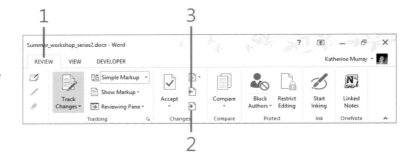

Accept changes

1 Display the change that you want to accept.

2 On the Review tab, in the Changes group, tap the Accept button.

3 Alternatively, tap the Accept drop-down arrow to view more options.

4 You can move through changes one by one, accepting each as you go, by choosing Accept and Move to Next.

5 Tap Accept All Changes to accept all changes.

6 Tap Accept All Changes And Stop Tracking to accept all changes and turn tracking off.

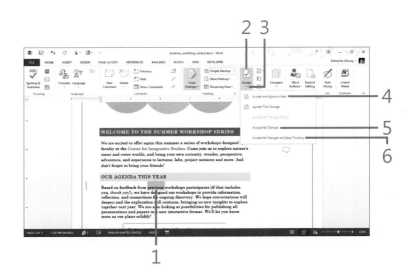

Reject changes

1 Display the change that you want to resolve. On the Review tab, in the upper-right side of the Changes group, tap and hold Reject And Move To Next until the square appears. Release your touch and a list of options appears.

2 To cancel the change at the cursor position and display the next change, choose Reject And Move To Next.

3 To remove the edits at the cursor position, choose Reject Change.

4 To cancel all edits in the document, choose Reject All Changes.

5 To remove all changes and turn tracking off, tap Reject All Changes And Stop Tracking.

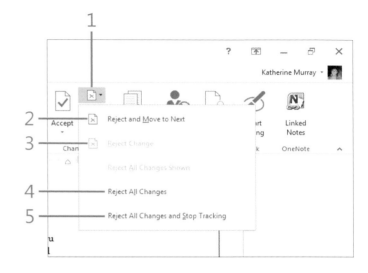

Presenting your document online

Another new sharing feature in Word 2013 makes it possible for you to present your document live online to colleagues, even if they don't have Office 2013 installed. The Present Online feature gives you the choice of using Lync 2013 or the free Office Presentation Service to connect to others and enable you to walk them through a review of your document. You can also share meeting notes you've prepared in OneNote 2013, and participants will be able to download a copy of your document if they choose.

Get ready to present

1 Open the document that you want to use in your presentation and then, on the ribbon, tap the File tab to display the Backstage view.

2 Choose the Share tab.

3 Tap Present Online.

4 Choose whether you want to use Microsoft Lync or Office Presentation Service to present your document online.

5 Tap Present Online. If prompted, tap Connect.

6 In the Present Online dialog box, tap Copy Link.

7 Alternatively, tap Send In Email or Send In IM to send the link by email message or instant message, respectively, to those you want to view the presentation.

8 When you're ready, tap Start Presentation.

Those people you invited to view the presentation can now view it live at the web address in the email invitation you sent.

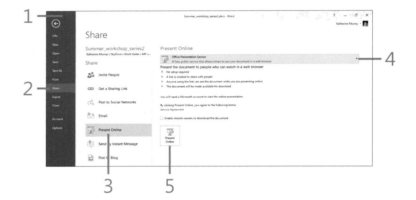

Present your document

1 To send additional invitations at the start of the presentation, on the Present Online tab, tap Send Invitations. Send the link to those whom you want to participate in the meeting.

2 Tap Edit if you'd like to change something in the document while you're presenting.

This pauses the presentation so you can make the change without others seeing what you're doing.

3 After you're finished making changes, tap Resume Online Presentation.

4 Share notes with participants by choosing Share Meeting Notes.

5 Find content in your document by tapping Find.

The Navigation pane opens on the left side of the presentation window so that you can enter the phrase you want to find. The Navigation pane isn't visible to those watching the presentation.

6 Scroll through the document, sharing the information you want to share.

7 When you're finished, tap End Online Presentation.

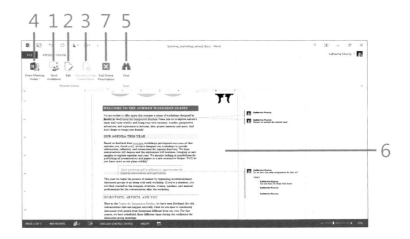

TIP The other people who are viewing your presentation do not need to have Office 2013 installed on their computers to view your Word 2013 document. Because you send a link and the presentation is hosted either by Lync or by using the Office Presentation Service, they can view the presentation in their browsers. Additionally, a Comment tab appears in the upper left of their browser window. When participants tap Comments, a Comments pane opens on the right side of the window so that they can read through comments added to the document.

Sharing and taking notes while you present

This is one of the places where the interconnectedness of the Office 2013 apps really shines. While you present your Word 2013 document to others online, you can share the OneNote notebook that goes along with the document (or you can create one on the fly if you haven't created one previously). This way, you can capture good ideas from the feedback you receive or add notes for follow-up later.

Others will be able to see and add to the notes, as well. To use this feature, tap Share Meeting Notes while you're presenting your document. Choose Share Notes With Meeting from the list that appears, and, in the Choose Notes To Share With Meeting dialog box, display the page or section where you want to add notes. Tap OK. Now, choose Share Meeting Notes again, but this time select Open Shared Meeting Notes. The Shared Meeting Notes tab appears at the top of the screen for those who are viewing your presented document so that they can see and add to the notes in your shared notebook.

> **TIP** Participants will be able to download a copy of the document you're presenting by clicking or tapping the File tab in their browser window and choosing Download in the Save As tab.

Designing, editing, and saving a worksheet in Excel 2013

9

If your work involves numbers—adding them, projecting them, managing them, or sharing them—the chances are good that you'll be working with Microsoft Excel 2013. Whether you need to create, review, or update simple or elaborate workbooks (Excel documents), you'll find the tools in Excel will help you zip through worksheets easily, no matter what device you use.

Excel 2013 includes new features that, similar to those you'll find in the other Microsoft Office apps, help you work basically anywhere, on any device. The new Excel Start experience makes it simple for you to choose a predesigned worksheet template, open an existing file, or whip up a blank worksheet, ready for data. This chapter introduces you to some of the key tasks you'll do with Excel.

In this section:

- Getting started with Excel
- Creating a new workbook
- Exploring the Excel window
- Adding and importing worksheet data
- Applying a theme
- Formatting worksheet data
- Inserting pictures
- Adding charts
- Filtering chart data
- Saving and protecting a workbook
- Sharing a worksheet
- Tracking changes
- Exporting worksheet data

Getting started with Excel

A number of the new features in Excel 2013 help simplify your work, whether you're on the road or sitting at your desk. When you start Excel 2013 in Windows 8, the Start screen appears in which you can choose the file you want to create or use.

The Excel 2013 window has a new, clean design that offers just the tools you need, when you need them. Minibars and galleries make finding those tools easy, and recommendations for charts and PivotTables to help you choose the right way to showcase your data. What's more, you can easily save your worksheet to the cloud and share it with others in a variety of ways.

Your first step involves starting Excel and creating a new, blank workbook. It's a simple task in Windows 8: just swipe and tap, and you're ready to go.

What's new in Excel 2013?

Here's a quick look at the new features you'll find in Excel 2013:

- **Get going quickly**   The Excel 2013 Start screen gives you immediate access to everything you need to create a new workbook, open an existing workbook, or begin fresh with a blank page.

- **Add data fast with Flash Fill**   If you need to enter a lot of information, Excel can help you do it. The new Flash Fill feature recognizes the pattern in the data you're entering and offers to complete the entries for you.

- **Discover the best way to show charts and PivotTables**   Excel now recommends charts and PivotTables to help you determine how to best display your data using those visual tools.

- **Easy chart tools within reach**   The new Chart Layout tools appear beside any chart you add, giving you the ability to fine-tune your charts quickly with a tap or two. You can change the look of chart elements, enter a title, and make other changes using these easy-to-use tools.

- **Save your workbooks to the cloud**   Because "in the cloud" is so much a part of Office 2013, you can save your workbooks to SkyDrive by default and you can share them with others easily if you like.

- **Share in the way that suits you best**   Excel gives you a number of options for sharing your worksheets. You can send links by email that others can click to display the worksheet or workbook, post it to a social network, or present your workbook online, even if those attending the online meeting don't have Excel 2013.

Start Excel in Windows 8

1 Swipe to display the app tiles off the right side of your tablet display.

2 Tap the Excel 2013 tile. The program opens on your Windows 8 Desktop.

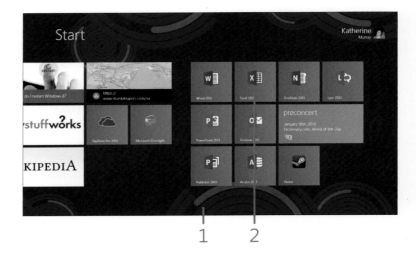

Creating a new workbook

The first thing you'll see after you start Excel 2013 from the Windows 8 Start screen is the Excel 2013 Start screen. This screen is designed to help you get started quickly, whether you're starting a new blank workbook, beginning with a template, or opening a file you've worked in previously.

Create a blank workbook

1 Display the Excel 2013 Start screen by launching the app.

2 Tap Blank Workbook.

TIP A blank workbook is just what it sounds like—a totally blank grid of columns and rows. If you have a unique worksheet in mind or you have something very simple that you want to add up, a blank worksheet can be just what you need. If your needs are a bit more elaborate, you might want to review some of the Excel templates, which provide ready-made worksheets with elements that you can use or adapt for your own data.

Start a worksheet from a template

1 If you've just started Excel, the Excel Start screen is displayed. If you are already working with Excel, you can tap the File tab to display the Backstage view and then tap the New tab.

2 Scroll down to view additional templates.

3 Or, tap a template category to display the specific templates it contains.

4 Alternatively, you can tap in the search box and type a word to describe the kind of template you want to find.

5 Tap the template that you want to use to start the new workbook.

✓ **TIP** If you choose one of the template categories in the Suggested Searches list beneath the Search box, a Filter By pane appears along the right side of the Start screen. You can use this list to choose the category of the template you'd like to find. You can choose multiple categories if you like (for example, tap Sales and Form categories to display forms related to sales). To clear the categories after you've selected them, tap the category at the top of the list to remove it.

→ **TRY THIS** In the Excel Start screen, experiment with searches for templates by using different words and phrases. Which styles do you like? Which ones will be helpful to you in the type of work you do?

Exploring the Excel window

You'll notice right away that the Excel 2013 window has undergone a makeover. Now, you'll see a clean design that thanks to Touch mode, gives you plenty to room for tapping and swiping. The Excel window gives you all the tools you need to create worksheets, enter and edit your data, format cells, add charts and tables, and much more. Contextual tabs appear when you select certain items in the worksheet—such as a range of cells or a picture you've added—giving you more choices related specifically to the item you've selected. What's more, when you add items like a picture, a chart, or a table, Excel offers tools beside the objects with which you can instantly make changes for that particular object.

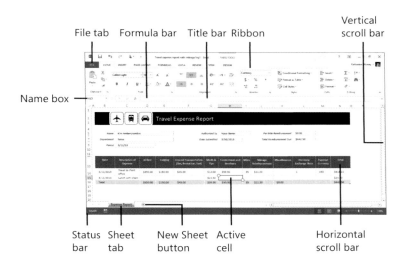

File tab   Formula bar   Title bar Ribbon   Vertical scroll bar

Name box

Status bar   Sheet tab   New Sheet button   Active cell   Horizontal scroll bar

TIP If you're already working in the Excel window, you can add a new worksheet to your workbook by tapping the New Sheet button, which is located to the right of the worksheet tab name along the bottom of the workbook window.

Adding and importing worksheet data

If you started with a blank worksheet, you might be typing data into the cells as you go. Depending on the amount of data you have, that can take a while. The Flash Fill feature in Excel can help you add information when that information follows a specific pattern. Excel can recognize and fill in data for you, which speeds up the process and reduces the likelihood of an inadvertent typo here and there.

Another nice thing about Excel is that you can easily import data from other programs. If you've saved information in another spreadsheet program, a database, or even a list in your word processor, you can bring it into your Excel worksheet where you can work on it with ease.

Type new data

1 Tap the cell where you want to enter text. The On-Screen Keyboard appears (if it doesn't, tap the keyboard icon on the taskbar).

2 Type the data that you want to appear.

3 Tap outside the cell.

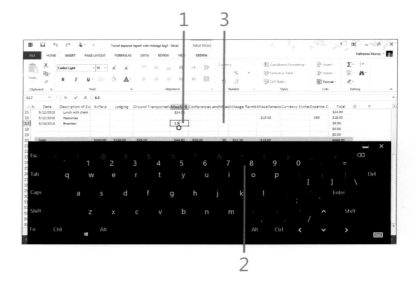

Enter data by using Flash Fill

1 Tap in the cell to the right of a cell that contains the data with the pattern you want to follow and type the part of the data you need.

2 Tap in the next cell down and begin to type the data you want to use. Excel shows you the pattern it sees in what you're typing.

3 Press the down-arrow on the On-Screen Keyboard or tap the next cell down in the list.

TIP If the original Flash Fill suggestions miss some aspect of the data, such as a middle name, edit the first example of that sequence to correct the Flash Fill values and Excel will pick up the correction.

Import worksheet data

1 On the ribbon, tap the Data tab. The Get External Data group lists the types of data you can import. Select From Access if you are importing data from an Access data table; choose From Web if you have a web query you want to use in Excel; select From Text if you have text data you want to organize in Excel; or choose From Other Sources if your data is from sources including an SQL Server, XML data, a Microsoft Query, and more.

2 For this example, tap From Text.

3 In the Import Text File dialog box, navigate to the folder that contains the text file that you want to import and double-tap the file to select it.

The Text Import Wizard opens.

4 On the first page of the wizard, click the Delimited option.

5 Tap Next.

(continued on next page)

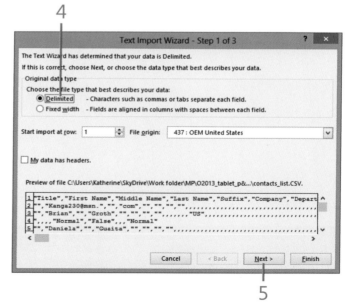

Import worksheet data (continued)

6 On the second page of the wizard, select the file's delimiter character.

A delimiter is the character used to separate one data item from another.

7 Verify that the data appears correctly in the Data Preview pane.

8 Tap Finish.

The Import Data dialog box appears, giving you choices for where the imported data will be placed.

9 Choose the cell on the existing worksheet where you want to place the data.

10 Alternatively, tap New Worksheet to place the data on a new worksheet.

11 Tap OK.

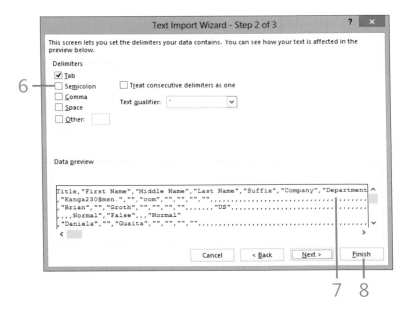

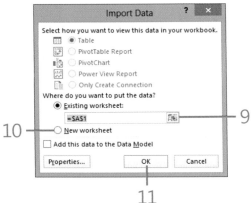

Editing your data

After you've added your data to the worksheet, you can edit it easily by correcting the information in the cells or by copying, moving, and pasting information to other places on the worksheet.

- To edit cell data, tap the cell to select it and then type the new data you want to include.

- To copy or move worksheet data, tap the cell or tap and drag a range of cells. Tap and hold until the rectangle appears and then release your touch. Tap Copy or Cut, depending on what you want to do with the data. If this is difficult to do, select the cells and tap Cut or Copy on the Home tab.

- To paste worksheet data, tap and hold the cell on the worksheet where you want the information to be pasted. When the square appears, release your touch and tap Paste.

Applying a theme

You can use themes in Excel 2013 to add designer color schemes, font families, and special effects to your worksheets. A default Office theme is applied to any new blank workbooks that you create, but you can use the Themes tool on the Page Layout tab to choose something different for your workbook. A theme coordinates a set of colors, fonts, and special effects that are applied to the various objects in your worksheet. Templates come with their own themes already applied.

Apply a theme

1 In an open Excel workbook, on the ribbon, tap the Page Layout tab.

2 In the Themes group, tap Themes.

3 In the gallery that opens, tap the theme that you want to apply.

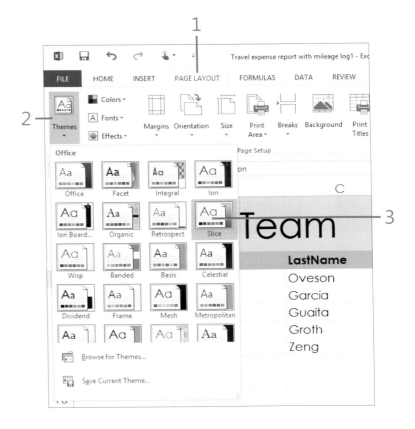

Modify and save a custom theme

You can easily tweak one of Excel's existing themes to create your own customized look and then save it and apply it to other worksheets you create. Begin by tapping the Page Layout tab and tapping Colors in the Themes group. Tap the color scheme that you want to use. Next, tap Fonts and choose the font family you'd like to include in the theme. Finally, tap Effects and select the way you want the theme to handle special effects such as lighting and shading.

Tap Themes and then, in the list that appears, tap Save Current Theme. In the Save Current Theme dialog box, navigate to the folder where you want to save your custom theme, type a name for the theme, and tap Save. Excel will display your new theme at the top of the Themes list on the Page Layout tab so that you can easily apply it to future worksheets.

Formatting worksheet data

Formatting the data on your worksheet is a pretty simple task, thanks to the tools available on the Home tab. You can simply select the cells you want to format and then tap the tool that you want to use, and Excel 2013 basically does the rest.

Format selected cells

1 Tap and drag to select a range of cells.

2 On the ribbon, tap the Home tab.

3 In the Font, Alignment, Number, and Style groups, tap the appropriate tools to apply formatting to the cells as you'd like.

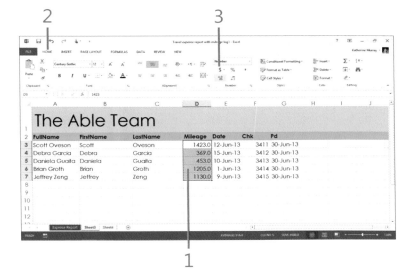

TIP You can change the width of columns and the height of rows on the worksheet by tapping and dragging. Tap the column header or row label. The entire column or row is highlighted and the pointer changes to a double-headed arrow. Drag the column or row divider in the direction you want to enlarge or reduce the column or row.

Inserting pictures

In Excel 2013, it's easier than ever to add pictures to your work-sheets. Whether you want to add a picture from a file on your local storage device or search for a new image on Bing, you can do it all within Excel. You can even find pictures you've saved on your favorite photo sharing sites or tucked away on SkyDrive.

Insert a picture file

1 On the ribbon, tap the Insert tab.

2 In the Apps group, tap Illustrations.

3 In the gallery that opens, tap Pictures.

The Insert Picture dialog box opens.

(continued on next page)

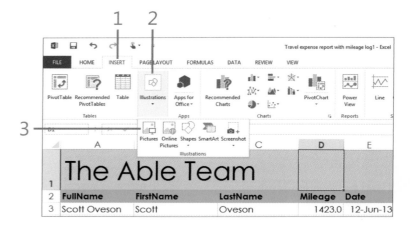

Insert a picture file *(continued)*

4 Navigate to the folder that contains the picture you want to insert.

5 Tap the desired picture.

6 Tap Insert.

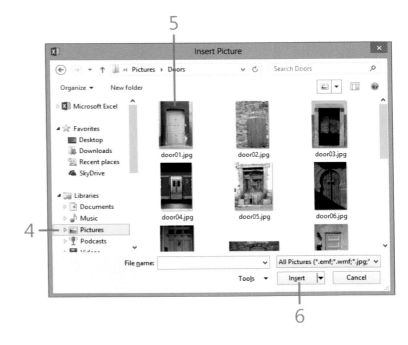

Insert online pictures

Another new feature in Office 2013 is the ability to search for online pictures and add them to your Excel 2013 worksheet while you're working. You can simply tap the Insert tab, tap Illustrations, and then tap Online Pictures. Then, in the Insert Pictures dialog box, tap the link that will take you to the online pictures you want to use. You might tap in the Office.com clip art box and enter a word reflecting the type of art you want to use, or do the same with the Bing search field to locate suitable images online. (Remember to tap the Search button after entering your search terms!) You can also access pictures you've stored in your photo sharing sites or posted in your SkyDrive account. This feature expands your illustrative reach and gives you a whole world full of images to use.

> **TIP** You can add a background image to your entire worksheet if you want to create a special effect. Tap the Page Layout tab and tap Background. In the Insert Pictures dialog box, tap Browse to add a picture saved either on your computer or on your SkyDrive account. Navigate to the folder that contains the image that you want to use as a background and tap the image. Tap Open and Excel adds the image to your worksheet.

Adding charts

Charts are important in Excel 2013 because they show non-numbers people what your data means in an easy-to-understand way. Now, with the Recommended Charts tool, you highlight the data you want to show, and Excel makes suggestions for the types of charts that would display that information best.

Add a new chart

1 Tap a cell in the data you want to summarize.

Handles appear on the selected cell.

2 Tap and drag the cell on the lower right to include the range of data you want to use as data in the chart.

3 On the ribbon, tap the Insert tab.

4 In the Charts group, tap the type of chart that you want to create.

5 In the gallery that opens, tap the subtype.

Excel adds the chart to your worksheet.

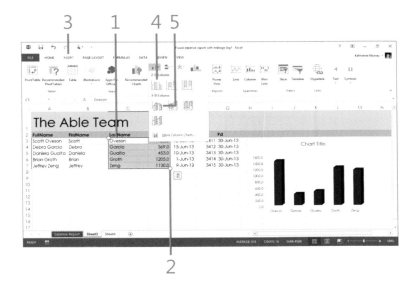

TIP After you add the chart to your worksheet, you can easily move it to a new location on the worksheet by tapping and dragging it to the new spot.

Performing quick analysis

Whenever you select information on your worksheet, Excel displays the Quick Analysis tool near the lower-right corner of the selection. When you tap the Quick Analysis tool, you'll see a palette of tools related to the information you've selected. For example, when you select data for a chart, the Quick Analysis tool displays a palette with the following choices: Formatting, Charts, Icon Set, Greater Than, Top 10%, and Clear Format.

You can tap each of these items to display additional choices related to them. You can learn more about these tools in Section 10, "Using Excel for data analysis."

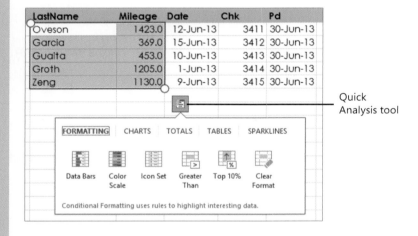

Quick Analysis tool

Use recommended charts

1 Select the data that you want to show in your chart.

2 Tap the Quick Analysis tool.

3 Tap Charts.

4 Tap the type of chart that you want to create. (You might only see one, or you might see several.)

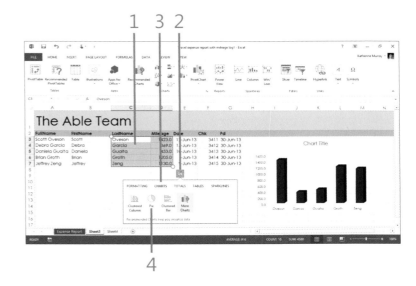

✓ **TIP** You can also display the charts Excel recommends for the data you've selected by tapping the Insert tab and choosing Recommended Charts in the Charts group. The Insert Chart dialog box opens and the Recommended Charts tab is displayed. You can scroll through the charts in the panel on the left and tap the one you want. Then, tap OK to add it to your worksheet. Of course, you don't *have* to choose a chart type Excel recommends for you, but it might be a good fit for what you're hoping to show.

→ **TRY THIS** Using a worksheet on which you've entered some data, select some cells and tap the Quick Analysis tool. Choose Charts and then choose a chart from the recommended charts that appear. (If no recommended charts appear, you'll need to select either different data or more data.)

Filtering chart data

In previous versions of Excel, when you selected data and created a chart, it was a done deal. Each time you changed the data on the worksheet, you needed to recreate the chart so that it would reflect your changes. But now, in Excel 2013, a chart is a kind of "living" display of your data, because you can change what appears in a chart by filtering the chart data to display only those values you want to include. Whether you change the filter once or a dozen times, each time you choose a new filter, the chart is redrawn to match your settings.

Filter chart data

1 Tap the chart whose data you want to filter.

2 Tap the Filter tool that appears to the right of the chart.

3 Select or clear the check boxes next to the data series that you want to display or hide.

4 Select or clear the check boxes next to the categories that you want to display or hide.

5 Tap Apply.

Excel displays the changes on your chart.

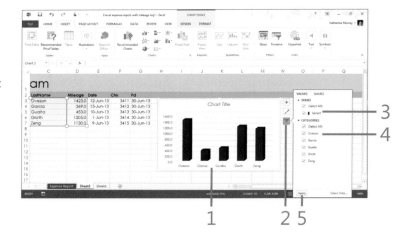

TIP You can change the display of data in the chart as many times as you'd like. If you have more complex charting needs, you can also create a PivotChart, with which you can rearrange the data displayed in the chart based on criteria you select.

Saving and protecting a workbook

Saving a file is a simple process, and if you've been working with computers for any length of time, it's a no-brainer. The big difference in Office 2013 is that now you have the option of saving your files—Excel or otherwise—to the cloud by default.

In addition to saving the file, you might want to protect your worksheet or your entire workbook by adding a password. These and other actions can help you safeguard important data and ensure that even your shared worksheets offer the measure of protection your data needs.

Save your workbook

1 On the Quick Access Toolbar, tap the Save button.

Excel saves your worksheet.

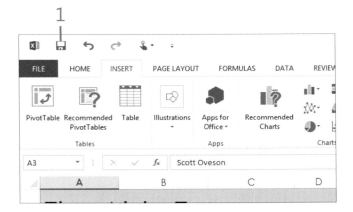

Protect the current sheet

1 On the ribbon, tap the Review tab.

2 In the Changes group, tap Protect Sheet.

3 In the Protect Sheet dialog box, select the check boxes corresponding to the protection options you want.

4 Tap OK.

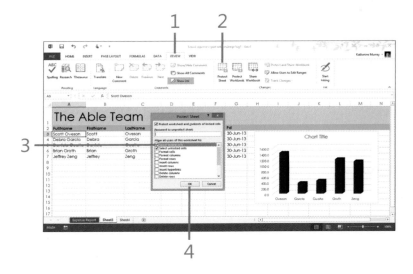

> ✓ **TIP** Another way to protect your workbook or the currently selected worksheet within it involves tapping the File tab to display the Backstage view. Then, tap the Info tab and choose Protect Workbook. Using the options in the displayed list, you can protect the current sheet, protect the structure of the workbook, or restrict access for others who might be viewing your workbook.

Add a password

1 On the ribbon, tap the Review tab.

2 In the Changes group, tap Protect Workbook.

   The Protect Structure And Windows dialog box opens.

3 Type a password for your workbook.

4 Tap OK.

   Excel displays the password box again so that you can retype the password and tap OK a second time to confirm.

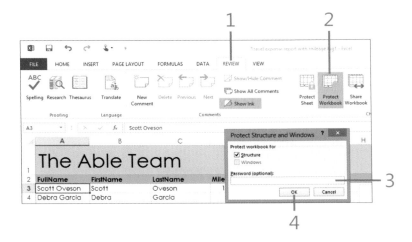

> **TIP** After you're finished creating and editing your worksheet, you can mark the file as final, which saves it as a read-only file. This means no further changes can be made to it, although you and others will be able to make a copy of the file and make changes to the copy. To mark the file as final, tap File to display the Backstage view and then tap the Info tab. Tap Protect Workbook. In the list of options that appears, tap Mark As Final. When prompted, confirm that you want to make the change.

> **TIP** Some of your worksheet features may be grayed out if you have previously shared your worksheet or workbook. If you want to use Mark As Final, for example, but the feature is unavailable, stop sharing the workbook by choosing Share Workbook in the Changes group on the Review tab, clearing the Allow Changes By More Than One User check box, and then tapping OK.

Sharing a worksheet

Today's work often takes us out of the confines of our own office and connects us with others down the hall or around the world. If you work with a team or need to get someone's sign off on your new report, you'll quickly realize that sharing your files can save you a lot of time and trouble. No more sending files by email from one place to another or going to great lengths to deliver a thumb drive to someone across town. In Excel 2013, you can use the tools in the Review tab to share your workbook by using either the Share Workbook or Protect And Share Workbook tools in the Changes group.

You can also use tools on the Share tab of the Backstage view to present your workbook online by using Microsoft Lync so that others can view and respond to your worksheet in real time.

Share your workbook with others

1 On the ribbon, tap the Review tab.

2 In the Changes group, tap Share Workbook.

3 In the Share Workbook dialog box, select the Allow Changes By More Than One User check box.

4 Tap OK to close the dialog box. The Save As dialog box appears so that you can save the file if necessary. Choose the folder where you want to store the file and tap OK.

Present the workbook online

1 On the ribbon, tap the File tab to display the Backstage view.

2 Tap the Share tab.

3 Tap Present Online. If you haven't previously saved the file to the cloud, you will be prompted to do so. After you save the file to SkyDrive or SharePoint, additional options become available on the Share tab.

4 Tap Present.

The Share Workbook Window appears, listing any current meetings you've joined in Lync.

5 Tap the meeting or conversation you want to join, if one appears in the list. If not, tap Start a New Lync Meeting.

6 Tap OK.

Lync makes the connection and displays the worksheet in the presenting window. Tools along the top of the screen enable you to switch the meeting control to another or stop presenting.

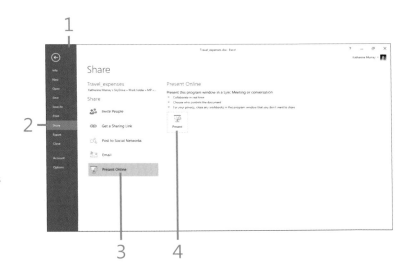

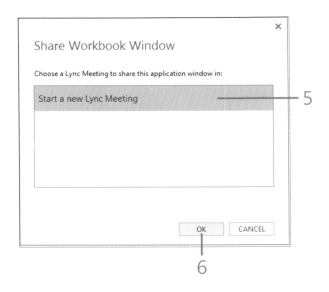

> **TIP** Sign in to Lync before choosing the Present Online option so that you don't have to stop and sign in before sharing your workbook.

> **TIP** When you're finished sharing the workbook online, tap Stop Presenting. You are returned to the Lync window, and you can continue your conversation as normal or close or minimize Lync.

Tracking changes

When you're collaborating on a workbook, it's important to be able to see what kinds of changes other are making on your worksheets. You can use the Track Changes feature in Excel 2013 to identify additions and changes made by others who are sharing your workbook.

Turn on Track Changes

1 On the ribbon, tap the Review tab.

2 In the Changes group, tap Track Changes.

3 On the menu that appears, tap Highlight Changes.

4 In the Highlight Changes dialog box, if necessary, select the Track Changes While Editing check box.

5 Tap OK and when the Save As dialog box appears, tap Save to save the workbook.

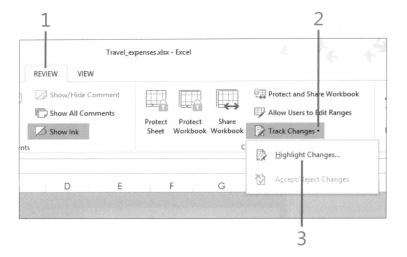

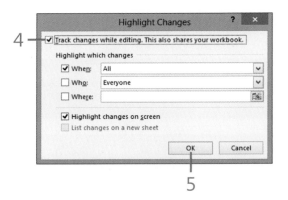

Review changes

1 On the ribbon, tap the Review tab.

2 In the Changes group, tap Track Changes.

3 On the menu that appears, tap Accept/Reject Changes. If the Excel message box appears, telling you the workbook will be saved, tap OK.

(continued on next page)

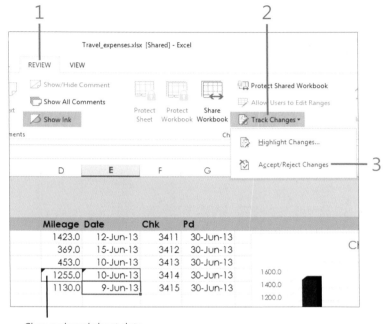

Changed worksheet data

Review changes *(continued)*

4 In the Select Changes to Accept or Reject dialog box, tap the check box of the items for which you want to search. To select further criteria, tap the drop-down arrow for the item.

5 Choose the timeframe of changes that you want to review.

6 Select the author of the comments that you want to see.

7 Indicate where in the worksheet you want to review comments.

8 Tap OK.

9 In the Accept Or Reject Changes dialog box, do any of the following:

- Tap Accept to accept the current change.

- Tap Reject to reject the current change.

- Tap Accept All to accept all the changes.

- Tap Reject All to reject all the changes.

10 Tap Close to stop reviewing changes.

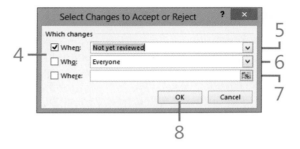

Exporting worksheet data

Excel 2013 is easy enough to use that you might find it makes sense to keep track of all kinds of data with it. You might keep the names and addresses of your book club members, sort the information for families in your neighborhood associations, or manage complex financial reports and such for all kinds

of work-related needs. No matter what the content of your workbooks, you can export them—and individual worksheets, as well—in formats that make it easy to share the data or work with it in other programs.

Create a PDF of your worksheet

1 On the ribbon, tap the File tab to display the Backstage view.

2 Tap the Export tab.

3 Tap Create PDF/XPS Document.

4 Tap Create PDF/XPS.

(continued on next page)

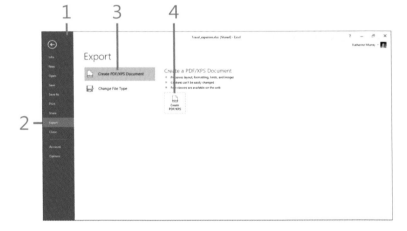

Create a PDF of your worksheet *(continued)*

5 In the Publish As PDF Or XPS dialog box, navigate to the folder where you want to save the workbook.

6 Type a name for the file.

7 Tap the Save As Type drop-down arrow and, if necessary, select PDF.

8 Choose the Optimize For option that you want to use.

9 Tap Publish.

Export the workbook in other file types

You can also export your Excel 2013 worksheet data in other formats, if you expect to use it with other programs. Tap the File tab to display the Backstage view and then tap the Export tab. Next, tap Change File Type and choose the file type you want from the list that appears. Tap Save As and select the folder where you want to store the exported information. Now, just type a name for the file and tap Save, and Excel saves the exported data in the folder and format you selected.

Using Excel 2013 for data analysis

10

If you're taking the time and trouble to add your data to Microsoft Excel 2013, the chances are good that you are interested in analyzing it, as well. Perhaps you want to show your management team the results of the most recent sales competition. Or, you want to talk about projections based on a number of different factors, which means you need to show your data in different ways by tapping a control or two.

Sound too simple? In Excel 2013, it's not. You can use Excel's new Quick Analysis tool to get a quick look at the trends in your data, and you can use slicers to change the data displayed on the fly. You can also use conditional formatting features to show data trends on the worksheet itself and add formulas and functions to extend the power of your data and perform calculations—simple or complex—in real time.

In this section:

- Applying conditional formatting
- Quickly analyzing your data
- Adding sparklines
- Understanding Excel formulas and functions
- Creating a formula
- Checking and revising a formula
- Using functions
- Sorting data
- Creating and modifying PivotTables
- Filtering your data by using slicers

Applying conditional formatting

In Excel 2013, you can add formatting to the cells on your worksheet that help others see at a glance what the trends in the data might be. For example, suppose your worksheet shows the weekly sales in your small bookshop. You can use conditional formatting to display values as data bars of different colors, which highlights changes in your data or presents it in a way so that you can easily compare data ranges based on the colors they represent. Or, you can display icons in the cells (such as an up arrow or down arrow), add greater-than or less-than symbols, highlight the top or bottom percent of values show, or clear the formatting altogether. Conditional formatting is fun to apply and easy to use, and it can help those who are unfamiliar with your worksheet to understand easily what your data shows.

Highlight data results

1 Open an Excel workbook and select the values that you want to format.

2 On the ribbon, tap the Styles group, tap the Home tab.

3 Tap Conditional Formatting.

4 On the menu that appears, tap Highlight Cells Rules.

5 On the submenu that appears, tap the type of rule that you want to apply.

6 In the dialog box that opens, if necessary, tap the Condition list box to change the value.

7 Tap the Formatting list box to display your conditional formatting choices and select the format that you want to apply.

8 Tap OK to apply the format to the cells.

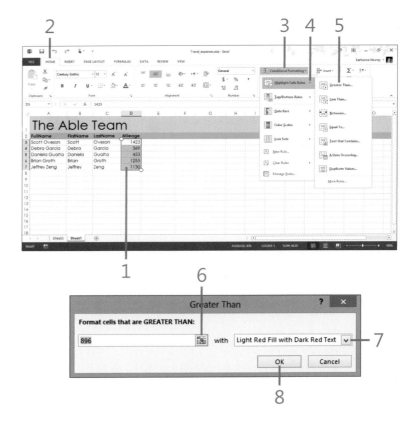

Display data bars

1 Drag to select the cells for which you want to display conditional formatting.

2 On the ribbon, tap the Home tab.

3 In the Styles group, tap Conditional Formatting.

4 On the menu that appears, tap Data Bars.

5 In the gallery that opens, tap the data bar style that you want to apply.

TIP You can also add icons to worksheet cells to display conditional formatting. You might, for example, add up-arrows or down-arrows to show data trends. Add icons to your cells by selecting the data on the worksheet and then tapping Conditional Formatting, tapping Icon Sets, and then tapping the icon set style that you want to add to the selected cells.

Quickly analyzing your data

Quick Analysis is a new feature in Excel 2013 with which you can apply different analysis tools to the data you've selected on your worksheet. It's easy to use and can show you at a glance what trends are appearing in the information you're gathering.

Apply Quick Analysis

1 Drag to select the cells that contain the data you want to analyze.

The Quick Analysis tool appears just below and to the right of the range you selected.

2 Tap the Quick Analysis tool.

A palette of tools appears, presenting the different options for analyzing the selected data. You can choose to apply conditional formatting tools, display the data as a chart, use Total functions, display the data in tables, or add sparklines, which are small, in-cell diagrams that show data trends in the cells you specify.

3 Tap the desired category, depending on what you want to do with the data: Formatting, Charts, Totals, Tables, or Sparklines.

4 Tap the analysis tool that you want to apply. For example, tap Sum. Excel adds the sum of the selected cells at the bottom of the selected data range.

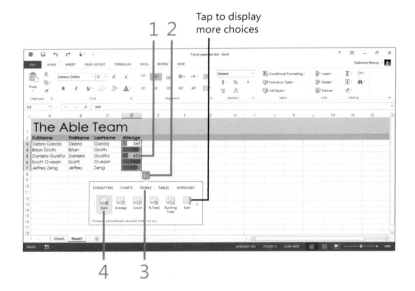

Tap to display more choices

Adding sparklines

You can use sparklines to show at a glance the data trends your data reflects. Sparklines appear in cells beside the data they represent so anyone viewing your worksheet can see easily what the values display. You can customize the sparklines so that they appear in different colors and styles.

Excel 2013 offers three types of sparklines: Line, Column, and Win/Loss. The Line option displays your data as a small line chart. The Column sparkline format shows your data as comparison values displayed as a small bar chart. The Win/Loss option displays values as a sequence of colored dashes that clearly indicate the variances in your data.

Create sparklines

1 Select the cells that you want to summarize. The cells must be in a single row or column.

2 On the ribbon, tap the Insert tab.

3 In the Sparklines group, tap the type of sparkline that you want to create.

The Create Sparklines dialog box opens. The data you selected already appears in the Data Range list box, and the cursor is positioned in the Location Range list box.

4 Tap the cell on the worksheet in which you want the sparkline to appear.

The cell address displays in the Location Range box.

5 Tap OK to add the sparkline.

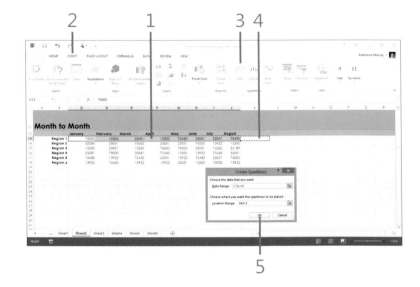

TIP You can also create sparklines for multiple rows or columns at once. Begin by highlighting all the data that you want to include, tap the Quick Analysis tool, choose Sparklines, and then tap the type of sparkline you want to add. You can then format all the sparklines at once while the range is still selected.

Edit Sparklines

1 Tap the cell that contains the sparkline you want to edit.

The Sparkline Tools | Design contextual tab appears, offering a number of tools that you can use to edit the sparklines.

2 In the Show group, select the desired check boxes to add data markers to your sparkline.

3 In the Style group, choose a style to apply to the sparkline.

4 to change sparkline color, tap the Sparkline Color button.

5 To change the color of the data markers that you added to your sparkline, tap the Marker Color button.

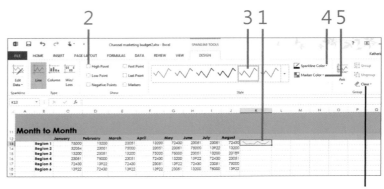

Clear sparklines

> ✓ **TIP** For best results, create one sparkline for a specific range of data, edit the sparkline to appear as you'd like, and then copy and paste the sparkline to other cells in your worksheet. Excel 2013 adjusts the data ranges automatically for you, and you get the benefit of adding the sparkline style that you just created to each series you want represented. To copy the sparkline quickly through contiguous cells, drag the small rectangle in the lower-right corner of the sparkline cell in the direction that you want to add the sparklines.

> ✓ **TIP** You can delete sparklines from your worksheet by simply selecting the cell containing the sparkline and tapping Clear on the Sparkline Tools | Design contextual tab. Choose whether you want to clear the individual sparkline or the entire sparkline group, and Excel does the rest for you.

Understanding Excel formulas and functions

Excel 2013 is a powerful worksheet program that gives you all kinds of tools for performing sophisticated calculations and data analyses. If you use worksheets only sporadically, you might not be too comfortable with formulas and functions. If this is the case, the following tasks are for you. Here, you'll learn about how Excel references cells and puts everything together with functions in formulas that you can use to perform calculations on the data in your worksheet.

Name box

Selected cell

Learning about cell references

Each cell in your Excel worksheet has its own unique address, which represents the intersection of the row and column where the cell is located; for example, C5 is an individual cell that falls at the intersection of column C, row 5. K23 is another, located in column K, row 23. You can easily determine the address of the cell by tapping in the cell. The Name box in the upper-left corner of the Excel window shows the cell reference of the selected cell.

When you select a range of cells, Excel describes that range by separating the individual cell references with a colon; for example, B4:B20 describes a range a cells that begins with cell B4 and extends to cell B20, which happens to define a group of cells that are all in one column. Excel uses the upper-left and lower-right cell addresses to describe a contiguous range selection, which is a single block of cells.

When you create formulas, the way the values are calculated will vary depending on whether the cell uses an *absolute* or *relative* reference. A formula with a relative cell address uses the data in the cells specified, relative to their position on the worksheet.

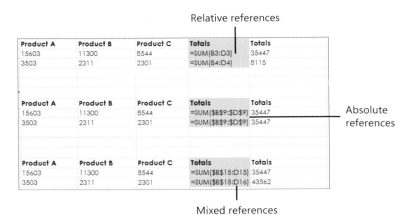

Relative references

Absolute references

Mixed references

For example, with relative cell references, if you are summing the data in cells A1 to D1 and showing the total in E1, when you copy the formula in E1 to E2, the formula recalculates the data based on cells A2 to D2. If the cells in A1 to D1 are absolute references, the formula you copy to cell E2 will continue to reference the cells in A1 to D1. In Excel, you add a dollar sign ($) to the beginning of any reference that is treated as absolute in a calculation. By default, cells use relative references, but if you want to make the references for cells absolute, select the cells you want to change in the formula bar and press F4 to switch from relative to absolute referencing.

Understanding formulas and functions

You need to understand cell references to use them properly in formulas. Formulas instruct Excel as to what calculations to perform on your worksheet. A formula always begins with an equals sign (=) and can be very simple; for example =3*5+2. A more common formula uses cell references to indicate to Excel where to find the data for the calculation, such as =D4+D5. In a formula, the standard *order of operations* apply, and any parts of the formula within parentheses are calculated first.

You use functions to perform common calculations on the cells you select in your worksheet. You include functions in your worksheet formulas. Some of the functions in Excel are very common, and you'll be at home using them right off the bat. Using functions such as SUM, AVERAGE, and COUNT, you can total values, calculate an average value, and display the number of elements in a data range. Some functions are available in the Quick Analysis tool and you can add them to your worksheet without crafting a formula by hand or using the Formulas tab in

the Excel window. You insert a function in a formula and specify to the function which cells you want to include in the calculation, for example:

=SUM(B3:E3)

In this formula, SUM is the function. A function returns the result of a calculation. The equal sign (=) informs Excel that what follows is a formula or function and should be calculated as such, not treated as worksheet data. The cell reference (B3:E3) points Excel to the values you want to use to produce the formula result.

The functions in Excel might have arguments that are required to perform the calculation. These arguments can be values or cell references or information that controls exactly what the function does. For example, the actual values of the cells used in a formula might look like this:

=15603+11300+8544

But they could also be written in cell notation like this:

=B3+C3+D3

And the formula, using the SUM function, could be written as

=SUM(B3:D3)

All three examples return the same result, but the first is static, meaning that it uses the numbers as they are entered. The second example is dynamic and allows the formula to change automatically if the data in one of the cells is changed. The third example uses the built-in SUM function and cell references and is the easiest and most expedient way to add formulas that can be copied and modified as needed on your worksheet.

You will probably use the Formula bar and the Insert Function tool most often to create and modify formulas in Excel. The Formulas tab also includes the tools you need to insert, manipulate, and modify formulas and functions on your worksheet.

Formula tab

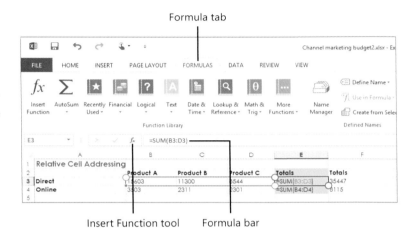

Insert Function tool   Formula bar

✓ **TIP** Excel formulas can be as simple or as complex as you need them to be. You can include multiple functions within a single formula, and you can also nest functions within functions for more sophisticated calculations.

✓ **TIP** The Function Library group on the Formulas tab also displays the various categories of functions you can add to your formula. You can add a function without using the Insert Function dialog box by tapping the category of the function you'd like to add and then tapping the function in the displayed list.

Creating a formula

Creating a formula is really a simple task, thanks to all the tools Excel 2013 gives you to create what you need and check the formula for accuracy. You can type a formula directly in the Formula Bar at the top of the Excel worksheet area, or you can tap and type it in the selected cell. Along the way, you can also type or select the function you need and type or drag to select the cells that you want to include. And, the program even provides you with on-the-spot error checking (the subject of the next task) to help ensure that your formulas are adding things up properly.

Type a formula

1 Tap the cell in which you want to enter the formula.

2 Either in the cell or in the Formula bar, type an equal sign (=).

3 Type the name of the function, followed by a left parenthesis character.

You can tap the Sum arrow to see a list of additional functions you can choose.

4 Type the cell addresses that you want to include in the function.

You can also tap the cells or range on the worksheet that you want to include in the formula, and Excel will add it for you.

5 Type a right parenthesis character and then tap outside the cell.

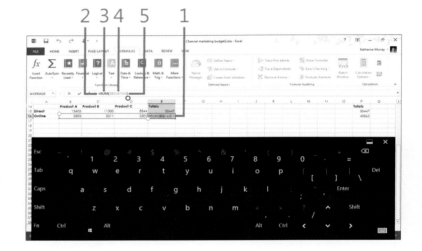

TIP If you need to edit a formula that you've already added to the worksheet, you can make changes easily. Double-tap the cell containing the formula that you want to change, type the corrected formula on the worksheet, and then tap outside the cell. Whether you make the edits in the cell or in the formula bar, after you tap away, the edits are added to the worksheet, and other cells depending on that formula are recalculated, as needed.

Checking and revising a formula

Excel 2013 includes a number of tools to help you troubleshoot the formulas in your worksheet. If things aren't working out properly or you're questioning the accuracy of a formula (or

Excel displays an error indicator in the cell that looks like an exclamation point, alerting you to a problem), you can use these tools to find the problem and correct it.

Check for formula errors

1 On the ribbon, tap the Formulas tab.

2 In the Formula Auditing group, tap the Error Checking tool.

3 On the menu that appears, tap Error Checking.

4 In the Error Checking dialog box, use the controls to change the formula or ignore the error.

5 Tap Previous or Next to view the preceding or ensuing error that Excel has found in the worksheet.

6 Tap the Close box to close the Error Checking dialog box and return to the worksheet.

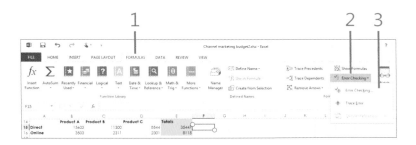

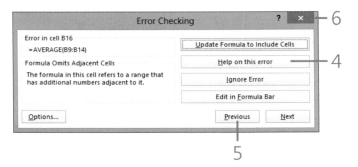

✓ **TIP** Excel has a comprehensive Help tool that can assist you in deciphering formula errors and correcting them. To get help with an error in a formula, Tap the Formulas tab and choose Error Checking. In the Error Checking dialog box that opens, Tap Help On This Error, which displays the Excel Help window.

Read through the entries related to the problem you're having. Tap the Pin tool in the upper-right corner of the Help window if you want to keep it open on your screen while you work through the problems. You can also search Help and read about related issues. When you're finished, tap the Close box to exit Help and then tap the Close box on the Error Checking dialog box.

Using functions

As you've already seen in this section, functions are the engines that drive your Excel 2013 formulas, returning the result of the formula's calculation. They do the actual processing, whether the formula calls for simple or complex calculations. When you add a function to a formula, the function needs to know which cells to use in the calculation.

Find the function you want

1 Tap the cell in which you want to add the function and then tap the Formulas tab.

2 On the Formulas tab, on the far left side of the Function Library group, tap the Insert Function button.

The Insert Function dialog box opens.

3 Tap the category list box to display the list and then select the function category that you want to view.

You can choose from All, Financial, Date & Time, Math & Trig, Statistical, Lookup & Reference, Database, Text, Logical, Information, Engineering, Cube, Compatibility, or Web categories. Upon choosing a category, the list of functions available in the Select A Function list changes.

4 Tap the function that you want to examine.

5 Tap OK to select the function.

The Function Arguments dialog box opens, in which you can specify additional information for your function. (Read on for more about working with function arguments.) For now, you can choose the settings appropriate to your formula and tap OK to close the dialog box.

TIP Some functions need further information before you can use them in the formula. If the function you select needs more information, the Function Arguments dialog box will open after you tap OK in the Insert Dialog box. Choose the settings that apply to the function you've chosen, and then tap OK to close the dialog box and insert the function and its arguments in the worksheet cell.

Sorting data

You can use Excel 2013 for more than just numbers. You might want to list products, client names and addresses, or create a worksheet to keep track of your store inventory. You can use Excel's Sort tool to organize the information in your worksheet and present it in a way that's meaningful for you.

Sorting is easy in Excel. You can choose an Ascending or Descending sort, or you can customize the sort process by sorting your information on the elements and in the order you specify. It's important that you select all data that will be impacted by changing the sort order on your worksheet, because it's easy to sort only a section of your data without realizing the ordering problem you're creating elsewhere. If you choose to sort a listing of customer records, for example, make sure you've included all relevant data for each customer in the rows and columns you've selected, so you don't inadvertently sort all the last names but not the first names, or accidentally separate customer names from the products they ordered.

Do a basic sort

1 Tap any cell in the column of data that you want to sort.

2 On the ribbon, tap the Data tab.

3 Follow either of these steps:

- In the Sort & Filter group, tap the Sort Ascending button.
- In the Sort & Filter group, tap the Sort Descending button.

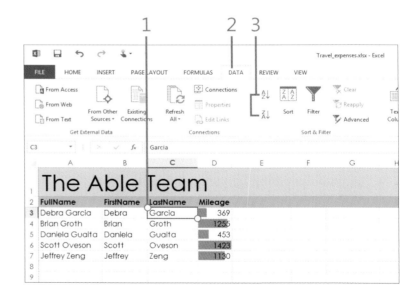

TIP You can undo the sort by tapping Undo in the Quick Access Toolbar immediately after sorting the data. You can also tap Descending (if your first sort was Ascending) to reverse the order.

Create a custom sort

1 Select a cell in the data range or Excel table that you want to sort.

2 On the ribbon, tap the Data tab.

3 In the Sort & Filter group, tap Sort.

The Sort dialog box opens.

4 Tap the Sort By arrow and select the criterion by which you want to sort.

5 Tap the Sort On arrow and select the criterion by which you want to sort.

6 Tap the Order arrow and then select the order in which the column's values should be sorted.

7 Tap Add Level.

8 Repeat steps 4–7 if you want to set additional sorting rules.

9 Tap OK.

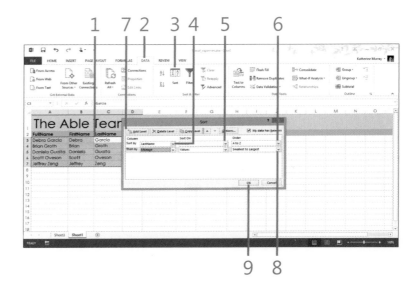

TIP If you want to include the headers in the sort range of the data you're asking Excel to order, select the My Data Has Headers check box in the upper-right corner of the Sort dialog box. If you want to exclude the headers, tap to clear the check box if necessary.

Creating and modifying PivotTables

PivotTables are powerful tools that can help you analyze your data in a variety of ways and from a variety of perspectives. They enable you to literally "pivot" your data to look at it in different views. Suppose, for example, that you are working with a worksheet that shows the sales of your top products in the first quarter. Your PivotTable can help you see, with a simple tap:

- Which products were the top sellers during the first quarter

- How quarter 1 sales compare to other quarters

- How a particular product has sold over time

You begin by selecting the data for the table, including a header row so that Excel knows how to categorize the data being shown. You specify to Excel how you want to display the data in the PivotTable and then—here's the pivot part—you can easily change the data items around to display the information in different ways within the same table.

Create a recommended PivotTable

1 Tap a cell within the range that you want to summarize.

2 On the ribbon, tap the Insert tab.

3 In the Tables group, tap Recommended PivotTables.

4 In the Recommended PivotTables dialog box that opens, tap the PivotTable that you want to create.

5 Tap OK.

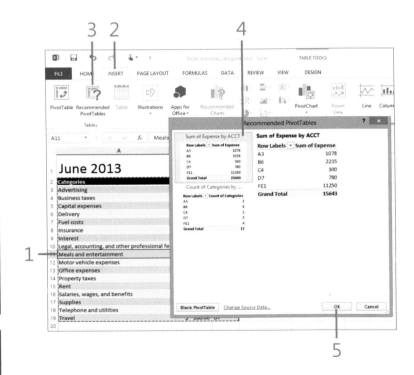

 TIP The great thing about adding a PivotTable to your worksheet is that you can pivot your data and look at it in different ways without creating a new table. Tap the arrow in the upper-left corner of the table and choose the field that you want to use as the pivot for the table. Select the check boxes of items that you want to include in the table; your data is filtered and displayed accordingly.

 TIP You can format your PivotTable by using the PivotTable Styles gallery on the PivotTable Tools | Design contextual tab.

Create a PivotTable

1 Tap a cell within the range that you want to summarize.

2 On the ribbon, tap the Insert tab.

3 In the Tables group, tap PivotTable.

4 Verify that the proper data range appears in the Table/Range box.

5 Tap OK.

6 Drag a field to the Values area. This instructs Excel to display the values for that field in the table.

7 Drag other field headers to the Rows and Columns areas, as needed. This shows Excel how to arrange the data in the table.

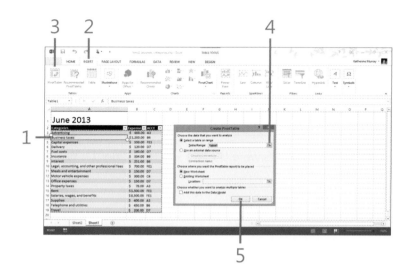

TIP To change your PivotTable, tap any cell in the data area of the PivotTable, and then on the PivotTable Tools Analyze tab, tap Field Settings in the Active Field group, and the Value Field Settings dialog box appears. If you want to change the format of numbers in the PivotTable, tap the Number Format button at the bottom of the dialog box and choose a different format in the Format Number dialog box. Tap OK twice to get back the worksheet.

TIP If you want to change the data source the table is using to create the PivotTable, in the Data group, tap Change Data Source and choose a different table to use as the basis for your PivotTable. When you're done making changes, test out the table to ensure that it shows your data to your satisfaction.

Analyzing data trends with Power View Reports

Excel 2013 includes a new feature called Power View Reports with which you can create custom reports in much the same way you put together PivotTables on your worksheet.

You'll find the Power View tool in the Reports group of the Insert tab. When you tap Power View, Excel prepares a new view, showing the Power View Fields in a pane along the right side of the Excel window. You can tap the Click Here To Add A Title area of the page to title your report, and then select the check boxes of fields in the Power View Fields pane to hide or display data in the report.

Filtering your data by using slicers

When you want to look at a subset of your data or display only data values related to a specific category of information, you can apply filters to that data. You use the Filter tool on the Data tab to instruct Excel as to how you want to filter the information on the worksheet. When you filter your data, the data items that don't meet the filter criteria are hidden temporarily so that you can view only the data you need.

Excel also includes features called *slicers* that you can use to filter your data in real time in a table format. Slicers are simple, graphical tables by which you can display your data in different ways without changing selections on the worksheet. Slicers easy to add and can be an effective tool for showing how your data looks when filtered in different ways.

Filter selected data

1 Tap any cell in the range that you want to filter.

2 On the ribbon, tap the Data tab.

3 In the Sort & Filter group, tap Filter.

4 Tap the filter drop-down arrow for the column that contains the data that you want to filter.

5 Select the check boxes adjacent to the values by which you want to filter the list.

6 Tap OK.

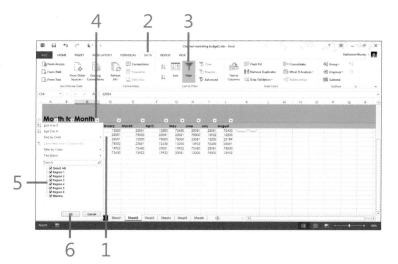

Use a slicer to filter a table

1 Mark the data that you want to use as an Excel data table by selecting the data range, tapping Insert, and then tapping Table.

2 In the Create Table dialog box, tap OK.

3 Tap any cell in the Excel table that you want to filter.

4 On the ribbon, tap the Insert tab.

5 In the Filters group, tap Slicer.

The Insert Slicers dialog box opens.

6 Select the check boxes adjacent to the fields for which you want to create a slicer.

7 Tap OK.

(continued on next page)

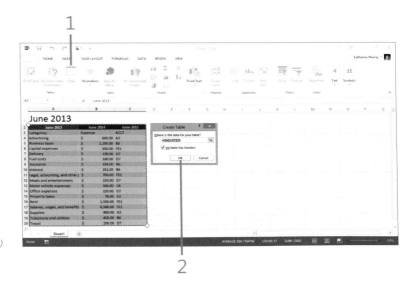

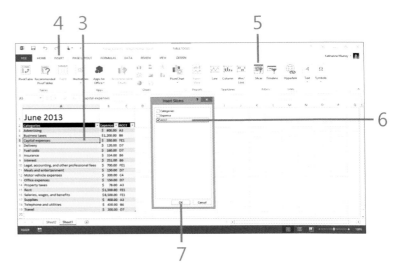

Use a slicer to filter a table (continued)

8 Do any of the following steps:

- Tap an item to display just that item's values in the table.

- Tap the Clear Filter button to remove all filters applied by the slicer.

- Tap and hold the slicer and tap the Remove menu item to delete the slicer.

Cancel the slicer and return to normal display

Creating, animating, and saving a presentation in PowerPoint 2013

11

Now, whether you need to plan a presentation quickly on the fly or put the finishing touches on one you've been working on for months, you can use Microsoft PowerPoint 2013 on your tablet to tap and touch your way to a great slide show. Using a number of new features, optimized for touch, you can create professional presentations, share them with others, and customize the elements, animations, and transitions to achieve just the right effect.

You create a new presentation or open an existing one by using the PowerPoint 2013 Start screen, which makes the whole process easier by appearing automatically when you tap the PowerPoint 2013 app tile to start the program. Likewise, the new redesigned PowerPoint window is clean and bright with plenty of room for swiping and tapping.

In this section:

- Getting started with PowerPoint 2013
- Starting a new presentation
- Selecting a presentation theme
- Choosing a slide layout
- Adding and formatting text
- Adding pictures to your slides
- Inserting slides
- Adding and editing video
- Animating slide elements
- Adding transitions to your slides

Getting started with PowerPoint 2013

The new features in PowerPoint 2013 follow along with the big changes you find in Microsoft Office 2013 overall: a new Start screen to get you going quickly, a clean new redesigned work area, and the ability to save to the cloud by default. You'll also discover some PowerPoint-specific features, such as a new wide-screen format for presentations, new themes with coordinated variants, and a way to present your presentation live online, even if those viewing the presentation don't have PowerPoint.

What's new in PowerPoint 2013

- **The PowerPoint 2013 Start screen** The Start experience makes it easy to begin a new or existing presentation. You can search for a template, choose a template style, open a recent presentation, or navigate to a previously created presentation on your local storage device or in the cloud.

- **Clean, open work area** PowerPoint, like all of Office 2013, now enjoys a minimalist look, leaving plenty of room on the screen for you to work with your content. A range of ribbon options makes it possible for you to display the ribbon or not, as your preference goes. You can also choose to auto-hide the ribbon so that it appears when you need to use it but disappears from view when you move the pointer back to the work area.

- **Improved touch capability** The new redesigned PowerPoint window makes it easy to navigate by touch. The new touch mode gives the display a roomy feel and makes it easy to tap the tools you want to use. New mini-bars give you galleries of options that are simple to select and navigate.

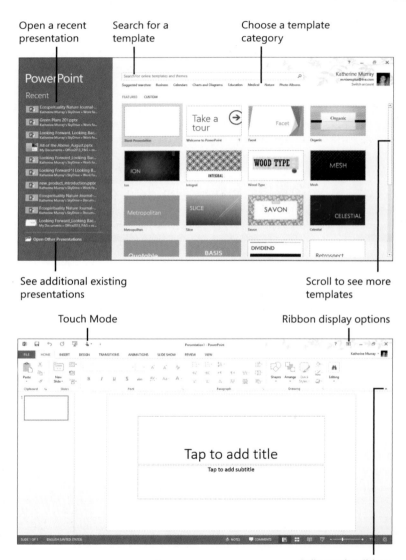

Open a recent presentation

Search for a template

Choose a template category

See additional existing presentations

Scroll to see more templates

Touch Mode

Ribbon display options

Collapse the ribbon

- **Improved commenting** The comments feature has been streamlined, and you can now read and respond to comments in the same comment balloon. Additionally, you can view comments in a Comments pane along the right side of your presentation.

- **New design tools** Now in PowerPoint 2013, in addition to applying themes (and you have new themes to choose from), you can choose variations of the theme in different color palettes.

- **Choose a widescreen format** Today many of the displays we use are in widescreen and high-definition formats, With PowerPoint 2013, you can use a 16:9 layout and select new widescreen themes, as well.

- **Simplify presenting** Now, Presenter View makes setting up and delivering your presentation easier than ever, whether you're using a single or multi-monitor setup. You can easily rehearse your presentation, and when presenting, you can use the Slide Navigator to move smoothly to the slides that you want to show.

Choose a theme   Select a variant   Choose a slide size

Change Presenter view display   View nest slide

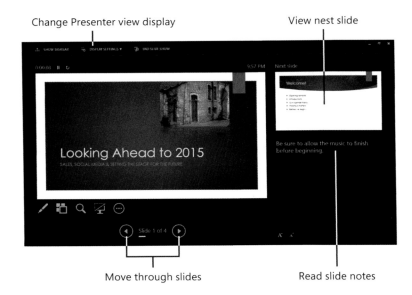

Move through slides   Read slide notes

Start PowerPoint in Windows 8

1 On the right side of the Windows 8 Start screen, swipe to display the app tiles.

2 Tap the PowerPoint 2013 tile.

The program opens on your Windows 8 Desktop.

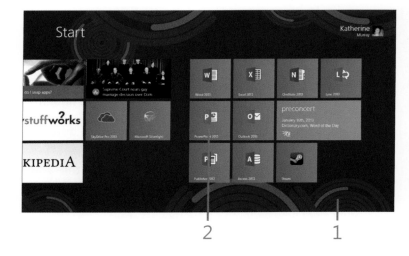

2   **1**

✓ **TIP**   You can pin the PowerPoint 2013 program icon to your Windows 8 Desktop taskbar by swiping down on the app tile and choosing the Pin To Taskbar icon in the apps bar at the bottom of the screen.

Learning the PowerPoint window

After you select a template or tap New Presentation on the Start screen, the PowerPoint window appears. The PowerPoint 2013 window has a new, clean design that maximizes your access to tools and gives you plenty of room on your screen to work. Here are techniques and tools you're sure to use regularly in the PowerPoint window:

- Choose the task you want to accomplish by selecting a tab on the ribbon.

- Tap a tool to select it.

- Unpin the ribbon so it appears only when you point to a tab or tool.

- Display the slide in Full Screen mode.

- See thumbnails of slides in your presentation.

- Add slide notes.

- Display the Comments pane.

- Change the slide view.

- Check slide spelling.

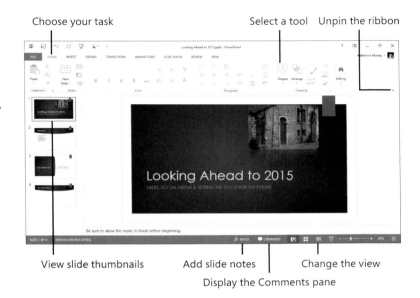

Choose your task Select a tool Unpin the ribbon

View slide thumbnails Add slide notes Change the view

Display the Comments pane

Starting a new presentation

Similar to other apps in Office 2013, PowerPoint 2013 makes your startup experience easier by displaying the Start screen when you first start the program. In the Start screen, you can choose from a sweeping array of templates to get you rolling on the type of presentation you want to create. You can also search specifically for a template that matches a style or approach you like. And course, if you'd rather start with a clean slate, there's always the standard Blank Presentation.

Start a blank presentation

1 Start PowerPoint 2013.

The Start screen appears on your display.

2 Tap Blank Presentation.

The PowerPoint window opens, and the slide area is blank, except for the title and subtitle prompts, where you can tap to add text.

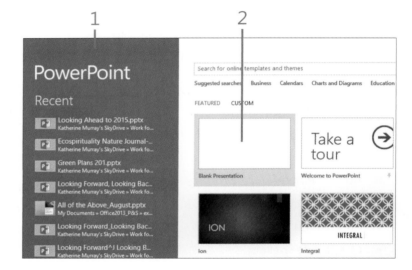

✓ TIP On the left side of the Start screen, you will see a list of recently opened presentations. If you want to open an existing presentation right off the bat, tap the presentation file you want to use. If you don't see it listed in the Recent list, tap Open Other Presentations to display the Open dialog box, in which you can navigate to the location where the file is stored, and then tap it to open it.

Start a presentation from a template

1 Swipe through the list to review the templates displayed by default.

2 Tap the template that you want to use.

3 You can also tap a template category that reflects the type of template you're looking for. The Category panel opens on the right side of the screen, listing the number of templates available online in each category.

4 Tap the filter category to see the templates in that group.

5 You can also tap in the Search box, type a word or phrase to reflect the template that you're looking for, and then tap Start Searching.

6 Tap the template that you want to use. A preview window appears, telling you more about the template.

(continued on next page)

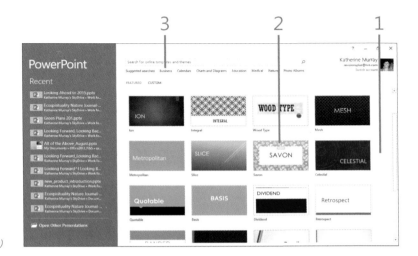

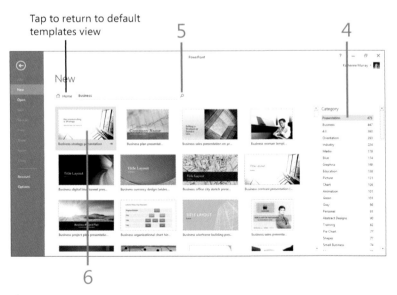

Tap to return to default templates view

Start a presentation from a template *(continued)*

7 Tap the arrows to view the pages in the template.

8 Tap Create to open a new file based on that template.

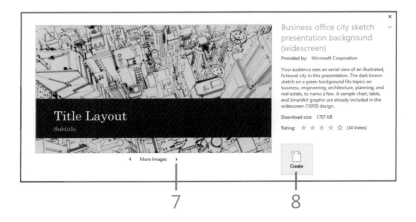

7   8

Opening an existing file

If you're like most of us, the chances are good that you will work on your presentation over a series of days. You create a presentation file, work on it a while, save it, and close it. Tomorrow you'll return and work some more on the presentation, invite feedback from others, and maybe work on the animations. This means you'll often be reopening the same file—one you've already worked on—and continuing your work. There are a couple of ways by which you can open an existing presentation in PowerPoint. If you've just started the program, you can tap the file you need in the Recent list on the Start screen. If you don't see the file in that list, tap Open Other Presentations to display the Open screen in which you can choose the location and file you want to open.

If you're already working in PowerPoint, you can open an existing file by tapping File to display the Backstage view and then tapping the Open tab. This also brings you to the Open screen in which you can choose the location of the file is store or tap Browse to display the Open dialog box and navigate to the file you need. When you find it, tap it and tap Open to begin working with the file.

Selecting a presentation theme

PowerPoint includes a number of themes that lend a coordinated look for the color scheme, fonts, and effects used in the presentation. If you like, you can get more specific with your design choices by choosing one of the new PowerPoint 2013 variants, which display the same theme but in a variety of colors that you can apply to the open presentation.

Apply a theme

1 Open a presentation.

2 On the ribbon, tap the Design tab.

3 In the Themes group, tap the drop-down arrow to display additional theme choices.

    A gallery of themes appears (not shown).

4 Tap the theme that you want to apply to the current presentation.

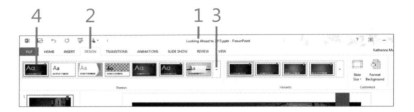

Choose a variant

1 After you select a theme, tap the Design tab if it's not already displayed.

2 In the Variants group, tap the variant that you want to apply to the presentation.

    Your selection is applied and all slides in your presentation show the new color of the selected variant.

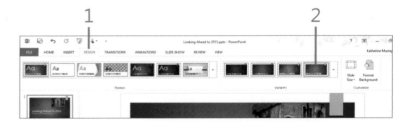

> **TIP** If you aren't sure which variant or theme you want to use, try one on for size. Tap a variant to apply it to the presentation, and if you don't like it, tap a different variant or, on the Quick Access Toolbar, tap the Undo button.

Create custom themes

You can create your own theme to apply to current and future presentations. On the Design tab, in the Customize group, tap the Format Background button to change the look of the slide background, and then tap Apply To All. Then, if you like, you can alter colors, fonts, and more by using the tools on the Home tab. To save your new theme, on the Design tab, in the Themes group, tap the Themes arrow and choose Save Current Theme. In the Save Current Theme box, type a name for your new theme and tap Save. The new theme will be available in the Custom area at the top of the Themes gallery the next time you tap the Themes arrow to view available themes.

Choosing a slide layout

PowerPoint offers you a number of different slide layouts that you can apply to create just the right look for your slides. You can choose from title slides, section slides, blank slides, pictures and captions, titles and captions, two-column, three-columns, and more. Whether you want to add bullet points or charts, video clips or animations, PowerPoint has a slide layout to create the slide easily. And after you create a slide, changing it to a different layout is as simple as tapping the one you want to use next.

Change a slide layout

1 In the Slides pane, tap and hold the slide that uses the layout you want to change. When the square appears, release your touch.

2 On the minibar that appears, tap Layout to open a gallery of layout choices.

3 Swipe up to scroll through the layout choices if necessary.

4 Tap the layout that you want to apply to the slide.

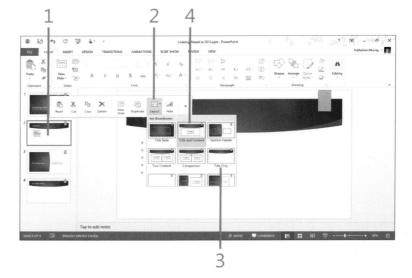

Working with slide masters

A slide master includes design elements that give a consistent look and feel to all slides to which it is applied. Every presentation by default has one slide master that is in place when you create the presentation file. If you want to add a header or footer to every slide, or add a logo to the background of all slides, you could add those items on the slide master and the elements will appear on all the slides that use that master.

To work with the slide master, tap the View tab and then, in the Master Views group, tap Slide Master. The slide master appears in the work area, where you can customize the design of the slide. When you tap Close Master View, any changes that you made are applied to all slides in your presentation to which that master is applied.

Adding and formatting text

The available PowerPoint slide layouts offer all kinds of different options with respect to how you add and work with content. Some slides include text areas and picture areas. Others include holders for text and media. Whatever layout you choose, you can easily add text to the slide by tapping in a text box and typing the content that you want to add. After text has been added, it can be edited easily: you can edit it or change the format and apply the font, size, color, and alignment you want.

Add slide text

1 When you start with a new presentation, PowerPoint displays the title page by default. In the Slides pane, tap the slide thumbnail to select the slide.

2 To add the first text, tap in the Tap To Add Title area.

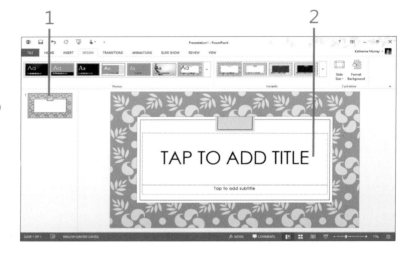

(continued on next page)

Add slide text *(continued)*

3 Type the title of your presentation.

4 Tap in the Tap To Add Subtitle area and add a subtitle for the presentation.

5 Tap outside the two text boxes.

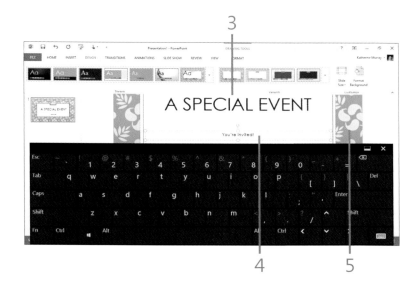

Format slide text

1 Tap the text box that contains the text you want to change.

2 Select the text by double-tapping a word or dragging the selection handle.

3 Tap the selection.

The formatting minibar appears next the selection.

4 Tap the formatting tool for the change that you want to make.

5 Alternatively, you can choose the formatting tool in the Font group on the Home tab.

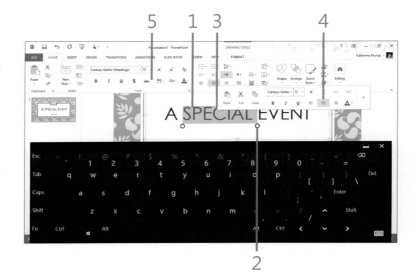

TIP If you like the format you've applied to an item on your slide and want to apply the same settings to other elements in your presentation, use the Format Painter to do the trick. You'll find the Format Painter tool in the Clipboard group on the Home tab. Highlight the text with the format that you want to copy, tap the Format Painter tool (which looks like a paintbrush), and then tap in the text to which you want to apply the format.

TIP If you tap selected text and expect the formatting minibar to appear, and it doesn't, check to make sure there's not a misspelling in the selected text. If PowerPoint detects a spelling error, the spelling correction options list will appear in place of the formatting minibar when you tap selected text.

Adding pictures to your slides

A long presentation full of bullet points can be ho-hum for your audience, especially if the topic you're presenting isn't the most exciting subject in the world. To liven things up and keep your audience interested, add compelling pictures to your slides. You could include pictures of your key staff members, stylized photos of your newest products, or images that simply inspire folks and help you make your point, whatever that might be. You can add pictures from your computer, cloud storage, or other connected picture sharing sites without ever leaving your PowerPoint 2013 slide.

Add a picture from your computer

1 In the Slides pane, tap the slide on which you want to add a picture. You can add a picture on any slide you like, but some slides display small Picture icons on the slide.

2 Tap the Picture icon on the slide.

The icon resembles the Pictures tool available in the Images group on the Insert tab.

3 Alternatively, on the ribbon, tap the Insert tab.

4 In the Images group, tap Pictures.

The Insert Picture dialog box opens.

(continued on next page)

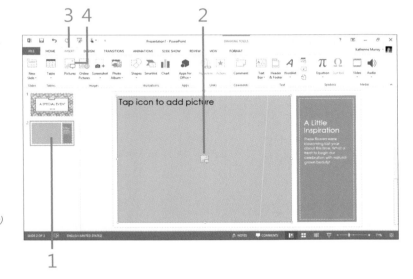

Add a picture from your computer *(continued)*

5 Choose the Folder that contains the picture you want to use.

6 Tap the picture.

7 Tap Insert.

5   6   7

> **TIP** If you want to add a picture that you've stored in the
> cloud, In the Favorites area of the Insert Picture dialog box, tap
> SkyDrive. Navigate to the folder containing the file you want to add,
> select it, and then tap Insert.

Add an a picture from an online source

1 In the Slides pane, tap the slide on which you want to add the picture from an online source.

2 On the ribbon, tap the Insert tab.

3 In the Images group, tap Online Pictures.

The Insert Pictures dialog box opens.

4 If you want to find clip art, type a word or phrase and tap Search.

5 To search for an image using Bing, type a description and tap Search.

6 Or, if you have connected Office 2013 to a photo sharing site (such as Flickr), choose an image from that source.

7 Or, browse your SkyDrive folders to locate the picture that you want to use.

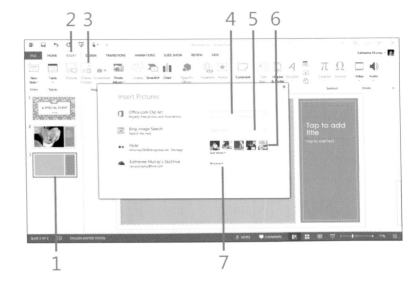

TIP You can also go online to search additional folders and albums in your photo-sharing site by tapping See More beneath the photos displayed. If you want to change settings for the account connected to Office 2013, tap the Manage link to the right of the service name in the Insert Picture dialog box.

Editing your pictures

PowerPoint gives you a number of tools with which you can edit your pictures after you've placed them on your slides. Using PowerPoint's built-in Corrections tools, you can adjust the light balance, sharpen the image, and correct the color tone. You can add special effects to the picture on your slide by choosing Picture Effects in the Picture Styles group of the Picture Tools Format tab. You can also add a number of special effects such as Shadow, Reflection, Glow, Soft Edges, Bevel, and 3-D Rotation by applying a picture style to a selected image. And if you want an even bigger impact, try applying artistic effects, which make your images look like paintings, drawings, pen-and-ink etchings, and more.

Inserting slides

The process of adding a slide to your presentation is just about as easy as it gets. The only trick is to tap the slide after which you want to insert the new slide. Then all it takes is a simple tap.

If you prefer to choose a layout while you're adding the slide, you can tap the New Slide button on the ribbon to show a gallery of layouts in which you can tap your choice.

Insert a new slide

1 Tap the slide after which you want to add your new slide.

2 On the ribbon, tap the Home tab.

3 If you want to add a slide with the same layout as the currently selected slide, in the Slides group, tap the upper portion of the New Slide button.

4 If you want to choose the layout for the new slide you're adding, tap the drop-down arrow on the lower portion of the New Slide button.

   A gallery of slide layouts opens.

5 Tap the layout that you want to use for the new slide.

6 Alternatively, if you want to make a copy of the currently selected slide, choose Duplicate Selected Slides.

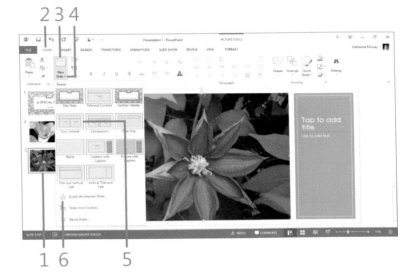

Reusing slides from other presentations

Recycling is a good idea, whether you're talking about newspapers, aluminum cans, or even presentations. You can easily reuse slides you've created in other PowerPoint presentations by tapping Reuse Slides at the bottom of the New Slides gallery. In the Reuse Slides pane, choose Open A PowerPoint File and navigate to the folder where the other presentation is stored, select it, and then tap Open.

The slides that are part of that presentation appear in the Reuse Slides pane. Add them to your presentation by tapping the ones you want to use. The theme used for your current presentation is applied to the reused slides, and you can edit the slides normally so that they fit well with the current presentation.

Correct picture sharpness and contrast

1 In the Slides pane, tap the picture that you want to correct.

2 Tap the Picture Tools | Format contextual tab.

3 In the Adjust group, tap the Corrections arrow.

The Corrections gallery opens.

4 Tap the thumbnail image that represents the sharpness that you want to apply.

5 Repeat step 3 and choose the Brightness/Contrast example that you want to use for your picture.

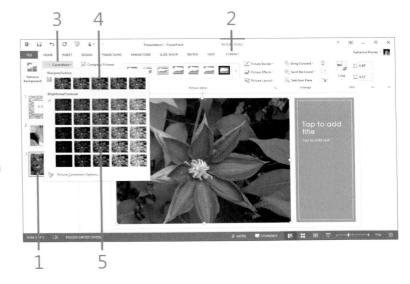

TIP PowerPoint 2013 now includes Smart Guides to help you line up the objects on your slides. When you tap an object, like a picture, and drag it around on the slide, you'll see a dynamic guide that shows you how the object aligns with the nearest object. The Smart Guide will change as you move the item, showing how the object lines up at the top, center, or bottom of another element. The Smart Guide can also show you the center of the page or the alignment with text boxes or titles.

Merge shapes on a slide

Another new feature in PowerPoint 2013 makes it easier to work with multiple shapes at once. After you draw shapes on the slide by using the Shapes tool in the Illustrations group on the Insert tab, you can combine the shapes into a single entity so that you can work with them as one object. Begin by selecting the shapes you want to merge and then, on the Drawing Tools | Format contextual tab, tap the Merge Shapes tool. Tap the merge option that you want to apply. You can select Union, Combine, Fragment, Intersect, and Subtract to create just the kind of effect you want from the resulting merged shape.

Adding and editing video

Using the Video tool in the Media group on the Insert tab, you can add video clips to your presentation, whether you're including an online video on your slide or adding a video file stored on your touch device. After you add the video to the slide, you can edit it to suit the topic and time you have available for it in your presentation.

Insert video

1 In the Slides pane, tap the slide on which you want to add the video.

2 On the ribbon, tap the Insert tab.

3 In the Media group, tap Video.

4 Choose either the Online Video or Video on My PC option. If you choose Video on My PC option, the Insert Video dialog box opens. Navigate to the folder containing the video clip you want to use, tap it, and then tap Insert to add it to the slide. If you choose Online Video, the Insert Video dialog box opens, and you can use one of the following steps to locate and insert your video.

(continued on next page)

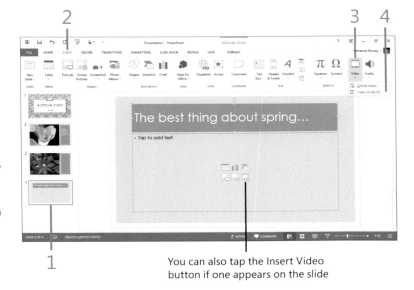

You can also tap the Insert Video button if one appears on the slide

Insert video *(continued)*

5 To open a video clip you have saved as a file, tap Browse.

6 Tap in the search box and enter a word or phrase describing the type of video you want to download and use in your presentation.

7 Tap to browse your SkyDrive for video files you have saved.

8 Tap to paste the embed code from an online video (for example, a YouTube video clip you have permission to use).

9 If you choose Video On My PC in the Video option list, the Insert Video dialog box opens. Tap the folder where the video is stored.

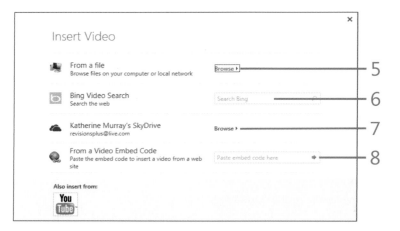

TIP PowerPoint might display a message that the program is optimizing your video clip for the latest media format. The update can take a minute or so. If you tap Cancel, PowerPoint won't insert the video, so if you want to use the selected video clip, let PowerPoint finish the optimizing. When the process is complete, your video is displayed on the slide.

Edit your video

1   Tap the video on the slide. The Video Tools contextual tabs appear.

2   Tap the Video Tools | Playback tab.

3   In the Editing group, tap Trim Video.

   The Trim Video dialog box opens.

(continued on next page)

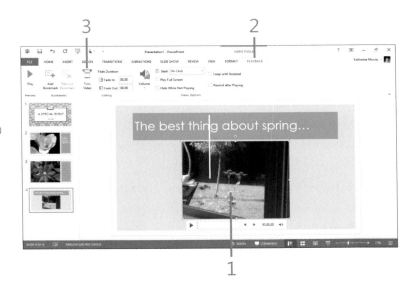

Edit your video *(continued)*

4 Adjust the Start slider to the point at which you want the video to begin.

5 Drag the End slider to the point at which want the video to end.

6 Tap to play the video clip.

7 Tap OK to save your changes.

8 If you want the video to fade in, In the Fade In box, enter a value.

9 Add a value, if desired, to the Fade Out box.

10 Control the volume of the video by tapping Volume.

11 Choose how you want the video to start and play.

12 Tap Rewind After Playing if you want the video to return to start after playing.

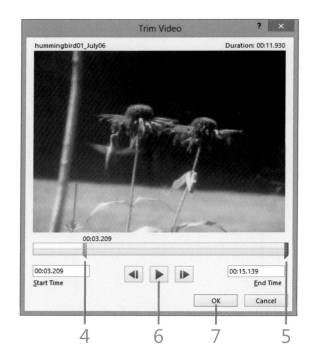

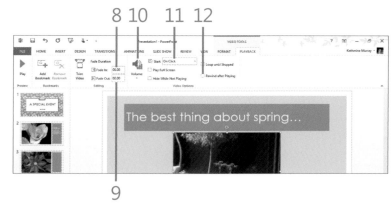

Recording narration

You can also add sound—separate from whatever sound plays in your video—to specific slides in your presentation. Perhaps you'd like to add narration that tells stories about your presentation for those viewers who will be reviewing it on their own. Or, you might want to add music clips or sound effects.

You can add audio to your presentation three ways. You can add audio to the current slide by using the Audio tool in the Media group on the Insert tab. To record narration and timings for your slide show, use the Record Slide Show tool in

the Set Up group on the Slide Show tab. And to add specific sound effects to animations or transitions, tap the Transitions tab and use the Sound tool in the Timing group to do the trick.

You can also add a sound clip you've already saved by using the Online Audio or Audio On My PC options in the Audio tool on the Insert tab. Navigate to the site or the folder where your audio file is stored and tap Insert to add it to the current PowerPoint slide.

Animating slide elements

Animation is a simple task in PowerPoint, and maybe even a little fun. You can bring your slides to life with just a few taps and ready-made animation sequences. The animation can be as simple or as elaborate as you'd like, and the entire process involves only a few steps: select the element on the page that you want to animate, choose the animation to apply, put the animated elements in the order you want, and then preview your work. Getting your animation just right might take a little trial and error, but with a little tweaking you can add extra interest to your slides that will keep your audience engaged.

Animate a slide element

1 Tap the text box, picture, or shape that you want to animate.

2 On the ribbon, tap the Animations tab.

3 In the Advanced Animation group, tap Add Animation.

   The animation gallery opens.

4 To display additional entrance effects, toward the bottom of the gallery, tap More Entrance Effects.

5 To see more exit animations, choose More Exit Effects.

6 Tap the animation that you want to apply to the object.

   The object is displayed on the slide with the animation you applied.

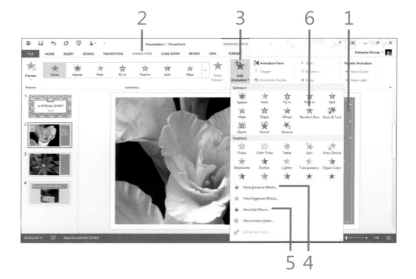

Choose a motion path

In PowerPoint 2013, you can animate objects on your slide by choosing a motion path to control where they go on the slide. Now, PowerPoint displays where your object will end up when you apply a motion path animation.

To add a motion path to your object, select the object and then, on the Animations tab, in the Advanced Animation group, tap Add Animation. Scroll down to the Motion Paths area on the Animation gallery and tap the motion path you want to use. You can also view additional motion paths by selecting More Motion Paths at the bottom of the gallery.

Choose animation effects

1 Tap the object that has the animation you want to change.

2 On the ribbon, tap the Animations tab.

3 Tap Effect Options.

A list of options related to the animation applied to that objet appears.

4 Tap the option that you want to apply to the animated object.

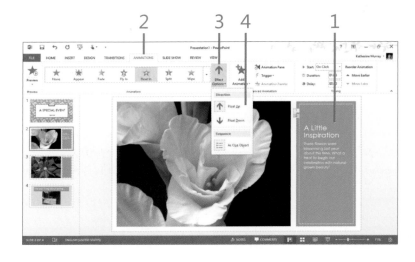

> ✓ **TIP** After you adjust animation settings the way you like them, you can use the Animation Painter, available in the Advanced Animation group on the Animations tab, to apply those same animation settings to other objects in your presentation.

Set timing and reorder animations

1 Display the slide with the animations you want to change.

2 Tap the Animations tab.

3 Select the item you want to change.

4 Tap the Start arrow. Choose whether you want the animation effect to be applied On Click, With Previous, or After Previous. On Tap means that the item won't be animated until you tap the mouse or tap the screen; With Previous means the animation will play with the animation of the previous object; and After Previous causes the animation to play as soon as that previous animation has completed.

5 Enter the duration you want to allow for the animation.

6 Specify a delay if you want a pause to be inserted before the animation plays.

7 Reorder the animation sequence by tapping or tapping Move Earlier or Move Later.

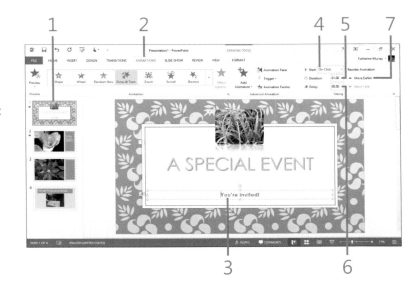

TIP Another way to control when the animation for an item plays is to set a specific trigger for the event. For example, you can tap the Trigger tool in the Advanced Animation group of the Animations tab and choose to play an animation when you tap one of the items on the slide.

Adding transitions to your slides

You might be surprised at how the way in which your slides change from one to the next can influence the feel of your presentation. PowerPoint calls that change from one slide to the next a transition. A transition that has a dramatic effect—like the Flip transition—shows a lot of movement and captures peoples' attention. A transition that is more understated, like Fade or Reveal, is a subtler way to keep things flowing smoothly from one slide to the next.

Choose a transition

1 Tap the Transitions tab.

2 Tap the More button in the Transition to This Slide group to see the full gallery of transitions and tap the transition you want to use.

3 Alternatively, if you see a transition you like without displaying the full Transition gallery, tap it.

4 Tap the Sound arrow to view a list of sound effects and tap the one you want. Built-in sound effects in PowerPoint include sounds like applause, a breeze, a chime, a drum roll, a typewriter, and more.

5 Tap the check box that reflects how you want to advance the slide. By default, PowerPoint chooses On Mouse Click, which means you must tap to display the next slide. If you want your slides to advance automatically, tap the After check box and enter the number of minutes and seconds you want the current slide to be displayed before the next slide appears automatically.

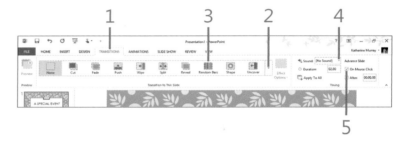

Modify a transition

1 In the Slides pane, tap the slide that includes a transition you want to change.

2 On the ribbon, tap the Transitions tab.

3 In the Transition To This Slide group, tap Effect Options.

   A list of options related to the current transition appears.

4 Tap the option that you want to apply, and PowerPoint displays the new transition with the option you selected.

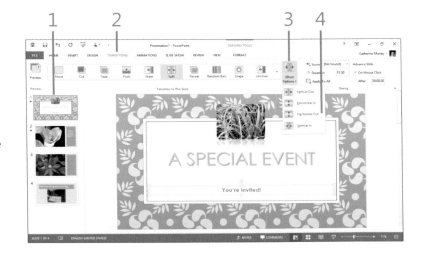

Collaborating and finishing your presentation

12

If you're working as part of a team, it is important for you to be able to share the presentation as it is developing. You might need to get buy-in from your department manager, or perhaps another person on your team will be creating the images you want to show on your slides. This kind of share-the-work ethic can make reaching deadlines easier (and faster), but it also means we need collaboration features in our favorite tools.

Microsoft PowerPoint 2013 includes a number of collaboration features that make it easy for you to work with others on a presentation. Whether you want to share a presentation you've created, work with others on a presentation in real time, or add comments to a presentation you're reviewing, the collaboration tools are straightforward and easy to use.

After you're finished making changes, you can finalize the presentation by previewing it and doing a practice dry-run. PowerPoint 2013 adds a big new feature to this end of things by introducing Presenter View. With this new view, you, as presenter, can navigate easily among slides and get additional information, like notes and sequence, as you present.

In this section:

- Sharing your presentation
- Commenting on a presentation
- Coauthoring presentations in real time
- Previewing the presentation
- Timing the presentation
- Printing presentation materials
- Using presenter view
- Broadcasting your presentation online
- Saving your presentation as a video

Sharing your presentation

Your first step in collaborating on a presentation involves sharing the presentation in the cloud. Because PowerPoint 2013 by default connects to your SkyDrive account, posting and sharing files you want others to see is a simple process. You can also send a shared file to others via email, which stores the master copy of the file in the cloud so that you can work on the file together online and then let PowerPoint synchronize all the changes for you.

Invite others to share your presentation

1 Make sure that you've previously saved the file to your SkyDrive folder. Then, on the ribbon, tap File to display the Backstage view.

2 Tap the Share tab.

3 Choose Invite People.

The Invite People pane opens on the right side of the Backstage view.

4 Type the name of people whom you want to invite to view the presentation.

5 Alternatively, tap the Address Book icon, choose the names of contacts from the displayed list, and then tap OK.

6 Tap the arrow to choose whether you want to allow invited participants to view and edit or only to view your presentation.

7 Type a message to send to those you are inviting.

8 If you want your colleagues to sign in before they view your presentation, select the Require Users To Sign-In Before Accessing Document check box.

9 Tap Share.

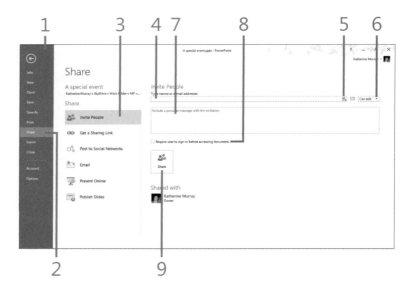

TIP When you tap Invite People on the Share tab of the Backstage view, if you haven't previously saved the file to your SkyDrive account, PowerPoint will display the Save To Cloud button. Tap the button and save the file to the cloud. The share options then become available in the Invite People screen.

Send the presentation to others via email

1 On the ribbon, tap the File tab to display the Backstage view.

2 Tap the Share tab.

3 Choose Email.

The Email pane appears on the right, offering you five different ways to send the presentation: Send As Attachment, Send A Link, Send As PDF, Send As XPS, and Send As Internet Fax.

4 Tap your choice. For example, choose Send As Attachment.

A blank email message window opens with your presentation displayed as an attachment.

5 In the To line, enter the email address of the people to whom you want to send the presentation.

6 Add a message if you like.

7 Tap Send to send the message with your presentation attached.

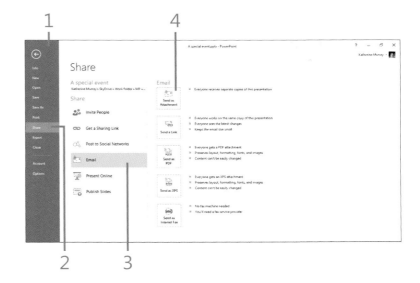

Commenting on a presentation

When you're collaborating on a presentation, you need a way to let your coauthors share their questions or suggestions about a slide. You can use comments to add notes, ask questions, and make suggestions that could improve the presentations you work on with your team. The commenting feature has been improved in PowerPoint 2013. The comment conversations are now threaded so that responses to comments indent within the original comment post, which makes it easy to see and respond to a specific comment. It also means the slide isn't littered with individual comment boxes, because comment conversations appear within a single comment thread.

Add a comment

1   In the Slides pane, tap the slide for which you want to add a comment.

2   On the ribbon, tap the Review tab.

3   In the Comments group, tap New Comment.

The Comments pane appears on the right side of the PowerPoint window.

4   In the text box, type the comment that you want to add.

Your profile picture appears to the left of the comment, making it easy for people to see at a glance who added the comment. PowerPoint uses the profile picture associated with your Microsoft Account. If you're not logged on to PowerPoint 2013 using your Microsoft Account, the image you selected for your Windows 8 user account appears there.

5   Exit the Comments pane by tapping Close.

> **TIP**   If you want to view the comments in the Comments pane, you can display it (and alternately, hide it again) at any time by tapping Show Comments in the Comments group on the Review tab.

Respond to a comment

1 In the Slides pane, tap the slide that has the the comment to which you want to respond.

2 In the upper-left corner of the slide, tap the Comment icon.

The Comments pane opens.

3 Tap the Reply box, type your response, and then tap outside the comment.

PowerPoint indents the response within the original comment so that you can easily read through all conversations related to the initial comment posted.

Navigate comments

1 On the ribbon, tap the Review tab.

2 In the Comments group, tap Previous to move to a previous comment in the presentation.

The comment opens in the Comments pane on the right side of the PowerPoint window.

3 Tap Next to move to the next comment in the presentation.

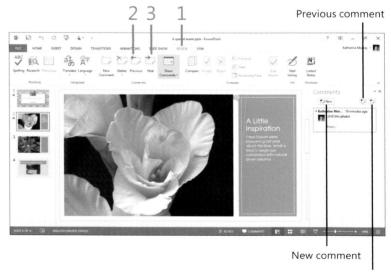

Previous comment

New comment

Next comment

Coauthoring presentations in real time

After you invite others to share your presentation, they can click the link to the file and open it, even if you're currently working in the file. Others can change the file as needed and Power-Point 2013 keeps track of all your changes automatically. When you or your coauthors save the file, others receive a notice in their status bars that an update is available. When each person saves the file, the changes from other coauthors appear in each person's file.

Open a shared presentation

1 On the ribbon, tap the File tab to display the Backstage view.

2 Tap the Open tab.

3 Choose the online location where your shared presentation is stored.

4 If necessary, tap Browse to look through folders and files in your cloud space.

(continued on next page)

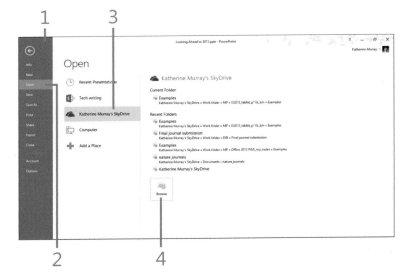

Open a shared presentation *(continued)*

5 Tap the folder that contains the file you want to use and then tap the desired file.

6 Tap Open.

The presentation opens on your screen. The coauthoring indicator on the status bar shows you how many people are currently working on the presentation.

7 Tap the indicator on the status bar of the PowerPoint window to see who else is working on the presentation.

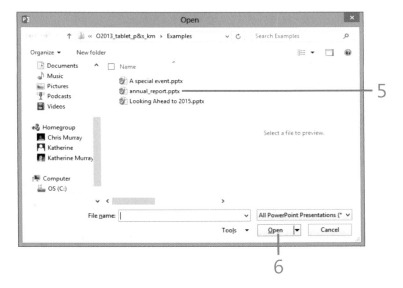

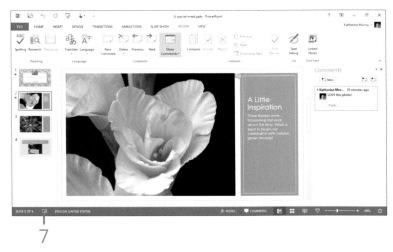

Coauthor a presentation

1 Make the necessary changes to the presentation.

When any other author saves changes, PowerPoint lets you know that updates are available.

2 Tap Updates Available.

PowerPoint displays a message box alerting you that when you save the document, it will be updated with the changes others have made.

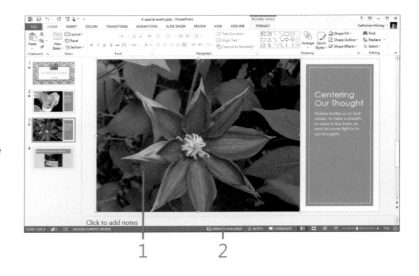

1   2

> ✓ **TIP** If your coauthor is online, you can contact him or her while you're working by tapping the name of the person in the indicator on the status bar. Your coauthor's contact information appears, and you can choose to send an instant message, email, or call the person directly by using Lync.

Previewing your presentation

You'll want to preview your presentation before giving it in front of a live audience. There are many ways to do this. You can choose to view the entire presentation or check out the slides from the current slide onward. You can also use Slide Sorter view to get a bird's-eye view of your slides and rearrange them as you like.

Preview your presentation

1 Open the presentation that you want to preview.

2 On the ribbon, tap the Slide Show tab.

3 If you want to display the entire slide show, in the Start Slide Show group, tap From Beginning.

4 To view the presentation from the current point onward, choose From Current Slide.

The presentation begins to play. The slides will advance depending on the method you selected: timed advancement or advancing only when you tap the mouse or tap the screen.

(continued on next page)

Preview your presentation *(continued)*

5 Tap in the lower-left corner of the preview window to display the navigation controls.

6 Tap Next to advance to the next slide or to play the next animation that is set to On Click.

7 Tap the Pen button to choose the tool to use during the presentation. You can choose Laser Pointer, Pen, Highlighter, Eraser, or choose a pen color.

8 Tap the More Options button to display additional options that you can use to display Presenter View, change the screen display, set arrow options, or get help.

9 To exit the preview, tap the Exit Presentation tool on the right end of the presentation toolbar or press Esc.

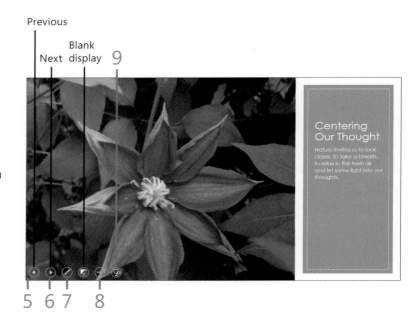

Previous

Next   Blank
        display   9

5 6 7   8

Reorder slides in slide sorter view

1 On the ribbon, tap the View tab.

2 In the Presentation Views group, tap Slide Sorter.

3 Alternatively, tap Slide Sorter in the view controls area in the lower-right corner of your screen.

4 Drag the slide that you want to move to a new location.

The other slides in your presentation adjust to accommodate the moved slide. Release your touch when the slide is positioned where you want it to appear.

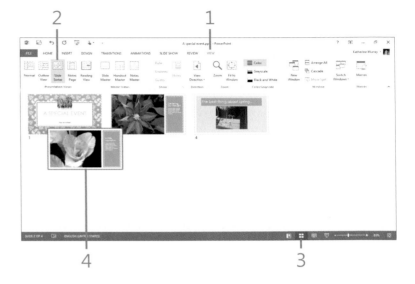

✓ **TIP** You can easily enlarge or reduce the size of the slides displayed in Slide Sorter view by pinching or zooming the screen display as desired. You can also tap the view slider control in the lower-right corner of the screen and drag the slider in the direction you want to resize the view.

Timing your presentation

Some people like presentations that advance automatically, and others like to control the advance of slides with a tap of the screen. Whatever your preference, you can use the Rehearse Timings tool to practice the amount of time you want to allow for each slide in your presentation. When you get the timing the way you like it, if you want to automate the presentation, you can record your settings and save them as part of your presentation file. If you just want to use the tool to rehearse, you can opt not to save the timing data.

Time the presentation

1 On the ribbon, tap the Slide Show tab.

2 In the Set Up group, tap Rehearse Timings.

The presentation begins to play and the Recording toolbar appears in the upper-left corner of the screen.

3 Tap Next when you are ready to advance either to the next animation or, if there are no animations on your slide, to the next slide.

4 Tap Pause to pause recording. This control and others appear in the upper-left corner of the screen.

A pop-up message box appears indicating that the recording has been paused. When you're ready to continue, tap Resume Recording.

5 Tap the Close button when you're done recording timings.

PowerPoint displays a message box asking whether you want to keep the new slide timings. Tap Yes to save your new settings or No to cancel the timing values.

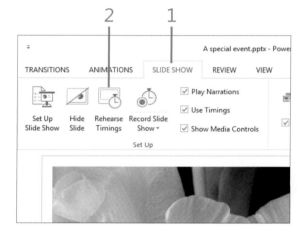

> ⚠️ **CAUTION** If you choose to save the timings you recorded during the rehearsal, any timing values you typed in the Timing group of the Transitions tab will be replaced with the new values.

Printing presentation materials

For presentations you'll be giving in person, you might want to prepare and print handouts your audience members can take home when your slide show is done. You can print your handouts in a number of ways, printing multiple slides on each page, printing slides and notes, or printing one slide per page, if that's your preference. You'll use the Print category in the Backstage view to get the job done.

Print slides

1   Save the presentation that you want to print and tap File to display the Backstage view.

2   Tap the Print tab.

3   Choose the printer that you want to use.

4   Choose which slides that you want to print.

5   Alternatively, enter the range of slides that you want to print (for example, 4–5).

6   If you're printing multiple copies of your slides, choose how (or whether) you want the pages to be collated, so different sets are arranged together on one set.

7   Select whether you want to print the slides in color, grayscale, or black and white.

8   Preview your slides in the print preview area.

9   Browse through the various slides.

10 Change the size of the previewed slide.

11 Scroll through the presentation.

12 Tap Print to send the slides to the printer.

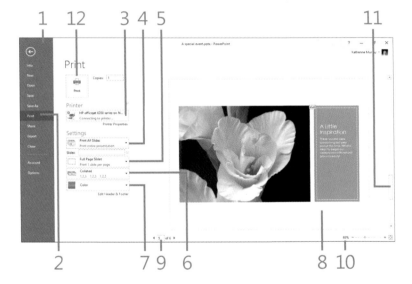

Prepare handouts

1 On the ribbon, tap File to display the Backstage view.

2 Tap the Print tab.

3 Tap the drop-down arrow to the right of Full Page Slides.

A gallery of options appears.

4 Select the way you'd like your handouts to display the slides in your presentation.

You can choose to have one, two, three, four, six, or nine slides on a printed page.

5 Choose whether you want to print the handouts in color, grayscale, or black and white.

6 Tap Print to print the handouts.

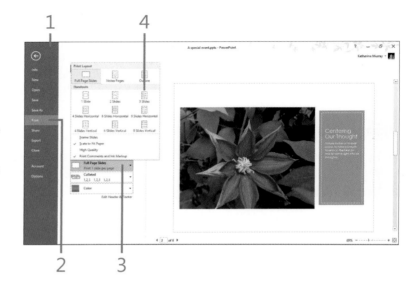

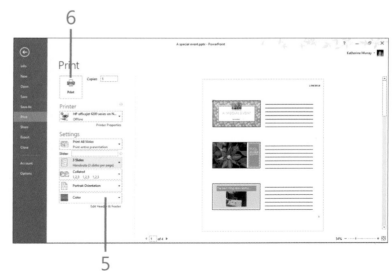

Using presenter view

PowerPoint 2013 makes it easier than ever to present with the introduction of the new Presenter View feature. Presenter View brings together all the elements you need in one handy interface that only you can see. You can see the slide your audience is viewing and write on the slide by using pen and laser tools. Also with Presenter View, you can move among all your slides easily, see which slide is next in queue, and review your slide notes while you present.

Display presenter view

1 On the ribbon, tap the Slide Show tab.

2 In the Start Slide Show group, tap From Beginning to start the slide show.

3 Tap the lower-left corner of the display to reveal the navigation controls.

4 Tap the More Options button (the ellipsis character) to display the Options list.

5 Tap Show Presenter View.

Presenter View opens on your screen, but it is not visible to your audience.

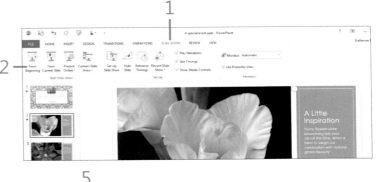

Use Presenter View

1 With Presenter View open, tap to select the Pen tool and tap Pen again so that you can draw on the current slide.

2 Tap the Pause The Timer button to suspend the presentation.

3 Tap to display the next slide.

4 Tap to display the previous slide.

5 Preview the next slide that will be displayed.

6 Read through your presentation notes.

7 Enlarge the font used to display slide notes.

8 Show the Windows taskbar so that you can switch between programs.

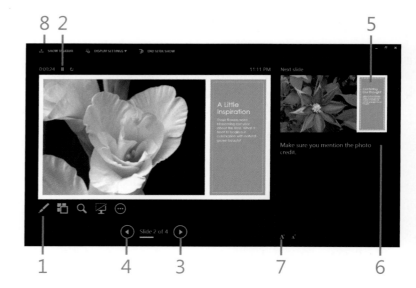

✓ **TIP** Using touch, you can zoom the presentation and return it to normal display by using the pinch and zoom gesture.

Using the navigation grid

Presenter View includes a tool called Navigation Grid that gives you an easy way to move directly to any slide that you want to display. The Navigation Grid displays all the slides together in one screen—similar to the way Slide Sorter shows thumbnails of your slides in the regular PowerPoint view. The Navigation Grid is not visible to your audience while you are presenting.

In Presenter View, tap Navigation Grid (the second tool from the left beneath the slide display). The slides appear in a grid format so that you can tap the one you want to view. You can zoom or reduce the size of the slides in the Navigation Grid by the pinch and zoom gestures.

⊘ **TIP** When you're ready to exit Presenter View and return to slide display, tap the Close tool in the upper-right corner of your screen.

Broadcasting your presentation online

Now, with PowerPoint 2013, you can share your finished presentation with people all over the globe by broadcasting it live online if you're logged on using your Microsoft Account.

Because people can view the presentation in their web browsers, they don't even need to have PowerPoint installed in order to view it.

Present your presentation online

1 On the ribbon, tap File to display the Backstage view.

2 Tap the Share tab.

3 Choose Present Online.

The Present Online pane opens on the right side of the screen.

4 Tap the drop-down arrow to choose the presentation service that you want to use.

Choose Microsoft Lync if your colleagues are all Lync contacts; choose Office Presentation Service if those viewing your presentation will be viewing your presentation in their browser windows. If you are not using Office 2013 as part of Office 365, you might see only Office Presentation Service for this option.

5 Tap Present Online.

6 If you choose the Office Presentation Service, the Present Online dialog box appears, displaying the link for the presentation.

7 Tap Copy Link to copy the link and paste it into an instant message to send to participants.

8 Alternatively, tap Send In Email to send the link in an email message to others.

9 Tap Start Presentation. PowerPoint launches the presentation and you can use the navigation controls to page through it normally. Tap Exit Presentation in the navigation controls when you're finished presenting online.

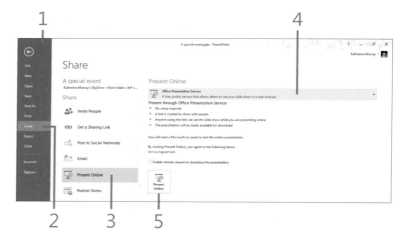

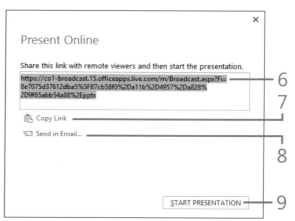

Saving your presentation as a video

If you plan to make your presentation available to others online so that they can go through it on their own time, you can save your presentation as a video others can view. This makes it possible for others to view the presentation without needing to have PowerPoint installed on their system or device.

Create a video

1 Save all changes in your presentation and tap File to display the Backstage view.

2 Tap the Export tab.

3 Choose Create A Video.

The Create A Video pane appears on the right side of the Backstage view.

4 Tap to choose the format for the video.

You can select Computer & HD Displays, which saves the file so that it can be viewed on a computer or other high-definition displays; Internet & DVD, which saves the presentation in a form suitable for the web or a standard DVD; or Portable Devices, which saves the presentation in a form optimized for devices running Microsoft Zune.

5 Tap to choose whether you want to use the timings and narrations you've included with the presentation.

6 If you opt not to use the timings saved with the presentation, you can specify the amount of time that you want to assign to the display of each slide. If you are prompted to provide your logon information, do so at the prompt.

7 Tap Create Video.

PowerPoint displays the Save As dialog box, in which you can choose the folder where you want to store the video.

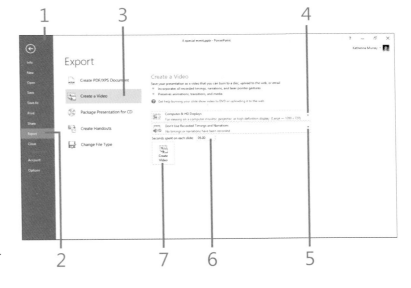

(continued on next page)

Create a video *(continued)*

8 Choose the folder for the video.

9 Enter a new name for the file, if necessary.

10 Tap Save.

PowerPoint saves the video to the folder you selected.

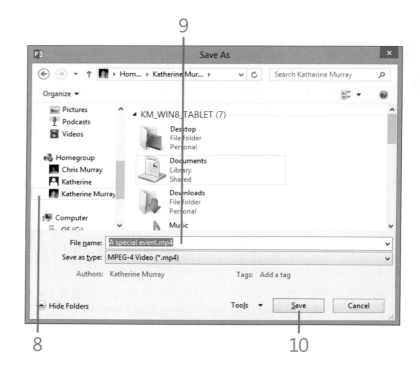

Organizing your research with OneNote 2013

13

Microsoft OneNote 2013 is the popular note-taking tool that is included as part of Microsoft Office 2013. Using OneNote, you can capture notes in whatever form you like best—text, pictures, audio, or video—and you can easily clip notes from the web, no matter what device you happen to be using. OneNote stores your information in the notebook you select, and helps you keep track of notes, organize and tag information, and easily find the notes you need later. You can also create shared notebooks that you can work on with colleagues anywhere in the world.

In this section:

- Getting started with OneNote 2013
- Creating a notebook
- Opening a notebook
- Capturing notes—anytime, anywhere
- Using note templates
- Searching for notes
- Sharing notebooks

Getting started with OneNote 2013

When you start OneNote 2013, you'll notice some similarities and some differences with the rest of the Office 2013 suite. For one thing, there's no OneNote Start screen to launch you into the notebook of your choice. Instead, the OneNote window opens, displaying some introductory information to help you begin taking notes. You'll see the familiar ribbon, however, and recognize common screen elements shared with other Office apps—so the basic lay of the land will probably feel familiar to you.

Starting OneNote 2013

1 Swipe or scroll to display the app tiles off the right side of the Start screen.

2 Tap the OneNote 2013 tile.

The app opens on your Windows 8 Desktop.

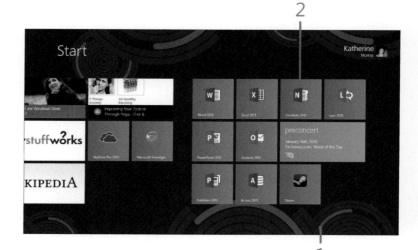

> **TIP** There are actually two versions of OneNote 2013 available. The one you installed as part of Office 2013 is the standard OneNote 2013 that can be used with Windows 7 or Windows 8. Another app, called OneNote MX, is available through the Windows Store and is optimized for touch. You'll discover some fun new features in OneNote MX like radial menus, which make choosing tools a snap. This chapter focuses on the standard version of OneNote 2013, but if you are using a Windows 8 tablet, check out OneNote MX—it's free!

Exploring the OneNote window

- On the ribbon, tap File to display the Backstage view, where you can change your notebook settings, share the notebook, print note pages, and more. Tap the back arrow to return to the OneNote window.

- Find common tools, such as Undo, Print, and Touch Mode, on the Quick Access Toolbar. You can also customize this toolbar to display the tools that you use most often in OneNote.

- By default, the OneNote ribbon display is set to hide automatically so that it doesn't take up screen space when you don't need it. When you tap a tab, the ribbon appears so that you can choose the tool you want to use. After you tap the tool, the ribbon disappears again. You can change this setting by tapping the Ribbon Display Options button in the upper-right corner of the OneNote window.

- Tap the + tab to add a new section to the current notebook. You can then title the new section and add note pages by tapping Add Page.

- The note pages you create are listed in the panel on the right side of the OneNote window. If you haven't added a note page title, the first line of text is displayed so that you can see what the note contains.

(continued on next page)

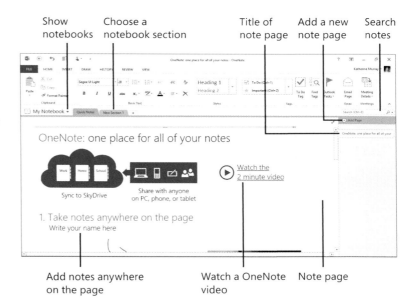

Show notebooks   Choose a notebook section   Title of note page   Add a new note page   Search notes

Add notes anywhere on the page   Watch a OneNote video   Note page

> **TIP** You can change the OneNote display so that the page tabs appear on the left side of the OneNote display if you prefer. Tap the File tab to display the Backstage view and then tap the Options tab. In the OneNote Options dialog box, tap Display and select the Page Tabs Appear On The Left check box. Tap OK to close the Options dialog box. All page tabs for the current section are now listed down the left side of the OneNote window instead of on the right.

- Tap the Insert tab to see the various items that you can add to your note pages, including tables, spreadsheets, files, pictures, audio, video, the date and time, equations, symbols, and more.

- Enter a word or phrase in the Search box, and OneNote's powerful search tool scours your notebooks and finds and displays results instantly.

Display Backstage view

Change ribbon display options

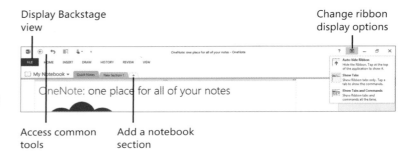

Access common tools

Add a notebook section

Creating a notebook

OneNote 2013 creates a new notebook for you automatically when you first start the app. You can use this notebook to learn about and experiment with OneNote, or you can begin using it to store your inspiring thoughts (or other data). When you're ready to create a new notebook, however, you can do that easily by choosing New in the Backstage view (tap the File tab) by tapping the Notebook selector in the tab row and choosing Add Notebook.

Start a new notebook

1 Start OneNote and your most recent notebook opens on the screen. If you are launching OneNote for the first time, the program creates the new notebook for you and displays an opening notes page with tips on using OneNote.

2 Tap the Show Notebooks drop-down arrow.

3 Choose Add Notebook. The Backstage view appears so that you can enter information about the new notebook you're creating.

(continued on next page)

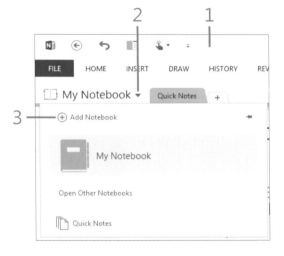

Start a new notebook *(continued)*

4 Tap the place where you want to store the new notebook.

You can choose a SkyDrive or SharePoint folder, which saves your notebook in the cloud, or a folder on your computer.

5 Type a name for the new notebook.

6 Tap Create Notebook.

A pop-up message box informs you that the notebook has been created and, if you selected SkyDrive or SharePoint as the place you wanted to save the notebook, OneNote asks you whether you want to invite others to share the notebook.

7 Choose Not Now and the new notebook opens in the OneNote window.

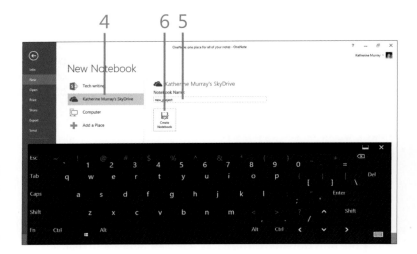

Opening a notebook

OneNote 2013 makes it easy for you to open existing notebooks, no matter how many you might have. You can access notebooks saved online in your cloud storage or stored in a folder on your device. You'll find the existing notebooks by choosing the File tab and then tapping the Open tab. You can choose a notebook saved in your SkyDrive account or at another online location you specify. You can also have OneNote update the folder display so that you can be sure you're viewing the most recent versions of the files.

Open a notebook saved online

1 Tap the File tab to display the Backstage view.

2 Tap the Open tab.

3 Tap a notebook saved on SkyDrive that you want to open.

4 If necessary, tap to refresh the folder display from your cloud storage.

5 Tap to display your SkyDrive folder if you like.

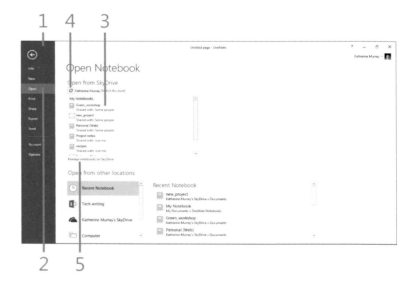

TIP   On the Open tab of the Backstage view, OneNote displays the notebooks that are connected with the Microsoft Account you used to log on on your computer, but you can change to a different account by tapping Switch Account at the top of the Open From SkyDrive list. In the Microsoft Account dialog box, enter the user name and password that you want to use to sign in to the other account and tap Sign In. The notebooks saved in the cloud space connected to that account then appear in the Open Notebook list.

Choose an existing notebook

1 On the ribbon, tap the File tab to display the Backstage view and then tap the Open tab.

2 Tap Recent Notebook.

   A list of notebooks you've worked with recently appear in the right side of the Open Notebook display.

3 Tap the notebook that you want to open.

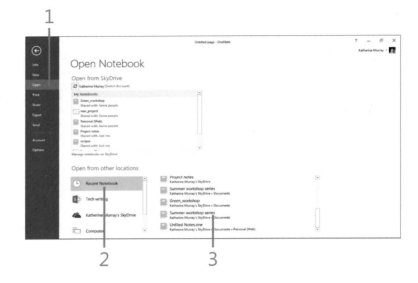

TIP You can also open a notebook when you're working with another notebook in the OneNote window. Tap the arrow to the right of the My Notebook tab and tap the notebook you want to use from the displayed list.

Capturing notes—anytime, anywhere

OneNote 2013 makes it easy for you to collect notes in whatever way feels most comfortable for you. If you like to take quick notes to yourself by using your tablet's microphone, you can record an audio note. You can sketch diagrams, post pictures to your notes pages, grab a video clip, or type text on the page. No matter how it occurs to you to collect your thoughts, OneNote gives you the tools you need to accomplish it easily.

Add a typed note

1 Open your notebook, if necessary, tap anywhere on the note page, and then, using the On-Screen Keyboard, type your note.

   As you type, OneNote expands the text box to make room for your text.

2 Press Enter to move the cursor to the next line.

3 Drag to increase or decrease width of the note box.

4 Drag to move the note box to another position on the page.

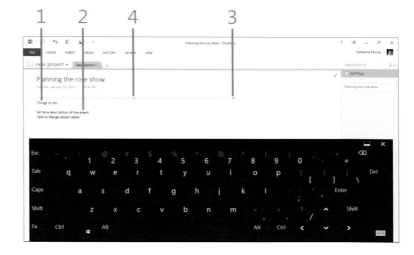

TIP To change the default font OneNote uses to display all text on your notes pages as you enter it, tap the File tab and then tap the Options tab. The OneNote Options dialog box appears, with the General tab displayed. Tap the Font arrow in the Default Font area and then tap the font that you want to set as the default. You can also change the size of the font and the font color. Tap OK to save your changes and close the OneNote Options dialog box.

Adding sections and pages

You can organize your notes by adding sections and then creating new notes pages within them. Tap the Add A Section tab (the tab with a plus sign in it) along the top of the OneNote 2013 notes area. Type a name for the new section and press Enter; OneNote saves it as a tab at the top of the display.

Add pages within the new section by tapping the section tab and then tapping Add A Page in the pane on the right side of the OneNote window. A new untitled page is added to the section so that you can add notes by typing, drawing, attaching files, or inserting audio and video notes.

Drawing your notes

1 On the ribbon, tap the Draw tab.

The ribbon displays drawing tools that can use to change the pen width and color, add shapes, erase lines, and arrange elements on the page.

2 To choose the color and line weight for the pen, tap the Color & Thickness button.

3 Tap the Color & Thickness tool to choose the color you want to use.

4 In the Color & Thickness dialog box, choose whether you want to apply the settings to a pen or highlighter.

5 Tap the thickness of the line.

6 Tap the line color.

7 Tap OK to save the settings.

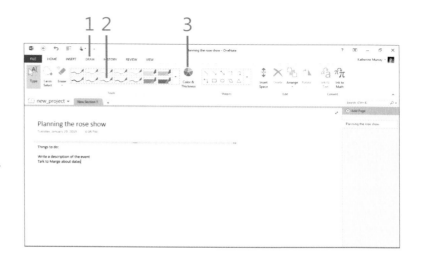

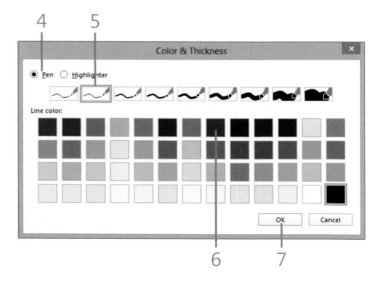

TIP You can add tags to your notes so that you can easily find them later. Simply choose the note that you want to tag, tap the Home tab, and then, in the Tags group, choose the tag that fits your needs. Whenever you want to locate notes that have a certain tag, you can use the Find Tags button in the Tags group on the Home tab to locate the notes with the tag you need.

Record an audio or video note

1 Tap the note page where you want to add the audio.

2 On the ribbon, tap the Insert tab.

3 In the Recording group, tap Record Audio to record a voice note or tap Record Video to record a video note.

The Audio & Video | Recording contextual tab appears, indicating that recording has begun. Record your content as needed.

4 Tap Pause to suspend recording.

5 Tap Stop when you're finished.

The Audio & Video | Playback contextual tab appears so that you can play back the recording you've captured.

6 Tap Play to listen to the recording.

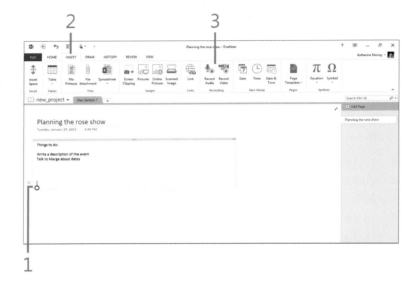

> **TIP** You can play an audio or video note at any time by tapping the object on your note page. A small playback toolbar appears beside the object, and you can tap Play to play the media on the page.

Attaching a file to your note page

Of course, not all the important information you want to capture in your OneNote 2013 notebooks will come from information you type or draw. You may also want to attach files to your notes so that you can collect the items you need all in one place. To attach a file, display the note page where you want to add the file, and then, on the ribbon, tap the Insert tab. In the Files group, choose either the File Attachment tool or the Spreadsheet tool. If you choose File Attachment, the Choose A File Or A Set Of Files To Insert dialog box opens, in which you can navigate to the folder containing the file that you want to add. Tap it and tap Insert.

If you choose Spreadsheet, two choices appear, giving you the option of inserting an existing Microsoft Excel spreadsheet or creating a new Excel spreadsheet. If you choose Existing Excel Spreadsheet, the Choose Document To Insert dialog box opens and you can then select the spreadsheet and tap Insert. If you choose New Excel Spreadsheet, a new worksheet is added to your OneNote page; you can then tap Edit and enter the values that you want to include. When you save the file, the data is stored with your OneNote notebook.

Using note templates

If you think more clearly when you have some kind of structure, you might like using the page templates available in OneNote 2013. You can choose from a number of different page designs to give your pages personality. You can choose from academic, blank, business, decorative, or planner templates or search for additional templates on Office.com.

In addition to templates, you can change the color and line style of your notes page by choosing the View tab and tapping Page Color and Rule Lines in the Page Setup group. Page Color displays a palette of 16 soft shades, and Rule Lines offers choices for adding various types of rule lines or grid lines to your pages.

Create a new page based on a template

1 Open a OneNote notebook.

2 On the ribbon, tap the Insert tab.

3 In the Pages group, tap Page Templates.

The Templates pane opens on the right side of the OneNote window.

4 Tap the category of templates that you want to view.

A list of templates appears.

5 Tap the template that you want to open.

6 Tap to display a list of templates from which you can choose a default template for all your new notes pages.

For example, you might want to choose Simple Lecture Notes if you use OneNote to take notes in class.

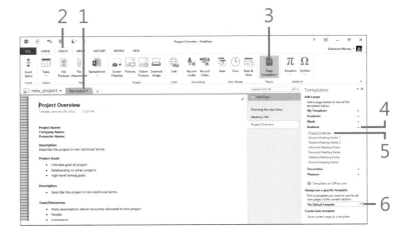

Personalize a page template

You might want to begin with a OneNote 2013 page template and tweak it to suit your needs. After you make the changes you want, you can save the page as a new template. To do that, on the ribbon, tap the Insert tab and choose Page Templates. Tap Page Templates from the resulting list, if applicable. At the bottom of the Templates pane, tap the Save Current Page as a Template link. The Save As Template dialog box opens, in which you can enter a name for the new template. To use the saved template as the default for all the new notes pages you add to your notebook, select the Set As Default Template check box. Tap Save to save the new template, and it will appear in the My Templates category at the top of the Templates pane, making it easy to choose in the future.

Adding lines to the page

1 Display the note page on which you want to add lines.

2 On the ribbon, tap the View tab.

3 Tap the Rule Lines button.

A palette of line styles and options appears.

4 Tap the line style that you want.

You can choose Narrow Ruled, College Ruled, Standard Ruled, or Wide Ruled.

5 If you choose to display a grid instead of horizontal lines, tap the grid style that you want.

You can select Small Grid, Medium Grid, Large Grid, and Very Large Grid.

6 After you choose a rule or grid line style, you can select a line color. Tap Rule Line Color.

7 In the list of color options that appears, tap the color that you want to apply to the lines.

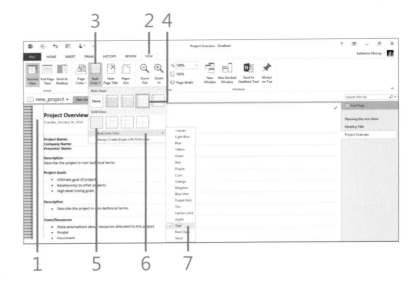

> **TIP** If you want to configure OneNote so that it always uses your line selection when creating new notes pages, at the bottom of the Rule Lines list, tap Always Create Pages With Rule Lines. A check mark appears to the left of the option name, and new note pages will include lines. If you want to turn off the lines feature at a later time, display the Rule Lists list again and tap the option again to remove the check mark.

Searching for notes

Tags can help you easily locate information related to a specific project, idea, or person. Whether you tag your notes or not, you can find them easily in OneNote 2013. OneNote has a lightning-fast search tool that displays results as soon as you begin typing in the Search box. You can add search criteria to find notes within a specific page, section, or notebook, and you can choose to search all notebooks at once. If you think you'll be using a certain search regularly, you can also set it as the default search so that you can use it again whenever you need it.

Search for note content

1 Tap the Search box on the right side of the OneNote window and type a word or phrase that you want to find.

2 OneNote instantly shows you where the word or phrase is found. The word is also highlighted if found on the current note page. You can tap a result to move to that item.

3 Narrow your search by tapping the Change Search Scope drop-down arrow. A list of options lets you choose to find what you're searching for on the current page, in the current section, in a group of sections, in the current notebook, or in all your OneNote notebooks.

4 Tap the scope that you want to define for the search.

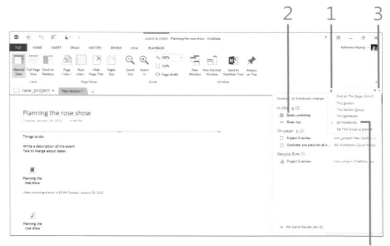

Sharing notebooks

Most of the Office 2013 apps are designed for sharing, and in OneNote 2013, sharing is even easier than it is in some of the other Office programs. When you first create a notebook, if you selected an online location to store the notebook, One-Note asks you whether you'd like to share it straightaway. If you choose not to share it at that point, you can go back and add sharing later. The process involves sharing the notebook to your SkyDrive account in the cloud and then inviting others to share the notebook.

Invite others to share the notebook

1 On the ribbon, tap File to display the Backstage view.

2 Tap the Share tab. If prompted, save your file to SkyDrive.

3 In the Share area, tap Invite People.

The Invite People pane appears on the right side of your screen.

4 Type the names or email address of those with whom you want to share the notebook.

5 Enter any message that you want to send with the invitation.

6 Tap Share.

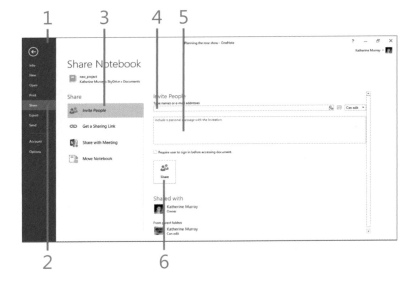

✓ **TIP** If you begin to share the notebook but haven't saved it yet, OneNote will prompt you to save it before you share it with others.

Send a link to a notebook

1 On the ribbon, tap File to display the Backstage view.

2 Tap the Share tab.

3 Tap Get A Sharing Link.

The Get A Sharing Link pane appears in the right side of Backstage view.

4 If you want others to be able to only view (but not change) the notebook, in the View Link area, tap the Create Link button.

5 To allow others to edit the notebook, in the Edit Link area, tap the Create Link button.

A link is displayed in that area that you can copy to share with others on your team.

6 The Shared With area shows what sharing permissions are in effect for the current notebook.

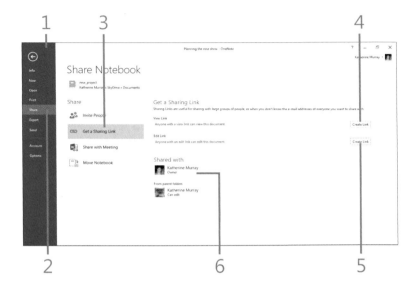

Share with a meeting

1 On the ribbon, tap the File tab to display the Backstage view and then tap the Share tab.

2 Tap Share With Meeting.

3 Choose the Share With Meeting button.

The Share Notes With An Online Meeting dialog box opens, in which you can choose a current conversation or meeting or launch a new meeting. If you are currently in a Lync meeting, that meeting will appear in the list. If no meeting has been started, you'll see the option Start A New Lync Meeting.

4 Tap your choice.

5 Tap OK.

The meeting information is added to your notes page and others who have the necessary permissions will be able to share your notes.

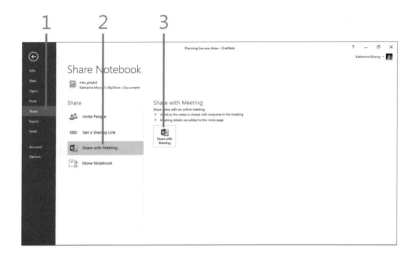

Exporting notes

You can easily copy and paste bits and pieces of your One-Note 2013 notes into Microsoft Word documents or Microsoft PowerPoint presentations, but you can also export your notes—in the form of pages, sections, or entire notebooks—in a number of formats. You can export pages and sections as OneNote files, Word documents, webpages, or PDF or XPS files. You can export an entire notebook as a OneNote package or a PDF or XPS file. To export your notes, tap File and choose Export. Choose whether you want to export the current page, section, or notebook, and then tap the format in which you want to export the selected item. If you choose Page or Section, you can export the content as a OneNote section, as a Word document, as a webpage, or as a PDF or XPS file. You can choose to export the notebook as a notebook package, a PDF, or an XPS file. Tap the format of your choice and tap Export to finish the task.

Creating, reviewing, and touching up publications with Publisher 2013

14

If you regularly create brochures, pamphlets, flyers, or invitations, you might be accustomed to whipping up or tweaking Microsoft Publisher documents on the fly. And if not, no worries—Publisher is easy to learn and use and offers a large slate of tools with which you can lay out publications of all types.

Publisher 2013 comes with a number of templates that you can use as the basis for your publications and then tailor to meet your needs. Or if you prefer, you can start from scratch with a blank page. Either way, you'll find it is easy to create professional looking reports, brochures, greeting cards, and more. This section introduces you to the basic features in Publisher 2013 and shows you how to put all the basics together to create an effective and inviting publication.

In this section:

- Getting started with Publisher 2013
- Creating a new publication
- Choosing and using a template
- Setting up pages
- Adding content
- Linking text boxes
- Inserting and replacing pictures
- Layering objects on Publisher pages
- Finalizing your publication

Getting started with Publisher 2013

When you start Publisher 2013 by tapping its tile on the Windows 8 Start screen, the app opens by displaying the Publisher 2013 Start screen. This screen helps you get started by offering templates for new files as well as access to files you may have worked in recently.

Start Publisher

1 On the Start screen, swipe left to display the app tiles off the right side of the screen.

2 Tap the Publisher 2013 tile.

The app opens on your Windows 8 Desktop, and the Publisher Start screen displays.

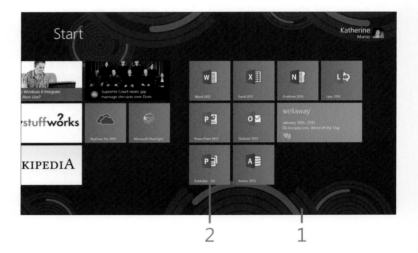

What's new in Publisher 2013

- **The Publisher 2013 Start screen**   Similar to other Office 2013 apps, Publisher includes the new Start screen to help you find the template or file you need quickly.

- **Access your recent publications anywhere**   When you log on by using your Microsoft Account, you can always access your most recently used publications that you've saved to the cloud. Your program preferences are also recorded with your account, so your Publisher screen will look similar from device to device.

- **New online templates**   New, professionally designed templates are available online in a wide variety of publication styles and personalities.

- **New effects for page elements**   Now, you can use new graphics effects to add soft shadows, glow, and reflection to text, pictures, or shapes on the page.

- **Add multiple pictures easily with thumbnails**   In the past, when you added multiple pictures to your page at one time, they all appeared as a big pile in the center of your page. Now, Publisher adds them as thumbnail images in the scratch area of your page where you can then drag individual pictures to wherever you want them to appear on your page.

- **Live picture swap**   Another picture feature makes it easier to preview a new picture in place of another. Simply drag the new picture to the place on the page where the existing picture that you want to replace appears.

- **Export content easily**   You can prepare your Publisher files for a commercial printer or export pages as image files that you can then print in high quality, using the tools on the Export tab in the Publisher 2013 Backstage view.

Creating a new publication

If you have a specific design in mind, you might want to begin with a blank page in Publisher 2013. You'll find three different options for blank pages on the New tab of the Backstage view or at the top of the Publisher 2013 Start screen. You can choose to create a blank page with a portrait (8.5 × 11") orientation or with a landscape (11 × 8.5") orientation, or you can choose More Blank Page Sizes to display a gallery of additional page sizes that you can use as the basis for your blank page.

Create a blank publication

1 On the Publisher Start screen, tap Blank 8.5" × 11" or Blank 11" × 8.5" to open a blank publication.

The new blank publication opens in the Publisher work area.

Tap to open a
recent publication

1

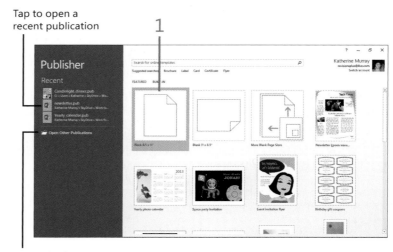

Tap to display the Open dialog
box to open other publications

Open an existing publication

The Publisher 2013 Start screen displays your most recently used publications along the left side of the screen. If you see the file you want to work on listed there, simply tap the file name and the publication opens on your screen.

If you don't see the file you want in the Recent list, tap Open Other Documents to display the Open tab in the Backstage view. Choose the place where the file you want is stored and tap the name of the publication you want to open.

Learn Publisher tools

Like the other Microsoft Office 2013 apps, Publisher strikes a balance to give you plenty of room on your screen in which to work while offering you the tools you need as you create and share publications:

- Choose the tab on the ribbon that reflects what you want to do next.

- Contextual tabs appear to offer tools related to the specific item you select

- Unpin the ribbon so that it appears only when you point to a tab or tool.

- Get a birds-eye view of the pages in your publication.

- Use the rulers to align and resize objects precisely.

- Use the scratch area as an extra workspace in which you can place objects nearby until you are ready to place them on the page.

- View the position and size of selected objects.

- Change the display to show a two-page spread and hide and display page elements.

- Zoom or reduce the display on the fly by using the view controls.

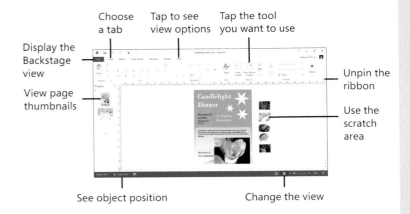

Tweak the Publisher display

You can use the tools on the View tab to change the look of the Publisher 2013 window. Begin by tapping the View tab to display set of related tools on the ribbon for configuring how your publication appears on your screen. Tap Boundaries to display the boundaries around the text and picture boxes on your page. Tap Guides to display guides around the edges

of page objects. Tap Baselines to see the baselines of text along the edges of the page so that you can align objects with lines of text. If you have added fields to your publication to include variable information—such as names and address information to be used in merge letters—you can select the Fields check box to display the fields on the Publisher page.

Choosing and using a template

Publisher 2013 includes a large library of templates from which you can choose when you're beginning a new publication. Whether you want to create a simple invitation, a flyer for your garage sale, or an elaborate, four-color business plan that you will have printed by a commercial printer, Publisher 2013 makes the entire process of starting a publication easy. After you open the template-based file, you can choose your own color scheme, select fonts, or add or change a page background for your file.

Start a new publication based on a template

1 Start Publisher 2013 and display the Start screen.

2 Scroll down and tap the template that you want to use to start a new publication.

3 The templates featured in the list are online templates. To see which templates are built-in to your version of Publisher, tap Built-In.

4 Alternatively, tap the Search box and type a word or phrase for the type of template that you want to find and then tap the Search button (the magnifying glass icon).

5 Tap the template that you want to use as the basis for your new publication.

(continued on next page)

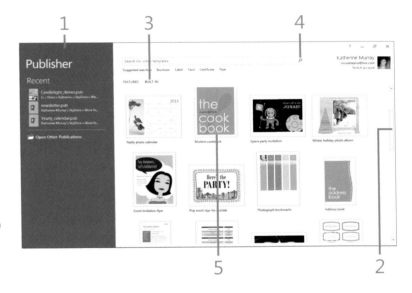

TIP If you search for a template by using the search tool at the top of the Start window, a listing of categories appears in the Category column along the right side of the display. Tap a category to display additional templates in the area.

Start a new publication based on a template *(continued)*

6 Review the description of the template.

7 If you want to cancel the template and return to searching, tap the close tool.

8 Tap the arrow to see the next suggested template.

9 To open a new publication based on the selected template, tap Create. The file opens in the work area, including the color scheme, font, and layout of the template file.

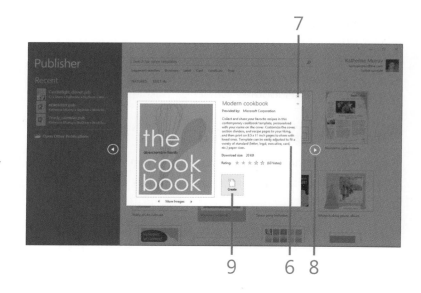

→ **TRY THIS** On the Publisher Start screen, tap the Search box and type a word or phrase to reflect a template that you want to find. Use the category selection to narrow your choices if necessary. Tap the template to learn more about it and decide whether to create a new publication based on it.

Modify the publication

1 With a publication open, on the ribbon, tap the Page Design tab.

Publisher displays tools with which you to set up the page, add layout guides, work with pages, and customize the color scheme, fonts, and background used for your file.

2 In the Schemes group, tap the Schemes drop-down arrow to display a gallery of color schemes.

3 Scroll through the list to see all available color schemes.

4 Tap the color scheme that you want to use.

(continued on next page)

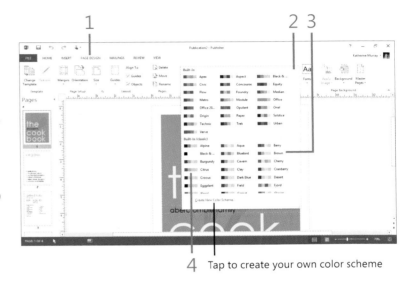

4 Tap to create your own color scheme

Modify the publication *(continued)*

5 In the Schemes group, tap Fonts to display a gallery of font selections.

6 Tap the font that you want to apply to the publication.

7 In the Page Background group, tap Background.

8 Tap the background style that you want to add to the publication.

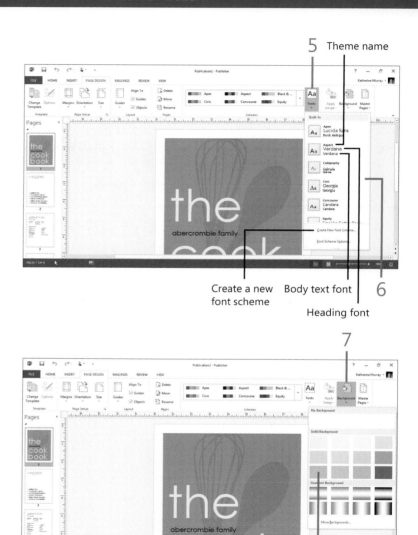

5 Theme name

Create a new font scheme

Body text font

6

Heading font

7

8

Setting up pages

When you create a new Publisher 2013 document, many of the page settings are selected for you by default. You can change the settings and set up your pages the way you want them to appear. The page size you select determines the size of the page that will be printed and determines how much content each page can hold. The orientation controls whether the page is created in a vertical or horizontal layout, and your margins affect the amount of white space that appears between the edge of the text and the sides of the page. You can change these settings individually or change them all together in the Page Setup dialog box. In the Page Setup dialog box you can also choose the overall layout type for your publication, whether you want a traditional one page-per-sheet selection or a booklet, envelope, website, or other project.

Choosing page setup options

1 With a publication open, on the ribbon, tap the Page Design tab.

2 In the Page Setup group, tap the Page Setup dialog launcher to display the Page Setup dialog box.

3 Tap the Layout Type list box to display your layout choices for the current publication. You can choose from One Page Per Sheet, Booklet, E-mail, Envelope, Folded card, Multiple Pages Per Sheet, or Web Page.

4 In the Page section, in the width and height boxes, tap the arrows or enter a specific measurement to change the dimensions of the page.

5 Tap to change the placement of margin guides along the top, bottom, left, and right sides of the page, or enter a specific measurement.

6 Review your changes in the Preview area.

7 Tap OK to save your changes.

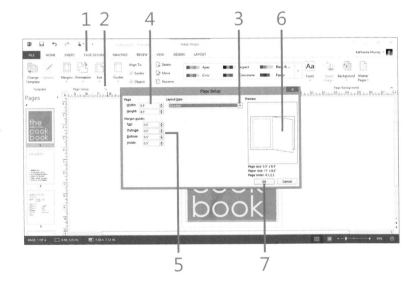

Naming pages

1 On the ribbon, tap the Page Design tab.

2 In the Pages group, tap Rename.

The Rename Page dialog box opens.

3 Type the new name for the page.

4 Tap OK.

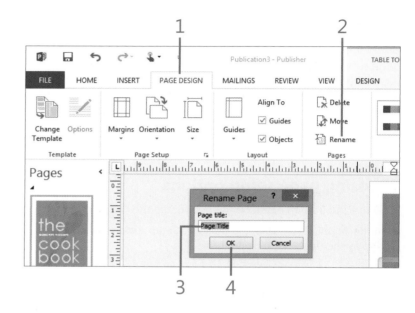

Inserting pages

1 On the ribbon, tap the Insert tab.

2 In the Pages group, tap the Page button.

A list appears, in which you can choose to insert a blank page, a duplicate page, or to display the Insert Page dialog box.

3 Tap Insert Page.

4 In the Insert Page dialog box, type the number of pages that you want to insert.

5 Tap to specify whether to add the pages before or after the current page.

6 In the Options section, tap to specify whether you want to add a completely blank page, a page with a text box, or duplicates of objects on the currently selected page.

7 Tap OK to add the page.

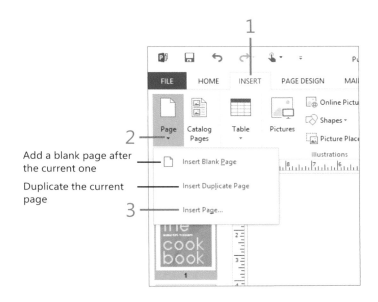

Add a blank page after the current one

Duplicate the current page

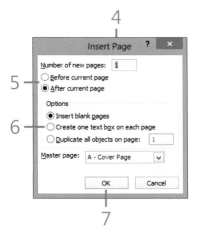

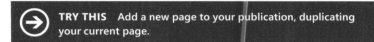

TRY THIS Add a new page to your publication, duplicating your current page.

Adding content

Adding text in Publisher 2013 is a little different from adding text in Microsoft Word. In Publisher, you flow text inside text boxes that you can move, resize, and link as you'd like. This enables you to flow text easily around various elements on your page. You can type text directly into Publisher or import it from another program, as well.

Type and format text

1 On the ribbon, tap the Insert tab.

2 In the Text group, tap Draw Text Box.

   The pointer changes to a cross-hair cursor as soon as you move the cursor over the current page.

3 Drag a rectangle on the page, and when it is the size you want, raise your finger.

   Publisher displays the text box on the page.

4 In the text box, type the text that you want to add.

5 Apply formatting as needed by tapping the Home tab and choosing tools in the Font group.

6 When you're finished adding text, tap outside the box.

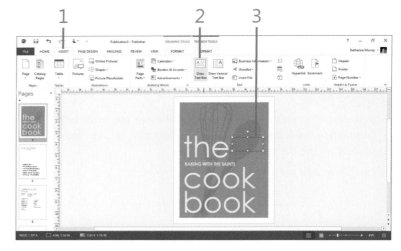

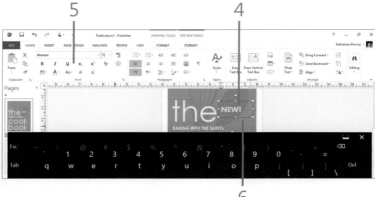

> **TIP** If you've been working in a view that makes it difficult to read individual characters, magnify the page by using the zoom gesture on the screen to enlarge the area in which you need to work.

Import content

1 Display the page where you want to add the new content.

2 On the ribbon, tap the Insert tab.

3 In the Text group, tap Insert File.

Publisher adds a text box on the page and displays the Insert Text dialog box.

4 Navigate to the folder that contains the text file you want to import.

5 Tap the file.

6 Tap OK.

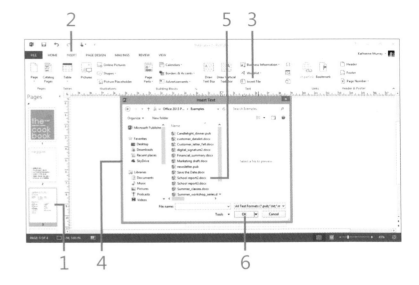

⚠ **CAUTION** Depending on the format of the text you import, you might have some reformatting to do after you insert the file.

✓ **TIP** Formatting text in Publisher isn't much different from formatting text in Word or Microsoft PowerPoint; you can select the text and use the formatting toolbar to make simple changes. You can also use the tools on the Text Box Tools | Format contextual tab (which appears when you are adding text or formatting it) to apply quick styles, change text color, adjust spacing, and employ higher-end typographical tools to fine-tune the appearance of your text.

Linking text boxes

Especially if you choose a multicolumn format or add columns to your publication, you need an easy way to flow the text from text box to text box. This comes in handy when you edit text in one portion of the publication, because the text in linked text boxes reflows automatically to reflect your changes. Publisher makes it easy to link text boxes, giving you control over the way text flows through your publication.

Link text boxes

1 When your current text box is full of text, Publisher looks for a place to put the overflow. Begin by creating a second, empty text box on the page.

2 Tap the first text box to select it.

The overflow indicator appears, letting you know that the text box has additional text that needs to be placed.

3 Tap the overflow indicator. The pointer changes to resemble a pitcher. Tap in the second text box to flow the excess text from the first box to that frame.

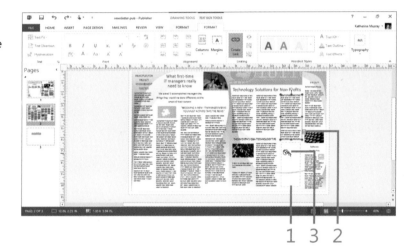

1 3 2

> **TIP** Use the Wrap Text tool in the Text Box Tools | Format contextual tab to control how your text flows around the pictures and shapes in your publication. Publisher offers a number of wrapping styles. You can also use Edit Wrap Points to create a unique shape for the text flow around the images on your page.

Create columns

1 Select the text box that contains the text you want to format in columns.

2 On the ribbon, tap the Text Box Tools | Format contextual tab.

3 Tap Columns.

A list of options appears. You can choose one, two, or three columns or select More Columns to display the Columns dialog box.

4 Tap More Columns.

5 In the Columns dialog box, in the Number box, tap to increase the number of columns you'd like to display, or type the number directly.

6 Change the spacing if necessary.

7 Review your changes in the Preview window.

8 Tap OK to apply your settings to the page.

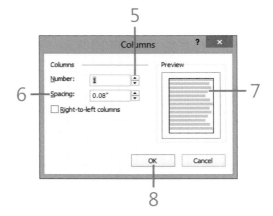

✓ **TIP** Why choose More Columns? If you want to create multiple columns on the page and control the spacing between each column, make your changes in the Columns dialog box. You can increase or decrease the spacing between columns to get just the look you want.

Inserting and replacing pictures

The picture capabilities in Publisher 2013 have been enhanced to make working with multiple pictures more easy as you choose and place them in your document. In earlier versions of Publisher, whenever you added multiple pictures, they were clumped together in a pile in the center of your publication and you had to drag them to where you wanted them to appear. Now, Publisher places your pictures in the scratch area alongside your publication where you can easily view and select the ones that you want to use on the different pages in your document.

Insert a picture

1 Display the page on which you want to add the picture.

2 On the ribbon, tap the Insert tab.

3 Tap the tool in the Illustrations group that you want to use. Choose Pictures if you have a picture on your computer you want to add; tap Online Pictures to download pictures from Bing, Office.com, your own picture-sharing sites, or your SkyDrive account. Tap Shapes to display a gallery of shapes that you can add to your publication.

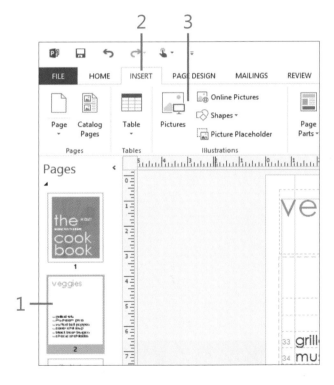

TIP Choose Picture Placeholder to add a picture placeholder box on the Publisher page, in which you can add a picture at a later time.

Inserting multiple pictures at one time

One new feature in Publisher 2013 makes things easier when you want to open a number of pictures that you plan to place on your Publisher pages. When you choose Pictures (in the Illustrations group on the Insert tab) to open the Insert Picture dialog box, you can navigate to a folder containing all the photos you need.

Select the files that you want to open and then tap Insert. Publisher places the images as thumbnails along the right side of your page, in the scratch area. You can then move the pictures to their respective locations within the document by simply dragging them to the new location.

If your pictures don't appear alongside your page, be sure you have the scratch area set to display. To do so, on the View tab, in the Show group, make sure that the Scratch Area check box is selected.

> **(→) TRY THIS** Use the Picture tool in the Illustrations group to add pictures to the scratch area of your page. Drag one of the thumbnails to your page to place the picture.

Replace a picture

1 Tap to select the picture in the scratch area that you want to use. Tap and hold the icon that appears on the image and drag it to the image that you want to replace.

2 When you see the pink outline appear around the image you're replacing, release your touch.

3 On the menu that appears, tap Swap to exchange the position of the two images.

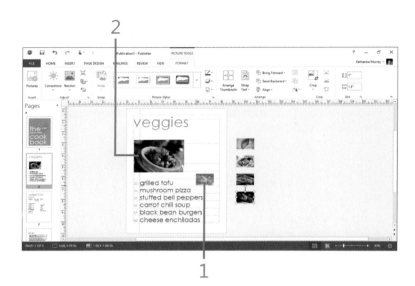

> **TIP** You can replace pictures with images that you haven't yet placed on the scratch area by selecting the picture you want to change, tapping the Picture Tools | Format contextual tab, and then tapping the Change Picture icon in the Adjust group. On the menu that appears, tap Change Picture, and the Insert Pictures window is displayed so that you can navigate to the picture you'd like to use instead. If you want to choose a picture from your computer, at the top of the window, tap Browse to the left of the From A File selection.

> **TIP** Another easy way to flip two pictures is to select both pictures on the page, tap the Picture Tools | Format contextual tab, and then tap Swap. Choose whether you want to swap the picture or swap only the formatting of the picture, and Publisher makes the change for you.

Layering objects on Publisher pages

Some of your publications might require a little more finesse of the elements on the page. You might want to overlap a heading with a picture, for example, or arrange page elements one on top of another. You can use the Arrange tools in Publisher to layer and arrange page elements just the way you want them. This is called reordering.

Arrange objects

1 Tap the object that you want to reorder.

2 If necessary, tap the contextual tab related to that object (for example, if you tap a picture, the Picture Tools | Format contextual tab appears).

3 In the Arrange group, tap either Bring Forward or Send Backward. A list of options appears.

If you tap the Bring Forward button, you can choose Bring To Front, which brings the selected element to the front of the page, or Bring Forward, which moves the selected object one layer up relative to the other objects on the page.

4 If you choose Send Backward, you can select Send To Back, which moves the object behind everything else on the page, or Send Backward, which moves the object one layer down relative to the other objects on the page.

⚠ **CAUTION** If you choose Send To Back and you have added a page background, your object might disappear completely! Don't panic—you can reverse the process by tapping to display the options list and tapping Undo Send Backward.

→ **TRY THIS** Tap an object on your page, tap the contextual tab, and then tap Send To Back. Where did the object go? Adjust if necessary.

Rotate items

1 Select the item that you want to rotate.

2 On the ribbon, tap the Picture Tools | Format contextual tab.

3 In the Arrange group, tap the Rotate Objects tool.

A menu appears that gives you the option of rotating the object in 90 degree increments, flipping the object vertically or horizontally, or dragging to rotate the object as you'd like.

4 Tap the tool that you want to use. If you tap one of the top four tools, the object is rotated automatically.

5 If you choose Free Rotate, handles appear at the corners of the object. Drag one of the handles in the direction you want to rotate the object. Release your touch when the object appears the way you want it on the page.

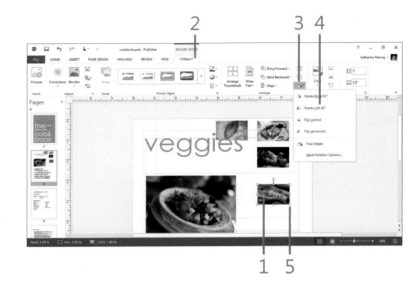

TIP If you are working with multiple objects on the page and want to rotate or layer them together, group them before you choose Bring Forward, Send Backward, or Rotate Objects.

Grouping and ungrouping objects

You can easily group items on the page so that you can work with them as one object. This can be helpful when you need to apply the same setting to a number of items—like rotating objects to the same degree—to get a particular effect on the page. Select the objects that you want to group and then tap the Picture Tools | Format contextual tab. In the Arrange group, tap the Group tool. The outlines of the objects combine, indicating that they have become one object.

If you decide later that you want to separate the group back to the original objects, tap the grouped object, tap the Picture Tools Format tab, and then choose the Ungroup button (just beneath the Group button). The objects are separated into their original configurations.

Finalizing your publication

Whether you plan to save your publication as a PDF and send it to friends; print the publication on your printer for posting in the office, proofreading, or saving as a backup; or have the publication commercially printed, Publisher includes a number of tools to help you prepare it for the last leg of its journey.

You can use the Design Checker to make sure the publication is ready to print, and use the Email Preview and Print tools to get a sense of any last-minute changes you need to make before sharing.

Run the Design Checker

1 On the ribbon, tap the File tab to display the Backstage view.

2 On the Info tab, tap Run Design Checker.

The Design Checker pane opens along the right side of the Publisher window.

(continued on next page)

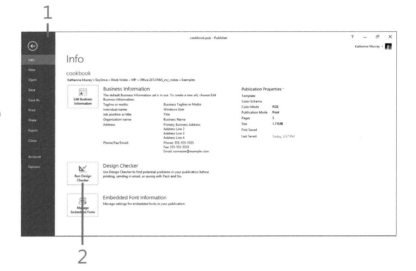

✓ **TIP** Remember to save your Publisher file after making changes with the Design Checker so your final file is as complete and ready-to-go as possible.

Run the Design Checker *(continued)*

3 Select the check box corresponding to the check that you want to perform.

4 Tap and hold an item in the list that you want to fix. A shortcut menu opens, offering ways to deal with the found issue.

5 Choose Go To This Item to move to the object in your publication that triggered the issue so that you can correct the problem.

6 Alternatively, tap Explain to see Help information on the topic.

7 Tap Close Design Checker to dismiss the Design Checker pane.

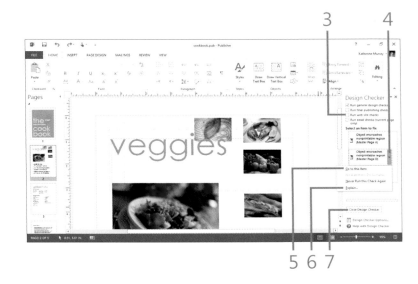

TRY THIS Tap the File tab and choose Run Design Checker to see if your publication is ready to distribute.

Preview as email

1 On the ribbon, tap the File tab to display the Backstage view.

2 Tap the Share tab.

3 Tap E-mail Preview.

4 Choose the E-mail Preview button.

Your publication opens in a browser window.

5 Scroll down through the document to view the publication.

6 Tap the Close button when you're through.

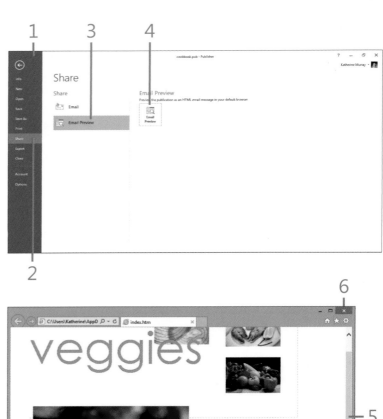

Preview and print your publication

1 On the ribbon, tap the File tab to display the Backstage view.

2 Tap the Print tab.

3 Review the publication in the preview window.

4 Browse through the pages in your document, if applicable.

5 Increase or decrease page size.

6 Hide or redisplay the horizontal and vertical rulers, if applicable.

7 Choose the printer that you want to use.

8 Choose print settings.

9 Enter the number of copies that you want to print.

10 Tap Print.

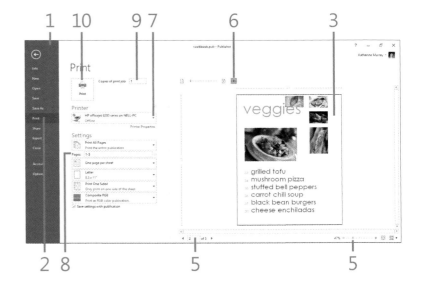

Prepare your project for commercial printing

You use Publisher's Pack And Go Wizard to prepare your Publisher 2013 files for commercial printing. Begin by displaying the Backstage view and tapping the Export tab. In the Pack And Go area of the Export screen, tap Save For A Commercial Printer.

The Save For A Commercial Printer options appear on the right side of the screen. Choose the size of file you want—Commercial Press (largest size), High Quality Printing, Standard, or Minimum Size. Choose whether you want Publisher to create PDF files, Publisher files, or both PDF and Publisher files. Tap the Pack And Go Wizard, choose a location for the file, and then tap Next. Publisher shows the status as the file is saved and displays a final screen that gives you the option of printing a composite proof of the file you've prepared for the printer. Tap OK to close the Pack And Go Wizard, and you're ready to take or send the final files to your printer.

Creating a web app with Access 2013

15

Apps are the big new story in Microsoft Access 2013. Now, if you have a Microsoft Office 365 account with access to Office 2013 Professional or your organization is running Access Services on Microsoft SharePoint 2013 Server, you can use Access to create a web app that collects information from others on your team, in your organization, and from the general public through the SharePoint web app. You create the basic structure for the data, by using data tables, and the gathered data plugs right in so that you can work with it in whatever way best fits your needs. Simple, right?

And with Access 2013, you can still create databases the old-fashioned way, with data tables, relationships, queries, and reports. Increasingly, however, we need to access and work with our data from multiple entry points and in a variety of ways. Microsoft recognizes that much of what we do is going to the cloud, and web apps that live online give you the option of gathering, managing, and sharing data in real time with people all over the world. You get to say who can access your data, of course, and you can customize your web apps to gather just what you need. Yet, the entire process is easier than you might think. And Access 2013 includes a number of predesigned templates with web apps in mind.

In this section:

- Getting started with Access 2013
- Exploring the Access window
- Adding tables for your data
- Adding data to the table
- Starting and using a web app
- Choosing the way you view data
- Changing an existing view
- Using your web app with a team site

Do I need Office 365?

You can use Access 2013 without an Office 365 subscription, but if you plan to create and use Access web apps through SharePoint, you'll need a way to connect to a SharePoint site, either through your organization's SharePoint account or by subscribing to Office 365. Office 365 is Microsoft's in-the-cloud Office platform that enables users to subscribe at different levels and access the Office 2013 programs they need by paying a monthly subscription rate suited to their situation. You can find out more about Office 365 at *www.office365.com*.

Getting started with Access 2013

After you start Access 2013, you can create your first Access web app based on a template designed to help you with the process, or you can go gung-ho and do it all from scratch. Either way, you'll have some simple choices to make about the type of information you want to gather and how you want to gather and work with it. Luckily, Access leads you through the steps, so getting started is fairly straightforward.

Start Access 2013

1 Swipe to the left to display app tiles on the right end of the Windows 8 Start screen.

2 Tap the Access 2013 app tile.

The Access 2013 Start screen appears.

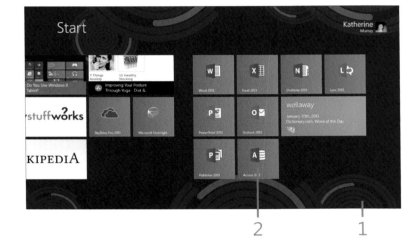

TIP Be sure to log on with either your Microsoft Account or your corporate user name and password (if you're using SharePoint 2013). You need to be logged on to create and work with web apps in Access.

Start a web app from a template

1 Display the Access 2013 Start screen.

2 Scroll through the templates to find a web app template that you want to use. Note that if a template name begins with the word "desktop," the template is not a web app template.

3 Tap the web app template that you want to use.

4 Enter a name for the app.

5 Tap a location at which to the new app.

6 Tap Create.

The web app opens in the Access window. The process takes a few minutes while Access creates the web app and adds tables and views for you to use. Your next step is to start using the application.

1   3   2

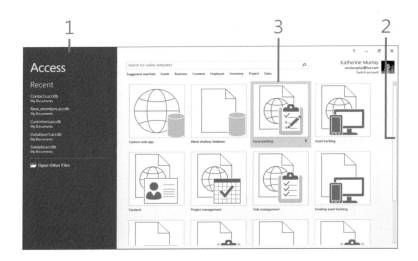

4

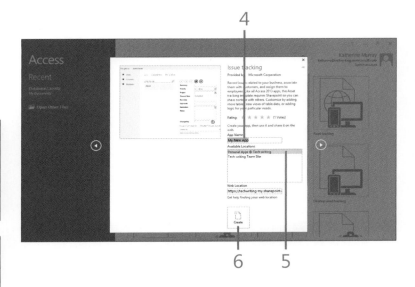

6   5

TIP When you select a template to create a web app, Access might offer you one or more suggestions for locations where you might store the web app. They might be SharePoint locations that you've used previously with an Office application. If you haven't used SharePoint or do not have an Office 365 subscription, you won't see the list of possible locations.

TRY THIS Launch Access 2013 and browse through the web app templates. Tap one that sounds good to you and choose a location for the app online. Tap Create to start developing the app.

Create a blank web app

1 On the Access 2013 Start screen, tap Custom Web App.

2 In the App Name text box, type a name for your app.

3 Choose the location where you want to create the web app.

4 Tap Create. If prompted, sign in to Office 365 with your User ID and password.

1

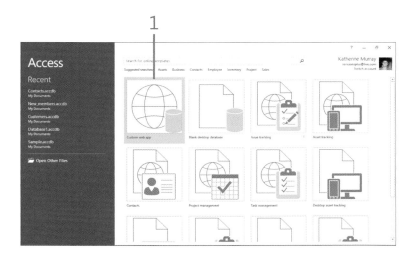

2 3

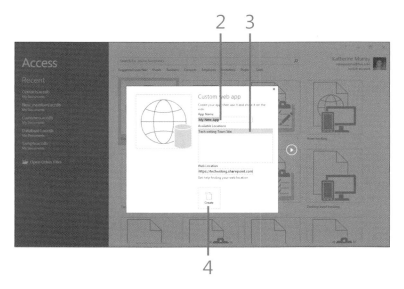

4

Exploring the Access window

The look and feel of the Access 2013 web app doesn't feel particularly "database-y." It feels more like a SharePoint app, something light and fun that you can work with and add data to easily online. The first window you'll see gives you the option of adding tables to your web app. Here's an introduction to the tools you'll use as you create your web app.

Click to display the Navigation pane

Search for a table to fit the type of data you want to collect

Import data from an existing data source

Add a new blank table

Adding tables for your data

When you're creating an Access 2013 web app, you have three options for adding tables. You can create a blank table, search for a table template that fits the data you need to manage, or open a table you've already saved in an existing file or list.

Search and find a table

1 Tap the Add Tables Search box and type a word or phrase reflecting the type of information you want to gather.

2 Tap the Search button (the magnifying glass icon).

   Results appear beneath the Search box.

3 Scroll through the results list.

4 Tap the table that you want to use.

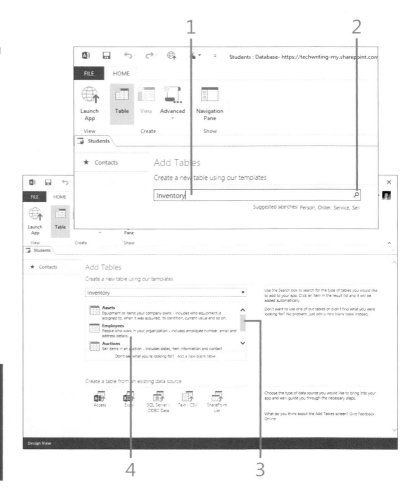

> ✓ **TIP** Depending on which table you select, Access might add multiple tables because it adds any related tables at the same time. You can determine by the icon to the left of the table name whether Access will add related tables. The table with the black outline means one table would be added (Employees, in this example). But, if you choose Assets, which shows a graphic indicating multiple tables, Access will add multiple, related tables.

Add a blank table

1 On the ribbon, tap the Home tab and then, in the Create group, tap Table.

2 Tap the Add A New Table link to add a new blank table.

(continued on next page)

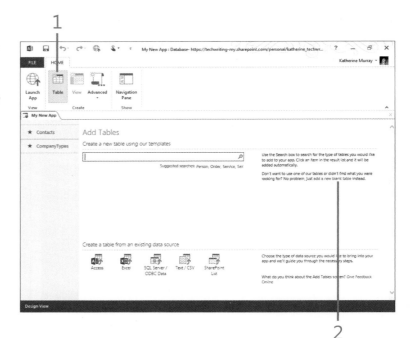

TIP After you save or create a new table, Access automatically creates at least two views called List and Datasheet, which you can use to display and interact with data in the table through the browser interface.

Add a blank table *(continued)*

3 Tap a blank line in the Field Name column and type the name that you want to assign to the field.

4 In the adjacent cell, in the Data Type column, select Short Text.

5 On the Quick Access Toolbar, tap the Save button.

6 In the Save As dialog box that opens, type a title for the Table name.

7 Tap OK.

8 Tap the View icon to display the table and enter data.

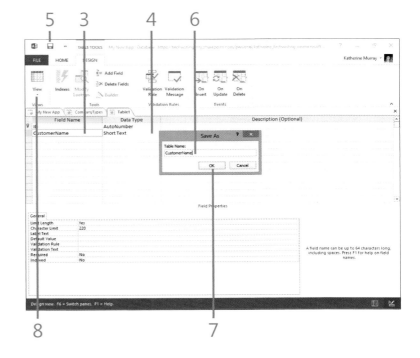

 TRY THIS Create a table for the web app, either by choosing a table template or creating a blank table.

TIP When you click on the View icon, you are seeing something called the Preview Datasheet (not to be confused with the Datasheet view). Using this special preview feature, you can work with data without needing to display the data in the browser.

Adding data to the table

You can add data easily while you're working with your Access 2013 web app. First, in Preview Datasheet, display the table to

which you want to add the information to in Preview Datasheet, and then tap and type the new information.

Add data to the table

1 Select the table that will store the new data.

2 Tap the Settings/Actions button.

3 On the menu that appears, tap View Data.

The table appears in Datasheet view.

4 Tap the first available field and type the information that you want to add.

5 Tap in the next field.

6 When you're finished adding data, tap the Close button.

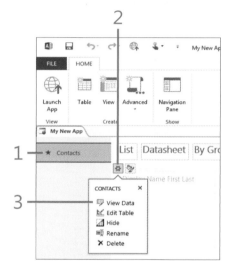

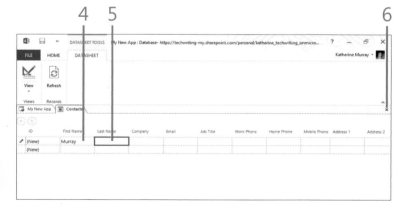

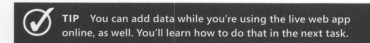

TIP You can add data while you're using the live web app online, as well. You'll learn how to do that in the next task.

Importing data

After you have your table set up the way you want it, you can import table data by tapping Table in the Create group on the Home tab. This displays the initial tables page, on which you can tap the icon at the bottom of the page that represents the type of data file you want to import. Access gives you the option of adding Access, Excel, SQL Server/ODBC Data, Text/CSV files, or SharePoint lists.

Starting and using the web app

After you've added tables and set them up as you want, you can start your web app and give it a trial run. You'll find the Launch App tool in the View group on the Home tab.

Launch the web app

1 On the ribbon, tap the Home tab and then, in the View group, tap Launch App.

If you're prompted to log on, enter the user ID and password you use with Office 365.

2 Tap the Add button (the plus sign) to add a new record.

The data fields become available on the form.

3 Fill in the details for the new record.

4 Tap the Save button (the diskette icon).

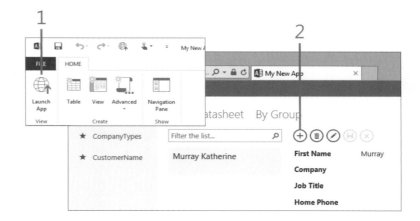

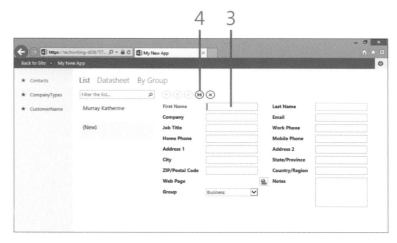

Choosing the way you view data

Access 2013 gives you different ways to view the data you gather in the Access web app. After you start the web app, you can use both List and Datasheet view to review and update your information. You can also create your own custom view so that you can view your data in the way that makes most sense to you.

Work with a List view

1 Tap a table that contains the information you want to view.

2 Tap a line item to display the details for the order line.

The data record for that item appears in a pop-up window.

(continued on next page)

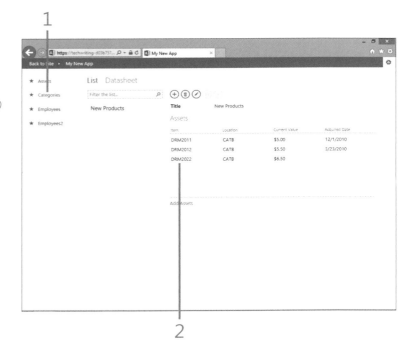

TIP When you added the template tables, because Access creates relationships between these tables, it can automatically create views that convey those relationships. These connections help you navigate to display related information that might be stored in different tables.

Work with a List view (continued)

3 Tap the Edit button (the pencil icon) to make the field available for editing.

4 Make the changes you need to make.

5 Tap Save to save your changes.

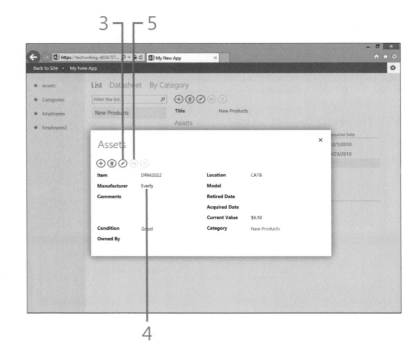

Work with a Datasheet view

1 Tap Datasheet.

2 Tap the Add button.

3 Enter data for a new record.

4 Tap another record to save the new record.

(continued on next page)

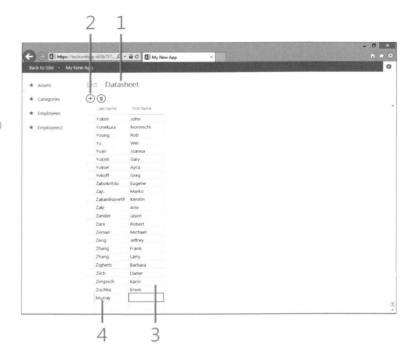

Work with a Datasheet view (continued)

5 To edit a record, tap in the field and start typing.

6 To delete the record, tap the Delete button (the trash can icon).

7 Tap Yes to confirm that you want to delete the record.

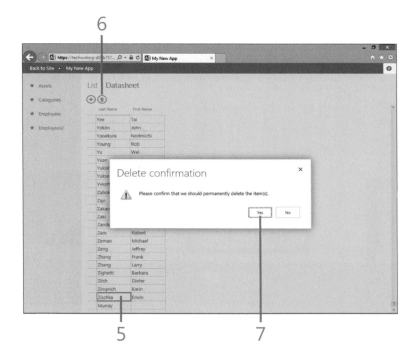

Changing an existing view

When Access 2013 creates a table, it automatically creates at least two views of the data, one called List and the other called Datasheet. You can use the method described here to alter the layout of the view.

Edit the view

1 Tap the table that you want to edit.

2 Tap Datasheet.

3 In the center of the web app window, tap Edit.

You can now change the design of the view.

4 Tap the field that you want to change. Three buttons appear, giving you the choice of changing Data, Formatting, or Actions. Tap Data to change the name, source, or value of the data field, which is called a control in Access web apps. Tap Formatting if you want to add a tooltip, hide or display the control, or add a caption. Tap Actions if you want to change the action assigned to the control.

5 Tap Data.

A pop-up box appears, displaying your options.

6 Change the control name, if you like.

7 Tap to display a list of other controls in the table. Choose your choice.

8 Enter a default value if you want to display one in the table.

> **TIP** Expression Builder is a fairly high-end feature that you can use to customize the expression that defines the value for the control property.

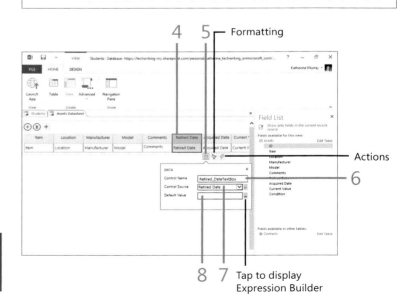

Create a custom view

1 In the Table Selector, tap the table that you want to use.

2 Tap the Add New View button (the plus sign).

3 Type a name for the new view.

4 Tap the View Type list box and choose the view that you want. You can choose from List Details, Datasheet, Summary, or Blank.

5 Leave the Record Source as it appears.

6 Tap Add New View.

The new view is added to the horizontal list of available views.

7 Tap the Settings/Actions icon.

8 On the menu that appears, tap Open In Browser to test the view.

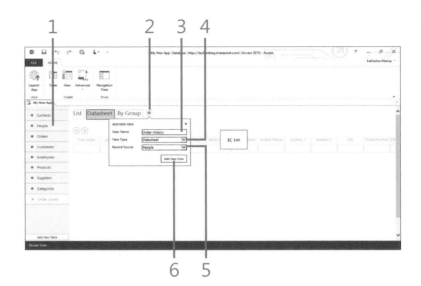

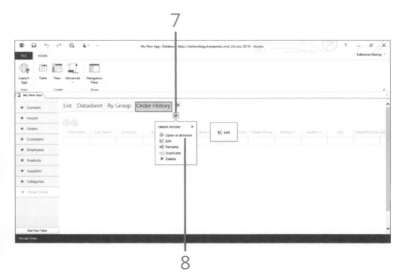

> **TIP** When you're creating a custom view, choose List or Datasheet view whenever possible, because Blank and Summary views will require a lot more work before they function effectively.

> **TIP** The Open In Browser option gives you a convenient way of displaying the results in a browser window with this particular view.

Using your web app with a team site

While viewing any webpage, you can tap the Back To Site link at the far left side of the navigation bar in the web browser to display your team site. From your team site, you have access to other files, blog posts, and more. You can also use the team site to open your Access web app in a local copy of Access 2013 to

change the design of the Access web app on a device which you have not previously used to work with the web app. You will need to have installed Access on that device before you can use this feature.

Open a web app in Access 2013 from a team site

1 Tap the Back To Site link.

2 At the bottom of the navigation bar, tap Site Content.

(continued on next page)

Open a web app in Access 2013 from a team site *(continued)*

3 Tap the More Options button (the ellipsis character) to display options for the application.

4 Tap the Web App icon once to open the web app in a browser window.

5 Tap the Customize in Access tool to open the web app in Access 2013.

4   3

5

Index

fonts
   changing default (OneNote), 329
   selecting for publications (Publisher), 352
formatting
   data in worksheets (Excel), 225
   Format Painter (PowerPoint), 280
   paragraphs, 167
   slide text (PowerPoint), 278–280
   styles allowed in restricted (Word), 195
   text in Publisher, 357
   text in Word, 158
   Word documents, 165–167
formulas, Excel
   basics, 252–253
   checking for errors in, 255
   creating, 254
functions, Excel
   basics, 252–253
   finding, 256
   Function Arguments dialog box, 256

G

Gallery View (Lync), 120
General tab (Options dialog box), 67
Get External Data group (Excel), 220
grouping
   contacts (Lync), 133
   and ungrouping objects (Publisher), 365
Guides option (Publisher), 348

H

handouts, printing (PowerPoint), 314
headers/footers in Word, 180–181
Help tool, 64–66, 255
hiding
   location information (Lync), 130
   menu bar (Lync 2013), 125

Highlight Changes dialog box (Excel), 238
Home tab (Outlook), 86
hosting meetings (Lync), 145

I

icons, adding to worksheet cells (Excel), 247
illustrations, adding to Word, 171
importing
   data to tables (Access), 381
   data to worksheets (Excel), 220–221
Info tab (Backstage view), 26
Insert Function (Excel)
   dialog box, 256
   tool, 253
Insert Picture dialog box
   Excel, 226
   Publisher, 361
   Word, 170
Insert Slicers dialog box (Excel), 263
Insert tab (Office apps), 47
Insert Text dialog box (Publisher), 357
Insert Video window (Word), 173
Inspect Document dialog box (Office
   2013), 57
inspecting files, 57
installing Office 2013 on multiple devices, 14
instant messages
   for coauthor collaboration (Word), 193
   responding to (Lync), 138
   sending (Lync), 136–137
Invite People option, 58, 302

J

jump lists of files, 51

K

keyboards
   displaying onscreen, 27
   display options, 4
   selection tool, 34
   types of, 34

L

Language group (Review tab), 63
Language tab (Options dialog box), 67
launching
   Access 2013, 373
   Lync 2013, 121–122
   OneNote 2013, 322
   Outlook 2013, 73
   PowerPoint 2013, 268
   Publisher 2013, 344
   web apps (Access), 382
layering objects on pages
   (Publisher), 363–365
layouts
   Layout Options toolbar (Word), 176
   for PowerPoint slides, 276
lines
   adding to note pages (OneNote), 336
   Line option (sparklines), 249
linking
   sending links to notebooks
      (OneNote), 339
   text boxes (Publisher), 358
List view (web apps), 383–384
Lock Tracking option (shared
   documents), 200
Lync 2013
   calls
      making, 138–139
      recording, 142
      video, 141

About the author

Katherine Murray has been writing about Microsoft Office since the earliest version was available, way back in the dark ages of DOS. She loves the new minimalist design in Office 2013 and is a faithful cloud enthusiast, sharing folders and files with editors, friends, and family all over the globe. She's also a "tech-everywhere" kind of person who enjoys the flexibility of being able to work on her desktop, laptop, tablet, or phone—no matter where she may be. In addition to her long-time tech writing, Katherine is the publications coordinator for Quaker Earthcare Witness (*www.quakerearthcare.org*), where she uses Microsoft Office and Adobe technologies to create, publish, and share print and online communications. Additionally, Katherine is a contributor to Windows Secrets (*www.windowsecrets.com*) and CNET's TechRepublic, and she is also the author of *Microsoft Office Professional 2013 Plain & Simple*, *Microsoft Word 2013 Inside Out*, and many other technical books.

What do you think of this book?

We want to hear from you!
To participate in a brief online survey, please visit:

microsoft.com/learning/booksurvey

Tell us how well this book meets your needs—what works effectively, and what we can do better.
Your feedback will help us continually improve our books and learning resources for you.

Thank you in advance for your input!